John Wallraff

From Drags to Riches
The Untold Story
of Charles Pierce

Pre-publication
REVIEWS,
COMMENTARIES,
EVALUATIONS . . .

"**J**ohn Wallraff has captured the essence of the golden age of nightlife. In his book, *From Drags to Riches,* Wallraff gets to the nitty-gritty of what went on backstage in the life of Charles Pierce, 'Male Actress.' Pierce, who garnered two full-page tributes in *Life* magazine, comes to life in this wildly effective story. This is raw and thrilling storytelling. . . . Wallraff tells it all. . . . Keeps you turning pages until you jump up with applause. The book digs down deep to the guts and the brains of Charles Pierce—an American classic. Wallraff brilliantly adds layer after layer of interesting characters—some famous and some disguised. It all adds up to rich drama with hilarious, slam-bang situations."

Lee Hartgrave
Journalist/Humorist;
Founding Member and Two-Term
President of the Bay Area Theater
Critics Circle

"**I**n *From Drags to Riches,* author John Wallraff 'lets it all hang out' as he chronicles Charles Pierce's life—personal, sexual, and theatrical. The book follows the ups and downs of Pierce's life; for years it was mostly the latter, but by the 1970s (the golden, pre-AIDS decade), he had established himself in LA, San Francisco, London, and New York, and developed his own theater circuit, often staying at one club for two- and three-month runs. Full descriptions of typical Pierce shows—from the dressing room to the final bows—are fascinating reading, particularly when the show's script is included, which is sometimes the case. The story of how Pierce developed a long, brilliant, and lucrative career, 'and lived his dream,' as Wallraff puts it, is a fascinating one indeed, particularly to those of us who only knew the public Charles Pierce, the entertainer who regularly brightened our lives."

Philip Elwood
Music Critic,
San Francisco Examiner
and Chronicle

From Drags to Riches
The Untold Story of Charles Pierce

HAWORTH Gay & Lesbian Studies
John P. De Cecco, PhD
Editor in Chief

One of the Boys: Masculinity, Homophobia, and Modern Manhood by David Plummer

Homosexual Rites of Passage: A Road to Visibility and Validation by Marie Mohler

Male Lust: Pleasure, Power, and Transformation edited by Kerwin Kay, Jill Nagle, and Baruch Gould

Tricks and Treats: Sex Workers Write About Their Clients edited by Matt Bernstein Sycamore

A Sea of Stories: The Shaping Power of Narrative in Gay and Lesbian Cultures— A Festschrift for John P. De Cecco edited by Sonya Jones

Out of the Twilight: Fathers of Gay Men Speak by Andrew R. Gottlieb

The Mentor: A Memoir of Friendship and Gay Identity by Jay Quinn

Male to Male: Sexual Feeling Across the Boundaries of Identity by Edward J. Tejirian

Straight Talk About Gays in the Workplace, Second Edition by Liz Winfeld and Susan Spielman

The Bear Book II: Further Readings in the History and Evolution of a Gay Male Subculture edited by Les Wright

Gay Men at Midlife: Age Before Beauty by Alan L. Ellis

Being Gay and Lesbian in a Catholic High School: Beyond the Uniform by Michael Maher

Finding a Lover for Life: A Gay Man's Guide to Finding a Lasting Relationship by David Price

The Man Who Was a Woman and Other Queer Tales from Hindu Lore by Devdutt Pattanaik

How Homophobia Hurts Children: Nurturing Diversity at Home, at School, and in the Community by Jean M. Baker

The Harvey Milk Institute Guide to Lesbian, Gay, Bisexual, Transgender, and Queer Internet Research edited by Alan Ellis, Liz Highleyman, Kevin Schaub, and Melissa White

Stories of Gay and Lesbian Immigration: Together Forever? by John Hart

From Drags to Riches: The Untold Story of Charles Pierce by John Wallraff

Lytton Strachey and the Search for Modern Sexual Identity: The Last Eminent Victorian by Julie Anne Taddeo

Before Stonewall: Activists for Gay and Lesbian Rights in Historical Context edited by Vern L. Bullough

From Drags to Riches
The Untold Story of Charles Pierce

John Wallraff

Harrington Park Press®
An Imprint of The Haworth Press, Inc.
New York • London • Oxford

Published by

Harrington Park Press®, an imprint of The Haworth Press, Inc., 10 Alice Street, Binghamton, NY 13904-1580.

Certain persons have been excluded from the narrative, in deference to their feelings, and here and there a name has been changed to conceal an identity.

Cover design by Marylouise E. Doyle.

Library of Congress Cataloging-in-Publication Data

Wallraff, John.
   From drags to riches : the untold story of Charles Pierce / John Wallraff.
      p. cm.
   Includes bibliographical references.
   ISBN 1-56023-385-0 (alk. paper) — ISBN 1-56023-386-9 (alk. paper)
   1. Pierce, Charles, 1926-1999. 2. Female impersonators—United States—Biography. I. Title.

PN2287.P539 W35 2002
791'.086'6—dc21
                                         2001051591

To all of Charles Pierce's fans:
"The Wonderful People Out There in the Dark"
who remained faithful to the end

ABOUT THE AUTHOR

John Wallraff began his theatrical career at the age of six as a child performer on a radio kiddie show hosted by "Uncle" Tom Murray. As a student at the famous Pasadena Playhouse, John Wallraff appeared in numerous plays while studying theater arts and playwriting. He was a fellow student, mentor, and longtime friend of Charles Pierce from 1946 until Pierce's death in 1999. For twenty-five years, the author worked as a graphic artist, as well as writing and performing in a musical revue in Hollywood and co-writing material with Charles Pierce for his comedy act. He also wrote and performed stand-up comedy at the Hollywood Purple Onion, The Opera Club in San Francisco, and in Charles Pierce's show at San Francisco's famous Gilded Cage Cabaret. Wallraff is now retired, living in San Francisco, and writing plays and novels.

CONTENTS

Acknowledgments

Special warm thanks go to many friends and relatives who encouraged me and helped me in so many ways. They are: Terrie and Phil Barsetti; the Bob Briggs family; Berenice Burrell; John De Cecco; Conrad Doerr; Roberto Friedman, Arts Editor, *Bay Area Reporter;* GLBT Historical Museum of San Francisco; Lee Hartgrave; Don Lee Kobus; Charlotte Martin; Dan Mills; Peter Mintun; Patsy Myers; Les Natali; Allen Ogi; Cheryl Pelton; Arlene Rogers; Jerry Royer; Ruth Rumpler; Bob Taylor, Curator, New York Public Library for the Performing Arts; Bill Thompson; Franklin Townsend; Curt Varnam; Betty and Fred Wallraff; Michael M. Yamashita, General Manager, *Bay Area Reporter*—and the kindly spirit of Charles Pierce himself, who, I'm sure, was very close by, guiding my hand! Thanks to you all.

I am not a drag queen! I am a Male Actress—a Master and Mistress of Disguise!

Charles Pierce

Prologue

"Cocksucker! Get down on your knees and suck me off!"

There was a strange urgency in David Hartley's voice commanding Charles Pierce to give him sexual satisfaction. The two teenaged boys had been showering together in the high school locker room in the basement of Watertown High School after practice on the athletics field. David at sixteen and Charles at fourteen were not close friends, but they were very aware of each other. David was on the football team and Charles went out for track.

Charles had a huge crush on David and he could hardly keep his eyes from David's naked body while they showered together, and Charles noticed that David cast furtive glances at him too.

David had a straightforward manner and a certain flirtatious way with his dark blue eyes, showing off his lean, well-muscled body, and flicking the dark hair from his handsome face.

On this afternoon, after they had stepped out of the shower room and were drying off and dressing, David gave Charles one of his sidelong, sexy looks. "Come on into the janitor's shop. I want to show you something."

Charles was curious and followed his handsome classmate along the dark passageway that led to the deserted shop area. Jake, the janitor, was busy with his other chores and wouldn't return to the workshop until school let out. Then he would come down to pick up his broom and cleaning equipment and perform his duties.

The shop was in semidarkness when the two boys entered. David led the way to a secluded area behind a ceiling-high stack of large cartons filled with paper goods. Charles' heart was beating fast, as he was anticipating that he and David were about to engage in some sort of sexual encounter.

David leaned back against a workbench facing Charles, unsnapped the waistband on his faded jeans, slid the zipper down, and let his jeans fall to the cement floor at his feet. He wasn't wearing underwear, so he was completely naked from the waist down, his full erection standing ready for action.

"Suck it!" David commanded, "Go on, you've been wanting it long enough, cocksucker! Get down on your knees and suck me off!"

This was not the action Charles had wanted from David. He wanted to kiss him and touch his hair and stroke his muscular body. He wanted David to want him, to hold him and kiss him back. But this was so crude, so bold, so shocking to Charles that he didn't know what to do. He wanted to run, but the sight of David, the almost angry look on his face, the demanding urgency in his voice, and David's naked body held him there.

"Get down on your knees, cocksucker, and put my cock in your mouth—now!" David looked dangerous and it frightened Charles, but he couldn't control himself. He was under David's spell, and he knew he'd do anything David demanded of him.

The room seemed airless and Charles had trouble breathing. A mixture of paint thinner and floor wax stung his nostrils, but when he caught the spicy scent of David's body as Charles knelt to face him, he surrendered and obeyed David's command.

Afterward, David pulled up his jeans, left the shop, and called over his shoulder as he walked away, "Gotta go—see ya." And he disappeared into the shadows of the basement.

Charles was devastated that afternoon as he walked home from school, and then he heard Aunt Carolyn call to him. No wonder she thought him distant and not himself. All he could think about was David and what had happened in the basement.

Charles cried himself to sleep that night. He had loved David so much, and he had done what David had wanted him to do. But David had been almost savage, calling him "cocksucker" and demanding rather than asking for what he wanted.

"Someday," Charles promised himself, "someday I'll be rich and famous—and then David will love me. I know he will . . . someday . . ."

"A Wonderful Idea"

"Charles! Charles, dear, come in. I have the most wonderful idea!"

It was the voice of Aunt Carolyn calling to him from behind the front screen door of her big, old, rambling Victorian house at 406 Franklin Street in Watertown, New York.

The fourteen-year-old boy she was addressing was a tall, lanky young fellow with an unruly thatch of bright blond hair, large, long-lashed sky-blue eyes—later, much later, to be called "Bette Davis" eyes—and a clear but pale complexion, free of acne, but slightly scarred from an operation performed at the time of his birth.

At first, he didn't hear his aunt call to him. He was thinking his own thoughts as he walked the familiar route from high school to his own home at 326 South Pleasant Street.

At five feet, ten inches, Charles Pierce was tall for his age, though he still hadn't reached his full height of six feet. In spite of his adolescence, he was not awkward. He was slender and moved with confidence and grace, and often he received compliments on his long, beautifully sculptured legs. But his hips were womanly, and later in his life he would call them "hips for childbearing."

"Too pretty to be a boy," some of the busybodies clucked as Charles glided past them on the street. The jocks at school teased him constantly when he showered with them, but Charles took it all in stride, his quick wit and humor usually diffusing the situation. But now Charles was thinking about a particular jock, David Hartley, the object of Charles' affection. David was the handsomest boy in school with his muscular body and even features. All the girls vied for his attention. When the boys showered together in the school basement, Charles couldn't help stealing sidelong glances at David in all his nakedness, and later, in bed, Charles couldn't get the image of David out of his mind. Then he'd touch himself, which would lead to sexual activity before he could drift off to sleep. Charles was in love with

David Hartley, and there was nothing he could do about it. At the moment, however, he was deep in thought about what he and David had done in the basement room at school—something he would never forget for the rest of his life.

Suddenly, he came out of his reverie when he heard his aunt call to him again. He was fond of his father's sister Carolyn, and next to his mother he loved her best. He hurried to her to hear what she was so excited about.

Charles Edwin Pierce was born in Watertown, New York, on Bastille Day, July 14, 1926. A thin, transparent veil of flesh, a membrane called a caul, covered his face, and when it was surgically removed it left facial scars that he bore until his death. At the time, a gypsy fortune teller told his mother that a child born with a facial caul was destined for prosperity and success.

Charles' parents, Gerald and Jessie Hickman Pierce, were overjoyed at their son's birth. They finally had a healthy child to love and cherish. Jessie had had several miscarriages prior to Charles' birth and had all but given up on having a family. She was a native of Ontario, Canada, had immigrated to Watertown as a young woman, and had met and fallen in love with Gerald Sloat Pierce, an ambitious young man who made his living as a traveling salesman.

The young couple set up housekeeping in the quiet, tree-lined streets of Watertown to be near Gerald's parents and sister Carolyn. Gerald's forebears can be traced back to United States President Franklin Pierce (1804-1869), our fourteenth president. Later, when Charles performed in drag, he would tell his nightclub audiences that if he were ever elected president he could save the country money by also being First Lady!

Because Charles was their "miracle child," his parents and his aunt Carolyn pampered him and gave him his own way. His mother, especially, catered to his every whim and gave him piano lessons; they were inseparable. She had the same bright blonde hair and blue eyes as her son, as well as the same bawdy sense of humor. She probably would have been successful if she had pursued a career on the stage. She loved decorating her home, and whenever she was slightly depressed, she'd buy a new hat or buy new wallpaper and redo the entire house. Charles said she must have studied at the Gypsy Rose Lee Institute of Interior Design because she was always stripping wallpaper and replacing it with paper covered with big, red cabbage roses. Of course, that was just a joke; Gypsy did favor cabbage roses on her walls, but stripping, in her case, had nothing to do with wallpaper.

Charles' father, Gerald, was a "good man," in Charles' own words, but "remote." The poor man wasn't well most of the time as he suffered with severe asthma, which eventually caused his death. In addition, he was forced to travel a great deal, and because of his absences, Charles really didn't get to know his father very well and turned to his mother and Aunt Carolyn for companionship.

Charles was an avid moviegoer and every Saturday afternoon he would be seated with a sack of popcorn in the local theater devouring a triple bill of everything from Bette Davis or Joan Crawford dramas to Errol Flynn swashbucklers, to Clark Gable and Jean Harlow films. One of his favorites was *Gone with the Wind* with Vivien Leigh as "Scarlett O'Hara." All of these images would one day be grist for his comedy mill. He loved all the great movie actresses, Bette Davis, Joan Crawford, Ingrid Bergman, Tallulah Bankhead, Katharine Hepburn, but he never dreamed that someday he would be impersonating them or that he would meet so many of them in person when they came to see his show.

Aunt Carolyn, who had been a vaudevillian, encouraged him to perform. "You've got the spark, Charles," she cajoled. "Someday you'll be a big star and tread the boards just like I did."

Often she led him up the narrow, creaky stairs to her attic, and they'd open the dusty trunks that held her old costumes. Charles loved the smell of the musty attic up under the eaves, and the smell of the costumes themselves, a mixture of sandalwood, stale cigarette smoke, and greasepaint.

What a treasure trove it was! Ostrich-plumed picture hats, brightly colored feather boas, bejeweled 1920s flapper gowns, shimmering with beaded fringe, countless wigs, bustled dance-hall dresses, sparkling rings and necklaces, and shoes of every description. Charles would shed his male attire, rouge his cheeks, apply eye shadow, lipstick, and powder, and arch his eyebrows with pencil. Aunt Carolyn would dust off the cracked, full-length mirror, play various old 78 r.p.m. records on a beat-up phonograph, and Charles would become a host of bygone characters, all totally different from himself, all exciting, and all female! Sometimes he was Mae West or Lillian Russell or even Carmen Miranda, or he'd slip into a slinky bias-cut silver lamé number and a platinum wig and be Jean Harlow. What fun they had!

Aunt Carolyn opened the screen door for her nephew as he slipped by her and sat down in a rocking chair by the living room window. It was a beautiful spring day, balmy after the winter chill.

"Now, Charles," Aunt Carolyn began, "help yourself to a glass of lemonade and some of those sugar cookies. I just baked them. You must be starved."

Charles filled a glass with the tart beverage and a couple of ice cubes that slipped over the lip of the pitcher. Then he took a sip, picked up a cookie, and sat back in the rocker.

"Is something wrong, dear?" Carolyn was concerned.

"No. Why?"

"You seem so far away—not like yourself at all. Did something happen at school?"

"No . . . no . . . of course not. Why would you think that? Everything is fine at school." Charles couldn't tell his aunt about what he and David Hartley had done in the janitor's workroom in the basement at school. He couldn't tell anyone.

"Very well, darling; I just worry about you sometimes. But now I must tell you my idea. It came to me this morning when I read the paper."

"I'm dying to hear, Aunt Carolyn." Charles leaned forward eagerly. "Don't tease me—tell me." He was always impatient. He hated to wait.

"Well, I read in the paper that Gertrude Lawrence is at the Alvin Theatre on Broadway in *Lady in the Dark,* and I've decided that we're going to go see her. What do you think of that? I've already called your mother and she thinks it's a great idea, so she and you and I are going to Manhattan and see ourselves some shows. You have a flair for performing, and it's high time you saw your first Broadway show."

"Oh, Aunt Carolyn, do you really mean it? When do we leave?" Suddenly, his current troubles vanished.

"I thought we'd go for a weekend when you have vacation in June. New York City is so hot then, but we'll survive. That'll give me time to arrange everything—tickets, hotel, and all. You know, I was in the chorus of Gertie's show *Oh, Kay!* when she first came over here from England. We'll go backstage and see her."

"I can hardly wait!"

* * *

The night they sat in the audience at the Alvin Theatre and the curtain rose on Act I of *Lady in the Dark,* Charles was completely spellbound. What a dazzling show, and such a talented cast. There was the brilliant Gertrude Lawrence, of course, bumping and grinding her way across the stage dressed in a simple gray business suit and singing "The Saga of Jenny," but in addition, there was the fluid-tongued Danny Kaye, and the "Gorgeous Hunk of Man" Victor Mature, all muscles and sex appeal, clad in form-fitting tights to portray movie star Randy Curtis.

When Charles read in the program that Victor Mature had studied at Pasadena Playhouse, he decided then and there that he would get a job, save his money, and enroll at that prestigious theater school. He had seen advertisements for the Playhouse in *Theatre Arts Magazine.*

The trio tried to go backstage to see Gertrude Lawrence, but they were turned away. Instead, they went on to see Carmen Miranda with Olsen and Johnson in *Sons o' Fun,* and Vincent Price as the villainous husband in *Angel Street.* Charles could see himself in the part, and it strengthened his resolve to go west and pursue a career on the stage. He just knew he'd become a big star, and then David Hartley would want him—everyone would want him because he'd be rich and famous, and he and David would be together always. But at the moment, he was completely captivated by the theater—the smell, the curtains, the lights, the roar of applause had hooked him forever. He was smitten till his dying day.

Charles was blessed with a clear, resonant, masculine voice, so, at the age of fifteen, he auditioned for and was employed part-time as the youngest radio announcer in the business at station WWNY in Watertown, New York, broadcasting news of World War II and performing organ solos and other entertainments. A photograph taken at the time shows a youthful Charles seated at the organ with sheet music on the rack titled "They're Either Too Young or Too Old," a song Bette Davis sang in the movie *Thank Your Lucky Stars.* Years later, his Bette Davis impression would be the highlight of his repertoire!

Charles enjoyed the work at the station and after six years on the job, and after graduating from high school, he had saved enough money for his train ticket to Pasadena and other expenses, including his two-years' tuition at the Playhouse.

He wrote to Margot Poley, head of admissions at the theater school, filled out the entrance forms she sent him, and was accepted. In August of 1946, he boarded the Santa Fe Super Chief, and it was "California, Here I Come!"

2

A Movie Star on Wheels

When Charles Pierce boarded the Super Chief in Chicago for his trip to Pasadena, California, that summer day in August 1946, he didn't know he would meet a glamorous movie star along the way!

It began on the sleek streamliner somewhere in the wild Southwest near Albuquerque, New Mexico. Charles had grown weary of sitting in his seat in the chair car, and he wasn't looking forward to another uncomfortable night of trying to sleep sitting upright. He had had dinner in the dining car, and now he was watching the sun slip slowly behind the jagged Sawtooth Mountains and the endless stands of saguaro cacti, sagebrush, and sand. He felt sticky all over in spite of the air-conditioning and the inadequate sponge baths he'd taken in the men's lavatory. God! What wouldn't he give for a shower!

Boring! The constant clickety-clack of the wheels on the rails was getting to him. Well, he could stand it—not too much longer and he'd be in Pasadena! Even so, he was homesick. He missed his mother more than he wanted to admit, but he had made his own decision—he wasn't his mother's little baby boy anymore, and he had no regrets about his plans for his future.

Pasadena Playhouse! He really was excited about attending classes there. So many stars had been discovered on its stages, and he just knew it would open up a whole new glamorous world to him. He could hardly wait to get started.

The club car was still serving. Why not saunter back, have a Coke or something, and he could do some observing from the observation car.

At first, he thought the club car was vacated except for the bartender, a pleasant black man who greeted him as he entered. Charles slid onto a barstool and ordered a Coke. The bartender set down the glass he was rinsing and poured the soda.

"Quiet tonight," Charles remarked, just to make conversation.

"Sure is," the bartender grinned. "Guess a lot of folks have turned in already."

Charles sipped his drink, and the bartender returned to his duties. Charles rose and walked to the very end of the car. Soft music drifted from the intercom as he seated himself in a large lounge chair. That's when he noticed he wasn't the only occupant in the club car after all.

She was so petite he'd walked right by her without noticing that she was half-hidden in a high-backed swivel chair facing away from him. Then a curl of cigarette smoke rose above the chair back, and he heard a slight, muffled cough.

She swung her chair around then, and suddenly she was facing him. She flicked a speck of tobacco from her pretty pink tongue with her thumb and forefinger, and took another drag on her cigarette.

"Dahling," she drawled. "Do you have the time? I left my watch in my compartment." Her voice was low—a whisky voice—but not unpleasant. He noticed her hair first, a bright orange-red, obviously dyed, then her breasts, obviously real, the two rounded mounds and deep cleavage visible in the snug, open-necked silk blouse and jacket. He recognized her instantly.

"It's just eleven-thirty," Charles replied, fascinated by the vision before him. They didn't make 'em like that in Watertown! With the music playing in the background, low and dreamy, and the sultry voice of Jane Froman caressing the lyrics to "Blue Moon," it made for a rather unnerving mood for the twenty-year-old from Upstate New York.

Now she was grinding her gold-tipped cigarette out in an ashtray.

"Dahling, would you tell the bartender I'd love another of his mahvelous mahtinis? I'm simply parched. Oh, and get one for yourself."

Charles walked to the bar and returned with two of the lethal concoctions, handed one to his new acquaintance, and returned to his seat.

"Thank you, dahling." She clinked her glass to his. "Cheers! Now, we really must introduce ourselves as long as we're stranded on this boxcar to oblivion! God! How I hate to travel!"

"I'm Charles Pierce. I'm from New York, and I'm on my way to Pasadena. I'm going to be an actor at the Playhouse."

"Oh, an actor. How divine. Yes, well, Charles dahling, I was hoping I wouldn't have to introduce myself. You do go to the cinema, I presume?" She let loose her trademark raucous laugh.

"Oh, yes, all the time. I'm a real film fan."

"Well, then, you must have seen my pictures? God knows I've made enough of them."

Was he dreaming? Lola Loraine, a real live movie star! And so beautiful, too. Of course he knew who she was. He'd seen her picture often enough in *Photoplay* and *Screenland,* as well as a number of her films. But he had been hesitant about revealing the fact that he recognized her.

"Oh, yes, Miss Loraine, I certainly know who you are." He took a big gulp of his martini. "I've seen a lot of your pictures. You're wonderful!"

"Thank you, dahling. At this stage in my career I'm always glad to know I'm still recognizable." That laugh again.

Several martinis later they were still seated in the club car, and Lola was putting the finishing touches on the story of her life.

"Well, of course, dahling, my name wasn't always Lola Loraine. The studio dreamed that up. After Alphonse died—my last husband—I've had five, dahling—all deadly bores, but rich—I headed for Hollywood. Fortunately, Alphonse left me very well off so I didn't have to take all the usual crap from the moguls. I marched right into the studio offices and I came right to the point.

" 'Listen, dahlings, I'll be brief. I already have the Rolls, the furs, the jewels, the pools, and the mansion in Bel Air, so I don't give a fuck if you hire me or not.' I didn't have an agent, so I left my card, and swept out.

"They were looking for a replacement for Clara Bow since sound was in and Clara was out. The poor dear hated the microphone— she'd beat it till her fists were bloody, and she couldn't stop raising her eyes to it during a scene, and the director had to call 'cut'—so they called a halt to Clara's career.

"I didn't have to wait long for a call. They tested me after dyeing my hair Clara Bow red, and turned me loose in front of the cameras. I wasn't terrified of the mike because I'd done some films in New York. Later, there were rumors they were stag films, but that wasn't true. They said I sizzled in my first film, *Manhattan Mantrap*—it caused a sensation. Then I starred in *Goat Girl*—my first musical. I played a Greek shepherdess among the ruins of the Parthenon. They dubbed all my songs. I was furious! The goats got great reviews and the whole mess bombed. Speaking of songs, dahling, you really should listen to a Cole Porter tune called 'Experiment'—good advice for a youngster just starting out. Don't be ashamed to try, go after what you want—experiment! I'm glad I did. I've tried everything I wanted to try and I have no regrets."

Charles was fascinated with Lola and her tale—no pun intended. They sat and talked, and she seemed to be genuinely interested in this eager young man full of dreams of being an actor.

"Now, Charles dahling, tell me—why do you want to be an actor?"

"Well, I've always enjoyed performing for my family at home, and then when I saw some Broadway plays, I thought, 'I can do that—that's what I want to do.' "

Suddenly, Lola became serious. "All very well, but you know, dahling, it's not enough to just want to do it. You must want it more than anything else on earth! You must have a burning desire to succeed! It has to be the only thing you'll settle for. You must put blinders on and focus everything toward that goal—never be discouraged by rejection or criticism. You must believe that you are the greatest actor in the world, and if you are told otherwise, you are right, and they are wrong!"

"Boy! That's a big order. I hadn't thought of it that way."

"Well, you must think that way—and begin at this very moment—because if you don't, you won't reach your goal, and you'll settle for something less, and all your life you'll wish you'd tried harder. What you need more than looks, talent, and a perfect speaking voice is that all-consuming desire that won't let you rest until you've reached your goal. You must either have the unshakable ego and faith in yourself and your ability or, if not that, then you must have a mentor, a friend, a parent, a teacher, someone who has that strong, unswerving belief in you to carry you to where you want to be! I didn't have to have all those things. I did believe in myself, and I had Alphonse's money, so I could afford to tell Hollywood to go to hell."

"I know you're right, but it'll be hard for me to follow all your advice. I will try though, because I have to be an actor! There's nothing else I want to be!"

The next morning over breakfast in the dining car, Lola had plans.

"We'll be in Pasadena at about noon today. My limo will meet me at the station, and I'll whisk you over to the Playhouse on my way home."

And that's what Lola did. After their luggage was stashed in the limo, the driver drove to 39 South El Molino Avenue and pulled to the curb. Charles retrieved his suitcase and leaned into the limo to say good-bye.

"Dahling, here's my card. Now, call me. I want to hear how you're doing, and maybe I can help." She gave him a quick peck on the cheek.

"Thanks, Miss Loraine. Thanks for everything, and I will call."

"Oh, call me 'Lola' for God's sake, dahling—and call me!" Her tiny hand waved from the window as the limo sped down South El Molino. Charles waved back, then picked up his suitcase and climbed the flagstone steps that led to the patio of the Pasadena Playhouse. He never forgot Lola Loraine nor the good advice she gave him.

3

Pasadena Playhouse—At Last!

Before he left Watertown, Charles had had plenty of time to read and reread the brochure that had arrived with his Playhouse application. The brochure had photographs of the interior and exterior of the building, the patio, administration offices, Main Stage Auditorium, the East and West Balcony Theatres where students performed their productions, the Patio Theatre used for experimental theater, and many photographs of students attending classes. At the back of the main structure, a six-story tower rose that housed rehearsal halls, the wardrobe department, and, at the very top, a snack bar and an open-air roof garden.

Charles was interested to learn that the Playhouse had been founded by Gilmor Brown, an actor-manager, who had brought his small touring troupe of actors to Pasadena in 1916. They were the Savoy Stock Company then, and later The Community Players, when they performed in a leaky-roofed building on North Fair Oaks.

By 1924, funds were raised to build the sophisticated theatrical complex at its present site at 39 South El Molino Avenue, just off and below Colorado Boulevard. Architect Elmer Gray, the man who had designed the world-famous Grauman's Chinese Theatre on Hollywood Boulevard, was commissioned to complete the Playhouse at a cost (over budget) of $400,000. Because of a shortage of funds, Elmer Gray had to use his ingenuity in order to meet Gilmor Brown's demand for a "beautiful building" and still keep the costs down. One of his cost-cutting inspirations was to paint the ceiling of the Main Stage Auditorium on canvas to resemble ornate and colorful Spanish tile. The illusion was, and is, perfect to this day. The Main Stage asbestos curtain depicts a Spanish galleon under full sail, and in full color, painted by artist Alson Clark.

In May 1925, the renamed Pasadena Community Playhouse opened its doors and thrived for the next forty years. In 1936, the Playhouse formalized its famous College of Theatre Arts. Among those who participated were Victor Mature, Tyrone Power, Robert Preston, Robert Young, Raymond Burr, Bob Cummings, Dana Andrews, Laird Cregar, Robert Taylor, Victor Jory, and Morris Ankrum.

Gilmor Brown was one of the first to experiment with theater-in-the-round. He created The Playbox, an intimate, flexible-staging area in his own living room, and membership was invitational. Later, he built a new, more elaborate Playbox behind his home on Herkimer Street, with a fireplace, French windows, a gallery, and a staircase leading to a balcony across one wall.

Many plays were performed at The Playbox, including the premiere of *Angel Street,* starring Judith Evelyn, which was eventually produced on Broadway, and *Manya,* the story of Marie Curie, dramatized by a young Pasadena Playhouse student named Bobker ben Ali. Gilmor Brown had invited ben Ali to do the play at The Playbox in 1938. Bill Beedle, a young Pasadena Junior College student, was recruited to play a small part in the play, and soon after he was given a screen test at Paramount Studios. He was signed to a contract, and his long screen career began after his name was changed to William Holden.

All of this history was churning around in Charles Pierce's head as he stood on the Pasadena Playhouse patio on that sunny August day in 1946. His eyes roamed over the scene before him. At last! Tall palm trees, like scaly brown pillars, lined the street. The theater building, designed in the Spanish style, had wide arched entrances, rough stuccoed walls, and terra-cotta tiled roofed structures that formed a U-shape on three sides of the spacious, open-air patio. Orange canvas umbrellas shaded rough-hewn wooden tables and chairs, and two dark-leafed Chinese elm trees stood in opposite corners of the space, one high over the ornate Spanish fountain, quietly splashing cool water into its tiled holding basin.

The patio was alive with students, some seated at the tables, some conversing in groups, others studying their lines or even rehearsing scenes. Instantly, Charles loved all this activity and excitement, and he knew he had made the right decision. He was in his element, and his heart raced as he made his way to the Office of Admissions, where he encountered Margot Poley, busy at her cluttered desk.

"Excuse me, Miss Poley. I'm Charles Pierce."

Margot Poley looked up from the papers on her desk and let her glasses, suspended by jeweled cords on each ear piece, drop to her chest. Admissions Director Margot Poley was a no-nonsense woman, but kindly, with her graying hair, lined features, and bright brown eyes. A slash of bright red lipstick was her only cosmetic.

"Ah, yes, Mr. Pierce. I received all your papers and your letter, and everything is in order. You've arrived rather early, but that's all right. Of course, you've made living arrangements?"

"Actually, no. I wasn't sure how to go about that. I was hoping you can help me."

"That's what I'm here for. We have several residence halls up the street where students are housed, but it will take a bit of time to arrange a room for you there. Meanwhile, you can stay across the street in 'The Little Gray Home in the West.' " She chuckled. "The students named it that. I call it 'The Little Gray Home' for short. It's a bungalow we've leased for overflow male students to put them up until permanent housing can be arranged." She handed Charles a key.

"The place is practically vacant—just one other student, Ty Raden. He'll be glad to have some company, I'm sure."

The bungalow was really quite spacious, with a small veranda, an entry hall, a large living room, a hallway that led to a dining room, a kitchen, a bathroom, and four small bedrooms. However, there was no cooking, so even the kitchen, living room, and dining room had been screened off to make sleeping space for the male students. Large windows let in the afternoon sunlight.

The place smelled musty, and it needed a good cleaning and airing out, Charles thought, as he walked down the hallway to Room 2, which had been assigned to him. Across the hall, the door to Room 1 was open wide, and seated on the bed was a man about thirty years old, bare-chested, and clad only in his Jockey shorts. When he saw Charles, he quickly put away the magazine he was holding.

Charles didn't think this fellow was an actor type, but then you never could tell. He had a slender, sturdy body, a hairy chest, and a real California tan, but he looked more like a construction worker than an actor. His dark hair was an unruly mop, and when his eyes met Charles', they were deep, almost purple, and he needed a shave badly.

"Hi, I'm Charles Pierce. The office sent me over here for a room. You must be Ty."

"Raden—Ty Raden." The man reached out his hand, but remained seated on the bed. His handshake was firm, and he held Charles' hand a moment too long.

Ty's room was spartan. Just a twin bed, a small dresser and mirror, and one wooden straight-backed chair. The floor was linoleum-covered, with a small rag rug by the bed.

Charles explained that he'd just arrived after a long train ride, and what he wanted most was a shave, a shower, and a good, long rest.

"The shower's down the hall." Ty retrieved his magazine from under a pillow.

Charles unlocked the door to his room and stepped inside. It was almost identical to Ty Raden's room except that the one window was larger. He opened it immediately to let in warm but much-needed air. A slight breeze fluttered the thin curtains. Hopefully, it would cool off toward evening.

After he had arranged his meager belongings in the chest of drawers, Charles stripped naked, but stopped to admire himself in the dusty mirror. Not bad, he thought. He'd reached his full height of six feet, and he was lean and strong. No bulging muscles, but his body was smooth and hairless, except for his long legs with their covering of blond hair that matched his shaggy mane. He tied a towel at this waist, picked up his shaving kit, and walked down the hall to the bathroom.

He shaved, then stepped under the warm spray of the shower, reveling in the scented soap that foamed over his body. How great to be thoroughly clean and refreshed after the long train ride! He thought about his showers with David Hartley, and he instantly became aroused.

"Not now," he said to his eager, upstanding erection. "I've gotta get some shut-eye first."

He toweled himself off, draped the towel around his waist again, and, with his kit in his hand, unlocked his door. Ty's door was still open, and Ty was still seated on the bed. He gave Charles a quick glance, then went back to his reading.

Charles entered his room, closing the door behind him. How tired he was! He walked to the window, closed the thin curtains that screened out most of the hot afternoon sun, whipped off his towel, threw himself down on the bed, completely naked, and sprawled on his back. Instantly, he was in a deep sleep.

Was he dreaming? It seemed like a dream. Fingers tracing gentle patterns on his chest and nipples, slowly moving down his body to his belly.

"David?—David?" he was still only half-awake, still in a hazy drowse.

The fingers continued, caressing his inner thighs, down even farther to his lower legs and feet. Then they were lightly, gently, massaging his thighs, and moving slowly to touch his aroused manhood. God! It felt so good! David really knew how to turn him on! He licked his dry lips, moaned, moved his hips slowly upward, and called David's name again.

Suddenly, he felt the thrilling sensation of moist lips and a hot mouth engulfing him, but he drowsed on, savoring the sensation. His hips began moving again, this time upward to bury himself in the hot, moist cavity that was taking him to places he'd never been before.

"Oh, David, David, it feels so good," he muttered. "Don't stop!" He was half conscious now, and the hot mouth became more insistent.

By now, he had completely surrendered to the driving force that had taken possession of him, and there was no turning back.

"Oh, God! Oh, God! Please take me! Suck my cock!" He was almost in tears, his heart racing. "I'm gonna cum—gonna cum! Oh, God!" He exploded then, and it was over. He awoke, sat upright, startled and confused. Where was he? Where was David? What had happened to him? He looked down at his naked body and saw that he was erect, and then, as his eyes became accustomed to the dark—only the light from a streetlight outside shone onto the bed—he saw the shadowy figure kneeling over him. It wasn't David! It was Ty Raden!

"What the hell? How did you get in here?" Charles was furious that this stranger had entered his room and had taken such liberties with him.

"Your door was unlocked." Ty's voice was calm. Charles wondered—had he really forgotten to lock his door? Evidently. He'd been so exhausted.

"Get outta here! What are you, some kind of queer?"

"No, I'm the real thing. I'm not 'kind of queer'; I'm really queer." Ty gave an amused chuckle.

"Well, I don't think it's funny, and don't try it again. You'll have to learn not everyone's like you."

"Oh, c'mon, Dorothy, it's not the end of the Yellow Brick Road. You'll survive. In a year or two you'll be cruising the tearooms just like me. You know the old saying—'this year's trade is next year's competition.' I'm sure you liked it more than you want to admit. I never knew a guy to say no to a blow job."

"Well, just keep your hands off me from now on. Okay?"

"How about my mouth? Seems to me you really dug it. Don't protest so much. You're gonna find I'm not the only one around this place that's gay. The woods are full of us fairies." Ty climbed off the bed and slid a hand into his shorts to arrange himself.

"Will you please get outta here? I'm starving, and now I've gotta take another shower."

Ty chuckled again, walked to the door, and turned to face Charles.

"Relax, Dorothy, you're not in Kansas anymore." He stepped into the hall and closed the door behind him.

Charles lay on the bed for a long time. He thought about what Ty had done to him, and he realized that, actually, it hadn't hurt him in any way, and to be honest, he'd found it to be pretty exciting and a fantastic release. Now he knew how David felt that day Charles had serviced him in the school basement.

"Well, it's true," Charles said aloud. "Toto, we're not in Watertown anymore!"

4

Extracurricular Lessons in Sex

It was still early evening when Charles set out to explore his newly adopted city. The air was cooler now, and it was dark along South El Molino Avenue, except for the glow from an occasional streetlight. He walked the short distance to Colorado Boulevard and the glare of neon and flashing signs, the sound of traffic, and the hubbub of pedestrians. An Albert Sheetz Restaurant, a chain that served plate specials, sandwiches, soups, coffee, and ice cream, stood on the corner of Colorado Boulevard and South El Molino Avenue. Across the street, catercornered from Sheetz, was Nardi's bar. Later, Charles would discover that both establishments were Playhouse "hangouts."

Albert Sheetz was crowded, so Charles turned left on Colorado and noticed the brightly lighted Broadway Pasadena Department Store, and farther down, across the street, a large Sears. He passed other cafes, clothing stores, and shops, until he came to Robert's French Restaurant, housed in a storefront building, and entered. The place was dimly lit, with a few white-clothed tables, an intimate, cozy atmosphere. Soft music was playing, and lace curtains screened the large front windows.

The dinner was excellent, and the place became one of Charles' favorite dining spots during his two-year stay at Pasadena Playhouse.

Charles continued his walk west on Colorado Boulevard until he came to the huge arched cement bridge that spanned the Arroyo Seco Canyon. Standing at the railing, he saw, through the high chain-link fence, the world-famous Rose Bowl, barely visible in the deep shadows far below. He didn't know at the time that he was standing on the notorious "Suicide Bridge," and that the fence was to prevent future suicides from occurring.

Walking back toward the Playhouse, Charles noticed that the movie theater across the street from Nardi's bar was showing a Bette

Davis picture, *A Stolen Life,* and, even though he had seen it in Watertown, he bought a ticket and went in.

After the movie, Charles stopped by Nardi's bar. Of course, at that time he didn't know that it was a favorite "watering hole" for Playhouse people. As he entered, the bar was on the right, with stools lining it, and a row of booths was along the wall on the left. The place had no theme or interesting Playhouse memorabilia on its walls. With the Playhouse so close by, it seemed strange to Charles that there were no photographs of students who had gone on to theatrical and movie fame. A few men were drinking and smoking at the bar, and the jukebox was throbbing out a Sinatra ballad, "I Fall in Love Too Easily."

Charles took a stool at the bar, ordered a draft beer, and when he glanced in the mirror, he saw Ty Raden just a few stools away. Charles pondered whether to join Ty—there was a vacant seat next to him—when Ty looked over at Charles and motioned for him to come over.

"Well, what are you up to?" Ty asked, taking a slug of his drink and a long drag on his cigarette.

"I walked down Colorado to the bridge, had dinner along the way, then saw the movie across the street."

"Oh, yeah, Bette Davis, the favorite of the fags. I dig her, too. She's got guts."

Ty gave Charles the lowdown on the "Suicide Bridge," the coming Rose Parade that would be the highlight of New Year's Day 1947, and that Sheetz and Nardi's were favorite spots for Playhouse students.

"You know so much about Pasadena and the Playhouse. You can't be a first-year student."

"No, I've done my two years, and now I'm beginning my third year—to get my master's." Frankie Laine's "That's My Desire" came on the jukebox.

"I guess that's the wise thing to do, but I'll have to wait and see if I'm invited back for a third year. First, I've gotta get my two years in."

"I figure if I get my master's, I can always teach. Some of the teachers at school are frustrated actors, and if a call comes through from one of the Hollywood studios and they're right for the part, they're just as eager and competitive as any first-year student. If they're not right for the part, they'll send one of their favorites. That's how it works."

"And how do the favorites get to be favorites? I would think that if you have talent and get good grades, you'd be eligible."

Ty chortled at that.

"You really are just off the farm, aren't you? I guess you can't grasp the fact that the old casting couch is alive and well, and that most of you first-year kiddies will do anything for a part. Of course, sleeping with the faculty is no guarantee that you'll get that part. Sometimes it works, but in most cases, it doesn't. I don't know of any surefire formula for succeeding in this business."

"Did you have any experiences on the casting couch?"

"No, I've never had sex with any of the faculty because they don't turn me on, and I won't do it just to get a part. Maybe I should, but I'm particular about who I have sex with, and maybe that will keep me from getting ahead, I don't know."

The bar was filling up, and the air was heavy with smoke. Charles didn't want his asthma to kick in, so he finished his beer and prepared to leave.

"Yeah, it is getting late. I'll walk back with you to the bungalow." Charles thought Ty was really quite handsome now that he had spent more time with him, and though he really was a stranger, somehow he was familiar, too. He had given Charles pleasure and had not demanded anything in return. Charles decided that he liked Ty Raden and was grateful for his company. The lyrics to Sinatra's song were still lingering in his mind: "I fall in love too easily. . . ." Was he falling in love with Ty? He was afraid, and still, he was excited and wanted something more to happen between them.

The two men crossed the street and continued into the darkness of the parking lot, and then to the entrance to the "Little Gray Home." Charles' heart was beating fast and his mouth was dry. His body was beginning to shake slightly, and he had a throbbing erection.

Charles followed Ty down the darkened hall to Ty's door. As they entered the room, Ty snapped on the bedside lamp, bathing the room in warm, seductive light. Ty seated himself on the bed and turned the knob on the clock radio, and soft background music came on.

"Come and sit here." Ty indicated the space next to him, and Charles joined him. "It's early—relax."

Ty lay back on the bed, his arms folded behind his dark head.

"I don't know about you, but I'm horny as hell." He reared up suddenly, took Charles' face in his large, strong hands, and kissed him full on the lips, forcing Charles' mouth to take his demanding tongue.

"It's time you learned a thing or two about sex, and I can teach you. I'm gonna give you the fucking of your life! Now, take your clothes off."

Charles slid off the bed and out of his clothes, and Ty did the same. The two naked men faced each other for an instant, embraced, and sprawled headlong onto the bed.

"You sure dug my giving you head this afternoon. Now it's your turn to do me. Ever suck a guy's cock?"

"Once—in high school." Charles gave Ty a brief account of his experience with David Hartley.

Ty was fully aroused. He broke away and sat on the edge of the bed with his legs wide apart, his full erection straining for relief.

"Come on, kneel down there between my legs and make love to my big dick. It's waiting for your hot mouth."

Charles rose from the bed and knelt before Ty. He leaned forward and let his mouth slide over Ty's erection, and suddenly, he wasn't afraid or nervous anymore.

Ty pushed Charles' head away.

"Get on the bed." Ty's voice was hoarse and urgent.

Charles did as he was told. He was curious and eager to learn what Ty would do next.

"Lie on your back."

Ty covered Charles' body with his own and they kissed again. Ty's body had a musky scent and his skin was moist and warm. His mouth wandered down Charles' body until it engulfed the large erection at the base of Charles' belly. Then he reached into a drawer of the bedside stand, squeezed lubricant from a tube onto his own erection, and ordered Charles to raise his legs and rest them on Ty's strong shoulders. Ty's fingers found Charles' opening and lubricated it deeply with a long, thick finger. Charles winced, then lay still.

"That pretty little ass of yours is just waiting for my big cock. Oh, man! I'm gonna fuck you silly!" With that, he slowly entered Charles' opening, and when he did, Charles cried out in pain. How could he take Ty's huge manhood? How could he get through this? Ty's body was insistent, and soon he had entered Charles completely, and a steady, pounding rhythm had begun.

Charles was moaning, half sobbing.

"No! I can't stand it—please stop—I can't—!" But Ty continued the steady rhythmic driving until Charles cried out again, but this time it was different.

"Don't stop! Fuck me, fuck me!" And then he came and soon after Ty cried out and burst inside the warmth that held him. Ty collapsed onto Charles' body and held him close, his manhood still embedded there.

Charles saw very little of Ty after that, until about a year later, when he began seeing a lot of Ty on the local movie screens. He had become one of Hollywood's most famous Western stars with a macho image—married, with two kids, and living on a ranch in Chatsworth!

5

"Make Me a Star!"

After the long night with Ty Raden, Charles felt he had learned the complete Kama Sutra of gay sex. It had opened his eyes to a lot of things, and now he knew more about what he wanted, and what he didn't want. In the heat of passion, he had cried out to Ty that he loved him, but Ty had said to forget it, that what they had done together was just sex, not love. Ty was not about to get involved in any kind of relationship. His career came first.

Charles realized that the experience he had with Ty was not unlike the one he'd had with David Hartley. He decided to put it out of his mind and concentrate on his studies.

He left "The Little Gray Home in the West" for a more comfortable room, which he shared with three other fellows at Tee's Residence Hall on North El Molino Avenue, about a block from the Playhouse. The windows of the large room gave a spacious view of the front lawn and the huge old magnolia trees that lined the street.

Charles settled in at his new home at Tee's and soon became friendly with his roommates. All were in the first year fall section, so he spent a lot of time with them when classes began after Labor Day 1946.

So many classes! He'd never been kept so busy, but he enjoyed every minute of them. Classes in makeup, voice, speech, introduction to Shakespeare, theater technique, history of the theater, manners and customs, costume design, radio and television, music appreciation, stage movement, dance, fencing, and elementary acting.

One of the first classes was stage movement; the students walked in a large circle while the instructor told them to place the balls of their feet down first, keeping the foot straight ahead, not pointing it to the side like a duck's waddle, then placing the heel on the floor. Charles was wearing a pair of soft leather Indian moccasins, and he was the only one in the class who walked the walk correctly. At the next session, the whole class attended wearing Indian moccasins!

In manners and customs, they studied how ancient people lived and dressed, what they ate, and diagrams of their houses, all of which were very important if you were in a play set in a bygone period.

Most of all, the students were eager to act in a play. The first student production was always a modern play, then a Greek one, and finally, a Shakespearean one, performed on the Main Stage for the faculty and students. After that, students were assigned roles in various plays set in various periods, by a number of different playwrights. Those productions would be performed in two student theaters, the East and West Balcony Theatres, for paying audiences.

Charles' grades were excellent and he was quickly assigned a Strindberg play in the East Balcony Theatre. Later, his best role was in *Engaged,* an English farce by W. S. Gilbert of Gilbert and Sullivan fame.

When *Engaged* opened, the word spread all over the Playhouse campus.

"Have you seen Charles Pierce in *Engaged?* He's a riot!"

His performance was brilliant, and the theater was sold out each night of the play's run. That was Charles' first taste of deafening applause, and he was hooked for life.

After Charles was so successful in *Engaged,* his fellow students, both men and women, suddenly found him to be "very interesting." He was often seen around campus surrounded by a group of laughing and chattering girls glancing up at him with smiling faces. Charles wasn't movie-star gorgeous, but he did have a manner and looks that attracted both sexes. He was now six feet tall, always tanned, and had those big, blue, long-lashed eyes, a mop of bright blond hair, and a wicked sense of humor. If he enjoyed a romp in the hay with the boys, nobody seemed to care.

At this time, Charles became acquainted with several students who remained his friends until the end of his life. There was Arlyne Gross, a pretty blonde, Bonnie Altman, a vivacious brunette, Bernie Wiesen, and Leonard Gumley, all from New York. Bernie Wiesen became a well-known producer/director and the head of talent at Twentieth Century-Fox Studios in Hollywood.

There were other successful students, most of them from Charles' fall section. George Nader, probably the most handsome man on campus, and a cinch to become a movie star, began his career at Twentieth Century-Fox. Later, Universal International Pictures signed him to a long contract, and eventually, he starred in a series of spy films in Europe. Two successful television series followed, *Ellery Queen* in 1958 and *Man and the Challenge* in 1959. His best known films include *Away All Boats, Carnival Story,* and *The Second Greatest Sex.* George Nader was the campus sex symbol, and it was rumored that some of the girls bored a peephole through the wall of the men's shower room, hoping to catch a glimpse of George in all his naked glory. Those who claimed success reported that the sight was most gratifying. Even some of the male students got more than their hopes up when they showered with George and caught a glance of his generous manhood.

Rose Mary Emma, the most beautiful girl in school, was also destined for stardom. Her big break came right after graduation when MGM Studios signed her to a contract and changed her name to Joan Taylor. Her lustrous dark hair and eyes convinced the studio to cast her as the Indian maiden in the remake of the musical *Rose Marie,* starring Ann Blyth and Howard Keel. Unfortunately, she played Indian maidens in most of the pictures that followed. She finally gave up acting when she married Leonard Freeman, a young student in the class after hers. He became one of television's most successful producers with shows that included *Hawaii Five-0* and *77 Sunset Strip.*

Leonard Gumley was cast as "Private Sid Stein" in the John Wayne film *Sands of Iwo Jima* in 1949. Elsie Holmes, also in Charles' fall section, a tall, striking-looking actress with a low, sultry voice and a resemblance to Diana Rigg of *The Avengers,* played the role of a spoiled rich girl in the Ray Milland film *Rhubarb,* the story of a cat that inherits a baseball team. She married James Hobson, the producer/director of *The Lawrence Welk Show.*

Cathedral Films, a producer of religious films, put out a call to the Playhouse for young men to audition for the role of a naive young fellow for a film they had in production. The plot concerned two mature bank robbers who dupe the young man into joining them on a heist. Charles won the part and the production was soon completed. The film was never shown commercially, but a 16 mm version was available for rental, and years later, Charles would show it at parties just for laughs. His performance was very amateurish, and he wisely chose a career in comedy after that.

In April 1947, the fall section students had completed their first year of training, and the class was in hiatus until November 1947, when they would return, complete their second year, and graduate in June 1948.

Charles decided to spend the summer with his parents and Aunt Carolyn in Watertown, and he was happy to be back again in all the old familiar places. He visited WNNY, the radio station where he had begun his radio career. His friends were eager to hear all about his California adventures and about the movie stars he had met.

Jessie, Charles' mother, was ecstatic to have her son home again. The bond between them was so special and so strong. Sometimes his being away from her was more than she could bear, but she knew he was doing what he wanted and loved. She knew he'd come home to her whenever he could, and he did write or phone every week. She had to face the fact that he was a grown man now. It was so close to the holiday season, and now it was time for him to leave. She couldn't hold back the tears as she clung to this son whom she adored with all her heart. Soon he was again on the train bound for Pasadena and, hopefully, a career of success and stardom.

6

Stars in My Eyes

I first heard about Pasadena Playhouse in 1941, when I was attending Santa Monica City College by day and working at Douglas Aircraft Company at night.

It was Occupations Day at the college, and the actor Morris Ankrum spoke on the subject of stage and screen acting, and the training to be had in that field at Pasadena Playhouse. He was an authority on the subject, having been a stage and film actor for many years, and a director at the Playhouse.

I still had theatrical ambitions that began when I was nine years old and my parents had enrolled me with an elocution teacher for lessons in drama and public speaking. After winning a medal in a speaking contest and appearing on the radio in a kiddie show, my "brilliant career" had ended when my father moved our family to the woods of Oregon.

Morris Ankrum pointed out the advantages of a theatrical career, but he also mentioned the negative side. I still remember his words:

> You can spend years studying at a drama school, learning everything about your craft, but then some guy who pumps gas down at the corner filling station, who's never taken an acting lesson in his life, but who just happens to be born with curly, blond hair, muscles, and a lopsided grin, will get the part.

How right he was! Of course, I didn't know that at the time, so I thought his pessimism was just sour grapes. Naturally, I thought that I'd be one of the lucky ones if I attended classes at the Playhouse. However, when Pearl Harbor was attacked that December, all thoughts of attending drama school vanished. My two-year hitch in the navy began soon after and ended in June 1946.

I returned to my job at Douglas Aircraft Company, but I continued to consider enrolling at the Playhouse. Finally, I filled out the application, was accepted, drove to the Playhouse to finalize my enrollment and to line up a place to live. I would have my two years of tuition paid in full under the GI Bill, which allowed all servicepeople to attend college, and I would receive $65 each month for living expenses.

When I walked into the entrance hallway at the Playhouse, I saw a small group of students gathered near the elevator to the tower, chattering away, and every time another student would join the group, they'd all shout, "Dahling!", hug, and give each other air kisses to the sound of "mmm-wah," then go on chattering again. It all seemed so artificial, theatrical, and rather fascinating.

The office sent me up El Molino Avenue to Hobart's Hall, a large, rambling, three-story residence run by Mrs. Hobart, a woman in her sixties, a bit overweight, and definitely the motherly type. She had a rare skin disease that caused scaling on her face, and it eventually killed her.

Mrs. Hobart showed me around the premises and told me how an actor named Richard Norris had been one of her tenants while he studied at the Playhouse, and that he had just finished playing the lead role in a new film version of *Abie's Irish Rose*. She didn't promise that she'd have a room for me, so I returned to Santa Monica and my job.

December 30, 1946, arrived, I said farewell to Douglas Aircraft Company, and, with stars in my eyes, I drove my 1929 Ford sedan to the Pasadena Playhouse to be ready for my first class in January 1947. Mrs. Hobart hadn't contacted me about renting the room, so I asked Margot Poley in the admissions office what I should do. She handed me a key to a room at "The Little Gray Home in the West."

"Just until we find you a permanent residence," she smiled.

I picked my suitcase up and headed across the street, but just as I reached the curb, I was hailed by Mrs. Hobart, her face a patchwork of tiny adhesive bandages.

"Where have you been? I've been looking all over for you." She was having difficulty breathing.

"But, Mrs. Hobart," I said, "I didn't hear from you, and I thought—"

"It's okay. Come along, I have a room for you."

I ran back to the office and returned the key. Mrs. Hobart led the way to her house on North El Molino Avenue, stopping occasionally to gulp in a large breath of balmy, but crisp, winter air.

We walked through the dark entry hall and up two flights of rickety stairs to an airless attic bedroom under the eaves. A pair of rain-stained dormer windows gave gloomy light to the space and offered a glimpse of the street below. Rag rugs barely covered the wooden floor and two twin beds stood side by side, separated by two matching nightstands. The rest of the furniture consisted of a forlorn-looking dresser, a desk, and a chair. An ill-smelling pile of unwashed clothes was thrown by the entrance to the cavernous walk-in closet, and the light switch was inoperable.

"He's gone out, I guess." She indicated one of the twin beds, piled with dirty sheets, pillows, and quilts. The room reeked of dirty laundry, stale cigarette smoke, and the remnants of a half-eaten enchilada on the bedside nightstand. An overflowing ashtray, heaped with smelly cigarette butts, candy-bar wrappers, and a jar of Vaseline were in complete disarray on top of the stand. I wondered what my roommate would be like, and from all appearances so far, I was pretty sure we weren't going to be compatible. I needed the room, so I'd have to give it a try.

"I'll be gone for a week, starting today. I'm going to visit my daughter in Pomona, so I'll settle with you when I get back." She went out the door and disappeared into the darkness of the stairs.

I had just gone to bed around midnight when I heard my door open and close, and I could see, in the murky darkness, the figure of a man enter and walk to the other bed. He disrobed down to his shorts, climbed into bed, propped himself up on the pillows and lit a cigarette. I could see the red glow of the tip and smell the acrid smoke as it rose above his head.

Eventually, I dozed off, but sometime in the early morning hours, perhaps 2 or 3 a.m., I was awakened by my roommate's deep voice speaking, in a hoarse whisper, a litany of sexual innuendo, just audible enough to awaken me, and to give me the creeps.

He went on and on, reciting his obscene monologue about what kind of sex acts he would perform on me and describing what my reaction would be. I'd never encountered anything like it before, so I thought it best not to confront him and to pretend to be asleep.

He finally crushed out his cigarette and ended his ramblings, and I fell asleep. The next morning he was fully dressed and preparing to leave when he noticed I was awake.

"Did I talk in my sleep last night? The other guy who just moved out accused me of it. By the way, I'm Bart—Bart Weldon."

I didn't say my name or shake hands.

"I didn't hear anything. I was pretty tired, so I slept right through." I knew he wasn't talking in his sleep because I saw him smoking his cigarette while he was babbling on. I knew I had to find another room, but Mrs. Hobart was gone, and I couldn't afford a hotel on my meager savings. It would be a month before my GI check would come through.

Fortunately, three fellow students had a vacancy in their room on the second floor, so I gathered my possessions and moved in with them. What a difference! So much light and air from the high windows, a large bathroom, a walk-in closet, a big round table and chairs, carpeted floor, and a twin bed for each of us. A radio playing classical music added to the calm and pleasant atmosphere.

The courses I took were identical to those of Charles, but because he and I were in different sections, we seldom saw each other. It's strange to think of it now, but in the two years we spent at the Playhouse, we never exchanged a single word.

About this time, one of the Playhouse directors asked me if I'd like to drive over to San Fernando Valley for a snack after classes. I agreed, and we drove in his car to a quaint beer garden set in the hills of Sunland. I didn't know Rory Vanderberg well, but he seemed pleasant enough, and when you're a student you hope that a director might want you for his next production. Rory was a rather roly-poly type, with a round bald head, a fringe of dark curly hair over his ears, a pointed goatee, and a face that was moist and oily. He was not an attractive fellow, but his reputation at the Playhouse was excellent because he had discovered a famous film actor, and he never let anyone forget it. But in spite of that, Rory didn't direct a single play during my two years at the Playhouse.

We talked very little as we drove to the Valley. Arriving at the beer garden, we ordered sandwiches and a couple of beers, sat awhile in the warm evening air, listened to the rollicking polka music on the jukebox, and watched couples dancing under the strings of colorful paper lanterns. It was very pleasant just to kick back after the hectic pace of the Playhouse classes. But Rory was silent and remote, and I finally gave up trying to converse with him.

On the drive back to Pasadena, Rory kept his gaze straight ahead on the road. Then, without looking at me, he blurted out a question he'd probably been mulling over for some time.

"How do you feel about sex?"

"Whaddya mean—sex?" I asked. His question did surprise me.

"You know, sex—going to bed with me."

I didn't want to alienate him, so I told him I was at the Playhouse to concentrate on my studies and that I didn't think it wise to have sexual relations with the faculty.

Immediately, Rory's face turned dark and furious, and he stepped hard on the gas pedal as we sped faster and faster toward Pasadena. It's a wonder that he didn't stop the car and put me out, but he drove on in silence. He was stone cold when he dropped me off in front of the Playhouse, refusing to look at me, and driving off in a fury.

After thinking it over, I've come to the conclusion that I sealed my fate at the Playhouse that evening when I rejected Rory's advances. Suddenly, I didn't get any acting assignments in student productions, only stage managing or performing some other technical chore. We were supposed to stage manage only one production, but I was getting one after the other, and I was missing out on roles I should have performed.

Finally, I confronted Dean Thomas Browne Henry, complaining about my assignments. He was a tall man with straight black hair slicked back from his forehead, snappy dark eyes, an intimidating, sarcastic attitude, and an enormous hatchet nose, not unlike Dick Tracy's in the comics.

After I'd finished my complaint, he smirked at me, his lip twisted in a sneer.

"Well, you know, John, you're very limited."

That remark made me furious, and I wanted to lash out at him that with his ugly nose he was more limited than I! I held it all in, but after that, when he called roll at assembly, he always called me some ridiculous name like "John Wharfrat" or "John Woof-Woof." Very amusing! The student assembly always laughed.

The interview with the dean did me no good, and I continued to get stage managing assignments. One of them was for *Blood Wedding,* the Lorca play performed at The Playbox with handsome George Nader in the leading role. Another time, it was Ibsen's *The Pre-*

tenders, and Charles Pierce had the small part of a heavily robed monk. We still had no contact with each other.

The "Powers That Be" must have finally decided they'd punished me enough for my refusal to sleep with Rory Vanderberg, because I was given the part of the sadistic prison guard in *The Last Mile.* The play was well-received and the director and my classmates complimented me on my performance. My best and final role before graduation was as "Simon" in Noel Coward's *Hay Fever,* and I again received compliments on my performance, and good grades.

Now I had completed my two-year certificate course, and I would graduate in June 1948 and receive my diploma. But what had I really learned? Was I prepared for a career in the theater or motion pictures after studying all the courses? Where would I go from here? The Playhouse had no program for placing or recommending students for acting jobs. It was up to the students themselves to make their own opportunities. Some of the classes had been very worthwhile, but many were a waste of time.

I remember in "Introduction to Shakespeare," the teacher spent each session reminiscing about his own stage career, then assigned us the memorization of Hamlet's advice-to-the-players speech, "Speak the speech I pray thee . . ." and we would stand and recite it. We should have been learning to read from a cold script as we would have to do at a "cattle call" audition. Listening to his account of his theatrical adventures was interesting but totally useless.

Once you have graduated and left the confines of the place you've called home for two years, and in which you have been exposed to an unceasing theatrical atmosphere, it's difficult to go out into the real world and sell yourself as an actor. Even George Nader, who had everything in his favor, became terribly discouraged. In an interview with *After Dark* in 1978, he recounted how he had contemplated suicide after many discouragements:

"One day when I was driving home from another disappointing interview I thought, 'Why don't you just step on the gas and not make this turn?' "[1] It's very difficult to keep your morale up after so many doors are slammed in your face.

Lola Loraine, the movie actress Charles Pierce met on the train, was so right when she told him he must have "a burning desire" to be a successful actor. One who had that "burning desire" was Paula Payson, a student actress in my class. She came from some desert town out near Mojave, and she had a hard-as-nails-coating you couldn't crack. Paula was not pretty, but she had a gorgeous figure and great legs, and she oozed sex. Her complexion was sallow and marred by acne scars, but with the proper makeup, those flaws disappeared. She was so hell-bent for stardom that she didn't wait to graduate, but headed straight for Hollywood. Small parts in low-budget films came her way and she began to appear in bigger and better roles.

When we were preparing our student production of a musical play we were assigned to, it was still to be cast. Paula stood up at the first meeting and told us that the most rewarding roles were in the chorus. It seemed odd to me that the director permitted her to take over and try to convince us that the minor roles were the best. When the play was finally cast, it was no surprise to me that Paula was playing the leading female role. I didn't end up in the chorus. I played the leading male role, and I got it legitimately.

As it turned out, it wouldn't have helped my career if I had gone along with Rory Vanderberg's advances. In spite of the fact that he had discovered that famous male star, he couldn't get a break for himself. The Playhouse seldom used his talents, and the last time I saw him he was sitting in his dilapidated old Plymouth parked in front of the Paramount Pictures gate.

"Hi, Rory. What are you doing here?" I asked as I approached his open car window. He looked puffy and sweaty, and he needed a shave.

"I'm waiting to see Bill." Bill was the famous actor he had discovered and helped. "I'm hoping he can get me on his picture as dialogue director."

"Good luck," I said, and hurried on my way.

One morning, Dean Henry called a special assembly in the Main Stage Theatre and told us that certain male students at one of the dorms were engaging in "shocking" homosexual behavior, and that it would not be tolerated. I'm sure most of the students would have laughed at that, because everyone on campus knew who was sleeping with whom, both male and female. One male couple actually wandered around campus holding hands and hugging.

A very handsome acting major named Dirk was involved in a "ménage à trois" with a male director and his wife. To look at them, you wouldn't think they were the least bit kinky. Dirk was every girl's dream of a gorgeous movie star, but offstage he was gay, gay, gay. I don't know why the director's wife stayed around—maybe she liked to watch, and being married to an important Playhouse director didn't hurt her career. She and Dirk played the leads in the director's next Playbox production. In addition, Dirk's mother contributed generously to the Playhouse coffers.

Gilmor Brown, the founder of the Pasadena Playhouse, was a quiet man who moved slowly around the campus due to his declining health. At the time I attended classes there, he was probably in his sixties. He would speak occasionally at the assemblies about his trips to see the plays currently on Broadway or about his annual tour of Europe. Each year he would select a young male student from the incoming class to be his companion on that journey. The young fellow probably thought that a trip to Europe with Gilmor Brown was a ticket to instant stardom. The two who were chosen while I was there were never heard of again.

Gilmor Brown's brother, Frank, spent a lot of his time at the Playhouse, but he never participated in any of the activities. He had a high-pitched voice, so he was never cast in a play. His wife, Arch Brown, was an interesting woman, as she, in her youth, had been Gilmor Brown's leading lady in his band of players, and she was known professionally as Virginia Likens. When I knew her she was in her late fifties, but she still had a lively personality that matched her mischievous blue eyes and her thinning snarl of dyed red hair. Each morning, when the students entered the building and took the elevator to the floors in the six-story tower that adjoined the back of the Main Stage building, Arch would station herself by the elevator door. She checked out everyone who passed to be sure they belonged there. Usually when I came by she would offer me a lozenge from a roll she always kept handy.

"They're the real rum," she'd say, and give me a sly, wicked wink. I wish there had been more Arch Browns at the Playhouse.

One morning, as I was walking down the hall to check my mailbox, a group of people approached, and I recognized one round-faced, smiling fellow with a mustache as the famous playwright, Tennessee Williams. He was visiting the Playhouse for the world premiere of his play, *Stairs to the Roof*. On opening night, the Main Stage Theatre was packed because Williams' *A Streetcar Named Desire* had recently caused a sensation on Broadway, and everyone was eager to see his latest effort. I had seen *The Glass Menagerie* in New York, and when I saw *Stairs,* I realized that, basically, it and *Menagerie* were the same play. The latter was a rewrite of the former, and it had become a hit. The Playhouse production of *Stairs to the Roof* was not well received, and I doubt that it was ever produced again.

Another well-known celebrity I saw at the Playhouse was Florence Bates, famous for her role as "Mrs. Van Hopper" in the Alfred Hitchcock film, *Rebecca*. She appeared in the Main Stage production of Zoe Atkins' *O, Evening Star,* a play based on the life of the great film star Marie Dressler.

Florence Bates was from Texas, where she had had a career in law. She was sponsoring a student in my class named William Leslie Butts. Bill was a very pleasant fellow with bright blond hair, blue eyes, a strong jaw, and a big dimple in his chin. He worked hard to overcome his thick Texas accent, and he eventually appeared as William Leslie in several films, including *Queen Bee* starring Joan Crawford and *The Long Gray Line,* a Tyrone Power film.

Burt Kennedy and Harp McGuire dropped out of school but went on to successful careers. Kennedy directed a long list of successful westerns, and McGuire played a pivotal role in *On the Beach,* the Gregory Peck and Ava Gardner film. Rudy Behlmer, who graduated in my class, went on to become a well-known Hollywood writer, coauthoring *The Films of Errol Flynn, Hollywood's Hollywood* with Tony Thomas, and *Memo from David O. Selznick.*

Graduation day finally came for me, and I was invited back for a third year. Perhaps I should have accepted the offer, as I could have tried for my master's degree in theater arts, but I was weary of trying to survive on $65 per month. Cooking cans of Franco-American spaghetti over my hot plate between checks was depressing, so I looked for a job, and decided to try my luck at the casting offices at the Hollywood studios.

At the Huntington Hotel in Pasadena, I took a job that supplied me with room and board, a small salary, tip money, and, most important of all, Thursdays off so that I could go over to the MGM casting department to show my 8 × 10 glossies to the casting director and hope to get a screen test or a part in a picture. It never happened! I needed an agent, but I couldn't get an agent unless I was in a picture or a play. I wrote a revue titled *Of All Things,* which a friend of mine produced and another friend directed. The cast consisted of three women and three men, and I had written all the best parts for myself. Nobody cared! The producer invited me to Albuquerque, New Mexico, while I was on vacation, and I played the doctor in a production of *I Remember Mama*. It was fun, but it led nowhere.

The Huntington Hotel put on a fashion show down by the pool, and two of the models were Caryl and Carolyn Seitz, twin sisters who had been in my class at the Playhouse. It was fun seeing them again, and they invited me to come to a rehearsal of a play they were doing at the now defunct Robert's French Restaurant, where Charles Pierce had had his first dinner on his arrival in Pasadena.

After work I walked down to the theater, which was arranged in arena-style much like The Playbox. James Leo Herlihy, author of the play *The Moon in Capricorn,* was putting the cast through their blocking. Still to be cast was the part of a policeman, and I was asked to play it. The play opened to mild success, but it folded quickly. The twins went on to do a Mike Hammer film and some stage work, but it was James Leo Herlihy who had the greatest success.

After a brief stay at the Playhouse, Herlihy took a room at a Playhouse annex in Hollywood called Orchard Gables, a rambling old mansion where theatrical hopefuls could reside for reasonable rent. Some Playhouse friends and I visited Jim there, but he was busy writing, so we didn't stay long.

Even though his *Moon* play failed, his later efforts were huge hits. His *All Fall Down* was filmed starring Warren Beatty and Eva Marie Saint, his play *Blue Denim* had a run on Broadway, and his most famous novel, *Midnight Cowboy,* became an Academy Award-winning picture.

I finally made a twenty-five year career as a technical illustrator, and I pretty much gave up on show business. I settled down in my comfortable apartment bordering the Hollywood Bowl and rarely thought about my crazy Playhouse days.

Then I met Charles Pierce.

7

Summer Stock and Shangri-La
for Awhile

"Look there, Al," Charles Pierce said, pointing to a bed of rose bushes that bordered the bricked path that led to the little theater building in Newport, Rhode Island.

"What?" Al Hedison was puzzled. There was nothing unusual about a bed of blooming roses.

"Why, that's where Tallulah Bankhead sprinkled the rose bushes."

"Oh, I didn't know she gardened." Al couldn't care less. He really wasn't interested in Tallulah Bankhead or her hobbies. Naturally, he'd heard of her and some of her escapades, but he'd never seen her on the stage or in a movie.

"She didn't garden, idiot. One night she was walking up this path and she decided she couldn't wait to relieve her bladder, so she hiked up her dress and let go—all over the rose bushes and in full view of passersby."

"They should put up a plaque; the roses seem to be doing just fine," Al glowered.

Charles was a Tallulah aficionado and continued on.

"You know, she had a very deep, masculine voice." Charles was eager to impart this trivia to his newfound friend. "Did you hear what she said to Noel Coward when he asked her if she had ever been mistaken for a man?"

Al gave Charles a "must you go on?" look, rolling his eyes heavenward.

"She said, 'No, have you?' " Charles roared with laughter at that one. "But the best one was what she said at a dinner party one night when someone asked her if Montgomery Clift was gay, and she answered, 'I don't know, dahling, he never sucked my cock.' "

"Where do you get this crap?" Al had other things on his mind and found Charles' anecdotes tiresome. Charles didn't answer, and the two men walked the rest of the way in silence.

After graduation from Pasadena Playhouse, Charles had flown home again in 1951 to Watertown, and, after a long visit with his parents and Aunt Carolyn, he returned to his former job at Station WWNY and eventually made his way to the bright lights of Broadway. He spent a lengthy time in Manhattan, going to auditions, and during that stay he wandered one evening into the bar of the famous Plaza Hotel. Later, as he crossed the lobby near the elevators, he encountered actor Charles Laughton and a male companion. The two men were in town in connection with the production of their hit Broadway show. When Charles Pierce approached Laughton for his autograph, Laughton invited him to join them in their suite. Pierce was young and handsome and fresh from the classrooms of Pasadena Playhouse, and Laughton and his companion, who was the husband of a famous Academy Award-winning actress, were both interested in the young man. Charles Pierce accompanied the two famous personages to their suite, where they all indulged in several rounds of drinks. Before the night ended Charles Pierce had not only anally satisfied the Oscar-winning actress's husband, but he had been serviced orally to boot! After that memorable night, he left Manhattan for a job with a little theater group in Newport, Rhode Island.

At first, it was fun helping to build scenery and running errands, putting up posters, and working in wardrobe. But he had done all those things at the Playhouse, and now he wanted to act. After performing a number of walk-on parts he was rewarded with the title role in a production of *The Man Who Came to Dinner*. It was a real stretch for the youthful twenty-five-year-old to create the cantankerous middle-aged "Sheridan Whiteside," but he came through with flying colors and enthusiastic reviews.

Soon the season was over, and he set his sights westward to California, where he felt he'd have more chances to make good.

Al Hedison, Charles' newfound friend, was also getting restless as nothing was happening for him in Rhode Island. He had tried his luck in New York City to no avail and had finally been glad to get the summer stock job. He, too, believed Hollywood to be the right move for him, so both men went west that year in 1952.

Soon after his arrival in California, Hedison was cast in the title role in *The Fly,* a science fiction film, also starring Vincent Price. He changed his name to David Hedison, and the film became a cult favorite until it was remade with Jeff Goldblum in 1986. Hedison's career never took off after that.

Charles Pierce returned to Pasadena and engaged a room at the Green Hotel, a once-fashionable establishment on Fair Oaks. He had been away from the Playhouse for four years, and his old alma mater was preparing the annual production of Dickens' *A Christmas Carol.* Charles auditioned for the part of Marley's ghost, performed it, and, in addition, was a jolly old Santa Claus at the Broadway Pasadena department store. It took a lot of padding to transform Charles' lanky frame into a rotund St. Nick, but he was convincing with his round belly, red costume, and flowing white beard. He "Ho, ho, hoed" his way through it all, and was having fun until one little girl became frightened, screamed, and wriggled, soiling Santa's lap. Charles leapt to his feet, yelled, "Enough," and ran for the showers. After that fiasco, he managed to talk his way into a job as clerk in a record shop, but that, too, was short-lived when he refused to trim his shoulder-length blond hair. Charles still had his savings from his employment back East, so he could afford to experiment for awhile.

The Playhouse agreed to sponsor him in a reading act in the East Balcony Theatre where, in *Engaged,* he had once trod the boards to much acclaim. Charles Laughton had had recent success reading selections from the Bible and other classical literature, so Charles Pierce, dressed simply in a sportscoat and slacks, read from the Bible, Shakespeare, Emily Dickinson, Noel Coward, and, in addition, gave a full-length recitation of the poem "Casey at the Bat." Only a few audiences were amused, so the show closed after only three performances.

Next, he tried reading only the Noel Coward selections at a little theater on Sunset Boulevard called Cabaret Concert. It was an atmospheric old Spanish-style stucco building that resembled a chapel, and to reach it one descended a long flight of stairs from the street level to an area just below Sunset Boulevard.

Two rather eccentric women, Kay Herbert and Miriam Schiller, operated Cabaret Concert, and because it was the era of the beatniks, they created a dark, shadowy atmosphere with candlelit tables and shows consisting of poetry readings, folksingers, and dancers in black leotards. At intermission, "mingle muffins" and hot coffee were served. The muffins were called mingle muffins because the audience was supposed to mingle while they munched. One of the dancers was Ruta Kilmonis, who danced with a male partner to a recording of "Night Train." Soon after, she appeared as one of the "seven brides" in the MGM musical *Seven Brides for Seven Brothers,* starring Howard Keel and Jane Powell. She changed her name to Ruta Lee and played a key role as Tyrone Power's mistress in *Witness for the Prosecution.*

Others who became successful after appearing at Cabaret Concert were Billy Barnes, who wrote and produced his revues there, some starring his wife, Joyce Jamison, and Jackie Joseph and Ken Berry, who later became husband and wife; Ruth Olay and Ketty Lester, both successful singers. I remember Ruth Olay singing "Any Place I Hang My Hat Is Home" and "The Gypsy in My Soul." She was a beautiful brunette with a haunting voice. Years later, Billy Barnes wrote a comedy song for Charles called "Doin' the Bette Davis," which Charles performed at the Plush Room in San Francisco.

Charles' stint at Cabaret Concert had been disappointing. He was unemployed and casting about for some sensible direction for his life. He knew he had talent, and he wasn't going to give up pursuing his dream of stardom, but he was at a loss as to where to begin.

There was a little bar on Beverly Boulevard in Hollywood called the Golden Carp, located not far from the famous Hollywood Ranch Market. With a name like that it might have been a Chinese restaurant. Now, it was a dark little boîte with a large oval-shaped bar allowing patrons to sit on all sides and cruise one another. Farther back, men played pool in an area that had once been a dance floor—dancing was no longer allowed—and a jukebox throbbed out the current hits of the day: the "Theme from a Place in the Sun," Kay Starr's "Wheel of Fortune," and Les Baxter's "Quiet Village."

Everyone hung out at the Carp: gays, straights, hustlers, and a sprinkling of actors and would-be actors, some from the Pasadena Playhouse.

One night in January 1953, I dropped by the Carp after work for a drink and the chance to see some of my ex-schoolmates from Pasadena to see what they were doing. I was now a full-fledged technical illustrator at Cannon Electric Company in Highland Park near Pasadena, although I lived in Hollywood. I was still curious about what others where doing in their pursuit of theatrical careers.

The bar was packed wall-to-wall, and the noise level was high with conversation, the clink of glasses, and the "Theme from a Place in the Sun" playing in the background. I was sipping a gimlet—all the rage at the time—when I looked up and saw Bernie Wiesen elbowing his way through the crowd at the bar. He wasn't alone. Trailing him was a tall blond fellow with a large white bandage plastered to his forehead, almost obscuring his left eye.

"Look who I found," Bernie called out to me over the noisy crowd. I didn't recognize his companion at first, probably because my eyes were on the bandage.

"Charles Pierce!" I cried out, finally realizing who he was. "What happened to you?"

"Don't ask!" he replied and pulled his mouth down in a grimace.

The two men ordered beers and we shouted across the bar at each other. We were finally able to make our way through the mass to the back of the room, where we settled in chairs around a tiny cocktail table. Charles and Bernie had just attended a performance of Arthur Blake's one-man show at the Bar of Music, a club close by the Carp. Blake was the toast of Hollywood at that time with his clever impressions of screen stars Bette Davis, Tallulah Bankhead, Gloria Swanson, Charles Laughton, Marlon Brando, former First Lady Eleanor Roosevelt, and many others. He had a clever way of becoming each personality. He would stand behind large, flat, headless, costumed, body-sized cutouts with sleeves attached so that he could slip his arms through the sleeves, rest his bewigged head above the neckline and do his routine. He could move his arms, but he had to remain stationary. The effect was stunning. Charles Pierce was so impressed with Arthur Blake's show and his talent that he talked of nothing else as we sat around the table that night at the Golden Carp.

I gave no more thought to that meeting, but one evening soon after, I visited the Pasadena Library to search for an old Isham Jones recording of "Frankie and Johnny" I had once borrowed for a Playhouse dance project. It was a rare recording with a rollicking rhythm, and I wanted to record it for my music collection. There was no record in the library files, so I suppose it had been stolen.

As I was leaving the library, who should walk in but Charles Pierce! Dressed in a dark suit, white shirt and tie, he had just come from another unsuccessful audition, and he no longer had the large white bandage over his left eye. Just a pinkish scar remained.

"Charles Pierce!" I shouted, and the librarian looked up with a "shush" and a frown.

"John Wallraff!" Charles shouted back. You'd think we were long-lost friends.

The librarian was giving us disapproving stares, and it was close to closing time. We exchanged phone numbers and addresses and went our separate ways, but suddenly Charles turned back and called out to me, "I'll be over for dinner tomorrow night."

That remark stopped me in my tracks, but before I could answer, he was gone. I was really shocked at his lack of manners, but then I thought that maybe he wasn't doing too well and needed a free meal. I had a steady job, and it wouldn't break me to help him out.

The next night, I had a skillet dinner of Pork Chops Creole simmering on the back burner—consisting of the chops, rice, bell pepper, onion, and a can of tomatoes—when the doorbell rang. There stood Charles, this time dressed casually in white sharkskin slacks, a blue and white striped pullover, sandals, and shades.

Over chilled glasses of Chablis with dinner we chattered away like two old friends who had reunited after a long absence. Our minds and our sense of humor were on the same wavelength and remained that way for all the years we were friends.

The next night after work I picked him up at his room at the Algonquin Hotel in Pasadena, and we drove to Cabaret Concert. Charles had decided to give it another try. The tables were crowded, the candles were glowing, and soft music drifted from the speakers. Charles went backstage to get ready, and I sat at a small table at the back of the room close by the plates of mingle muffins and the coffee urn.

After performances by a folksinger, a dance act, and another female singer, Charles gave a reading by Noel Coward about a shepherdess named Flannelette and her flock of sheep, which got a smattering of polite applause, but was not well received.

Back at his hotel, I didn't comment on his performance as I felt embarrassed for him, and, fortunately, he didn't ask. As I was leaving, he stopped me at the door.

"Let's go see Bette Davis in *The Star.* It just opened. How about tomorrow night?"

I said, "Okay," and the next night I was back again to pick him up. After a quick dinner at the YWCA cafeteria in Pasadena—the men's Y didn't serve food—we walked to the theater.

Charles phoned me at work the next day.

"Stop by after work. I want to show you something."

Of course I was curious, wondering what he had come up with, so I drove to his hotel and knocked on his door.

"Sit on the sofa," he said as I entered the room. "You'll be surprised."

In the film *The Star,* Bette Davis has a scene where, as has-been actress "Margaret Elliott," she has to take a screen test in order to audition for a small part in a film. She's supposed to be a dowdy, older, dishabilled scrubwoman on her knees, scrubbing the floor. Instead, before the test, "Margaret/Bette" changes her makeup and hairstyle to look more sexy and ties a scarf at the waist to show off her figure. She proceeds to do the test as a seductive siren. Of course, the test is a flop, and she loses the part.

I took my place on the sofa in Charles' hotel room as he had ordered, waiting for the "surprise," when out of the bathroom came Charles as Bette Davis on his hands and knees with a bucket at his side, holding a scrub brush and wearing a loose, sloppy kimono, with a band of toilet tissue tied across his forehead!

I gasped when I saw him, and he began a monologue as Bette Davis, a parody of the movie dialogue, batting his big blue Bette Davis eyes and giving an imaginary character sexy sidelong glances and smirks.

I fell off the couch, screaming with laughter. I'd never seen anything so hilarious, or such a dead-on impression of a famous movie star. When I could speak, I got up from the floor and shouted.

"Charles! This is what you should be doing! Forget Flannelette and get her flock the hell outta here! That was absolutely, fabulously, uproariously funny, and you've gotta do more of it."

Charles didn't say anything, but I knew he was pleased with himself and my comments.

About this time, a young fellow who had known Charles at the Playhouse told him he had a key to the wardrobe department at the Playhouse because he had been helping the wardrobe mistress, Betty Flint, sort through a pile of old costumes. He and Charles waited until 2 a.m. when the wardrobe department was deserted, then unlocked the door and helped themselves to a treasure trove of apparel. Among the items Charles took was a voluminous, black, fur-trimmed, floor-length robe, something to be worn by the Doge of Venice, Italy, during the Renaissance. They locked the door and slipped quietly away, laden with their ill-gotten garments and props.

Laguna Beach was a fun town in those days, and I had often passed through it when I hitchhiked during my navy days. Later, a friend and I had gone down for the weekend, and he introduced me to a lively bar/restaurant right down on the beach called Las Ondas.

"Let's drive down to Laguna Beach this weekend," I said to Charles soon after his impromptu Bette Davis performance in his hotel room. "There's a fun bar down there that I think you'll like, and we can relax on the sand."

"Sounds great. Let's go!"

I had recently purchased a light green Nash Rambler convertible, so when the weekend came, we put the top down, turned on the radio, and we were off.

Saturday night at Las Ondas was the busiest time, and the place was always packed. Even though it was lunchtime when we arrived, a steady stream of suntanned bodies milled around the bar. Casual dress was the order of the day, with most of the patrons clad in shorts or Speedos and little else. The jukebox was blaring out the hits of the day, including Jane Powell's "Too Late Now," from the film *Royal Wedding,* and Lena Horne's plaintive "Where or When."

The building was divided into two rooms by an open-arched partition that afforded a full view of both areas, which, in turn, faced a sweeping view of the ocean and a stretch of white sandy beach. When evening came, the tables were aglow with lighted candles and the place took on a magical atmosphere that seemed to transport one to exotic locales like Capri or the Playa del Sol in Spain.

We found a room at a weathered old frame hotel up near the slope of the mountains, but we were back in town for breakfast on Sunday morning. We put on our trunks, spread our towels on the sand, and spent most of the day "bagging some rays."

Charles began to tell me how he wanted to write a sketch based on the Gloria Swanson movie *Sunset Boulevard,* called "The Return of Norma Desmond." I thought it was a great idea, but we didn't have a pad to write it on. He did have a pen, and we found an old discarded cake carton half-buried in the sand. On it we wrote our first collaboration—material that he would use in his show until his last farewell performance. The following is, word for word, the sketch we created that long ago day in the hot sun on the sands of Laguna Beach:

"The Return of Norma Desmond"

Norma Desmond! Back with you all you wonderful people out there in the dark. You don't come to see me anymore to buy popcorn, chewing gum, peanut brittle. Why? Don't you want to know why? I'll tell you why. People who remember me can't chew.

Oh, yes. They sent me away for shooting my friend, William Holden. He fell into my swimming pool. I had two—one to rinse off in.

They sent me away to a tropical island—Alcatraz. My prison sunsuit was by Edith Head, ball-and-chain by Cartier. I had tile on the floor of my cell, so I could tango with the prison matron whenever I wanted to.

I couldn't stand it anymore. I tried to escape. As I was scaling the prison wall in my hip-boot flagellation wedgies, I fell 400 feet to Mother Earth. Suddenly, the prison spotlight hit me. I bowed. It was Paramount calling me back to show biz.

Now I am back with you, all you wonderful people out there in the dark. Mr. DeMille, I'm ready for my close-up. The one part of my body that hasn't wrinkled—my teeth.

We'll make another picture, and another picture, and another picture. . . .

We thought it was a scream, and we laughed our heads off at what we'd created. Years later, I found out the truth about what Charles had in mind when we wrote it. In 1986 he gave an interview in which he said, "I wrote a lengthy monologue titled 'The Return of Norma Desmond' for an impressionist named Arthur Blake, who was appearing at the Bar of Music in Hollywood, but he rejected it, saying it was too long, so I decided to perform it myself."[1] He didn't mention that I had helped him write it, just "I wrote." I suppose if Arthur Blake had paid Charles for it he would not have shared that with me either. At the time I didn't know that, so I continued to give him lines. I knew he was tremendously talented after seeing his Bette Davis impression, and I thought if he had success, I might share in it as his co-writer. It never happened!

Charles had discovered an intimate little gay bar in Altadena called Club La Vie, and it was there that he met a charismatic, campy, gay waiter named Joseph O'Sullivan who worked evenings at a fashionable Altadena restaurant. Because Charles was unemployed and was having trouble paying his rent at the Algonquin Hotel, Joseph invited

Charles to share his small apartment, which was also located in Altadena. As soon as Charles was settled in, he phoned me to drop by to see his "new digs," as Joseph called his living quarters.

It was like entering a little corner of Shangri-la when I walked up the driveway to the high wooden gate in the fence that screened Joseph's apartment from the street. A mass of deep-red roses clung to a trellis over the gate as I entered. A small, low, rambling building took up space to the right with a solid wall of French doors that could be folded back so that the entire space was open to sunshine and cool breezes. A cement slab served as a patio and adjoined the full length of the building. The air was pungent with the scent of night-blooming jasmine and orange and lemon blossoms. Tall cannas, purple iris, and a riot of pink and red geraniums were everywhere. A lone banana tree rattled its broad leaves in the wind. Across a patch of lawn, in a corner of the yard, to the left, was a round, home-built swimming pool, bowl-shaped and surrounded by a necklace of smooth field stones, set in cement. The place had a certain enchantment about it, especially at night when Joseph floated pad-shaped, lighted candles on the surface of the pool, and a crystal wind chime tinkled in a tree. Soft guitar music came from the hi-fi. I tapped on the door frame, and Charles walked toward me from the bedroom. He introduced me to a wren-like woman who moved about the tiny kitchen quietly but efficiently.

"Audrey, this is John. We went to the Playhouse together."

Audrey gave me a quick look and smiled, but kept on with her domestic duties and didn't say a word.

Just then a rather strained Tallulah Bankhead-ish voice called out from the bedroom.

"Buckets of coffee, Audrey—buckets of coffee."

It was the voice of Joseph O'Sullivan, who had just awakened and was in desperate need of his morning "fix."

Audrey hastened to place the mug of hot coffee on a tray and rushed it to Joseph's beside table. Charles and I followed behind her.

Joseph O'Sullivan, a fragile little creature with a pixie face, lay almost hidden in a pile of pillows and bedclothes. He stretched, rubbed his puffy eyes, and greeted us with a merry grin.

"Thank you, dahling," he said as he gave Audrey a grateful look. "You absolutely saved my life. I'm simply parched!" He took a quick sip and invited Charles and me to sit on the edge of the king-sized bed. After introductions, Joseph wanted to know the latest news and gossip, so we spent about an hour bringing him up-to-date.

Audrey was just a friend to Joseph. He hadn't hired her as a house-keeper and cook. She waited on him slavishly because she absolutely adored the man. In gay jargon, Audrey was a "fag hag," a "fruit fly," a straight woman enamored of a gay man. Even when she knows he's gay, she won't give up her dream that someday he'll return her love. It was a perfect setup for Joseph, as Audrey waited on him just for the pleasure of his company.

Joseph told Charles that he could get him a busboy job at the restaurant where he was employed. On the night Charles debuted clearing tables and carrying trays to and from the kitchen, Audrey and I went to the restaurant for dinner and to lend Charles moral support. Joseph was our waiter, and it was a revelation to watch that lithe figure, with his bleached blond head, weave in and out among the crowded tables, like a graceful ballet dancer going through his paces.

All was going well until Charles tripped and spilled a tray of dirty dishes, making a resounding crash. He didn't say a word or attempt to clean the mess up, but walked out the door, never to return. His career as a busboy was over—permanently.

Charles and I continued to visit Laguna Beach practically every weekend and to write material for his act-to-be. In addition to his Bette Davis and Gloria Swanson sketches, he now had an Eleanor Roosevelt routine, Katharine Hepburn aboard *The African Queen,* Tallulah Bankhead in *Lifeboat,* and a hilarious character of his own invention, Tallulah Bankhead's grandmother, Pocahontas Bankhead. Dressed in the shaggy black robe Charles had "borrowed" from the Playhouse wardrobe department and a stringy dark wig, "Pocahontas" began "her" routine by croaking in a Tallulah-ish voice:

"We were driving down Hollywood Boulevard today in Tallulah's new car—an oxcart convertible. . . ."

As we drove along one day, I turned to Charles and told him I had thought up a joke while I was on vacation in Arizona. I'd seen Indian women selling their beadwork along the edge of the Grand Canyon, and it had inspired me.

"Maybe you'll think it's too dirty. . . ."

"Let's hear it."

"Well, there's this royal Indian, and she's selling her beads on the edge of the Grand Canyon—she's a rim queen."

"It's perfect for Eleanor Roosevelt," he screamed. "I love it!" And it became a staple in his show for years after. Of course, he told me years later how he had thought up the "rim queen" joke! Oh, well, that's showbiz!

I don't mean to imply that I wrote all of Charles' material. Far from it. He had a fertile, clever mind, and he did create most of his own material. However, he did give me credit for cowriting one of his best routines that he actually wrote with someone else.

It was his "Scarlett O'Davis" sketch, where Bette Davis as "Scarlett" is in Atlanta in *Gone with the Wind,* and Prissy, her slave girl, is supposed to help birth Melanie's baby.

"Don't you remember, we were driving down Sunset Boulevard, and we wrote the *Gone with the Wind* routine?" Charles was adamant.

"Not me, Charles. It was someone else." I wish I could take credit for it because it was one of Charles' funniest bits, with him playing all the parts, and it went like this:

(Strains of the "Theme from Gone with the Wind" are heard in the background)

BETTE: Tah, tah, tah, tah,—tah, tah—big deal. Fiddle-dee-dee. Great balls of Rhett Butler. Here I am, Scarlett O'Davis, girl midwife. I want you all to look over here at Melanie on the bed. Look at her. She's so large and lumpy. If she doesn't give birth to Judy Garland, a star will never be born. I wonder where my little slavette Prissy is. Probably over at her relatives', always fretting and worrying about them. She's such a mother-fusser. I must raise my window and see if I can find her. Raise window, push back lace curtains— they have tiebacks. Push back Confederate flag. The South will rise again—probably on me. Oh, look! There's Prissy in the courtyard laying on the grass with nothing over her but a thin boy. Prissy! Get up here!

PRISSY: Hi, Miss Scarlett—Sir. Look, I'm on my picket fence. You can't see it—I'm a method actress. *(Sings)* 'Jest a few mo' days for to tote the weary load—'tis Summer, the old folks are gay.' Hey, you old folks. Git off Miss Scarlett's porch.

OLD FOLKS: We're going, Mary.

BETTE: Prissy! Live and let live.

PRISSY: Jest so's they don't do it in the street and frighten the horses.

BETTE: Prissy! Get up here. There you are. You took so long. I'm going to have to hit you. Prepare yourself. *(Hits her)* Um, um, um, um! How does that grab you?

PRISSY: It grabs me! *(Sings)* 'Oh, do it again. I may say, oh, no, no, no—'

BETTE: Oh, shut up! Now, Melanie's going to have a baby, and you've got to help. I'll need string, rubber gloves, sutures, a jack, grappling hooks, a bathroom plunger, and two cans of Drano. Now shag ass outta here!

PRISSY: Lawsy, Miss Scarlett—I don't know nuthin' 'bout birthin' babies. I'm a lesbian.

BETTE: That's not true! You were in the stables the night I gave birth to Fury. Now go, and leave Barbara Stanwyck alone in the kitchen.

PRISSY: I dig her all-leather slack suit, Miss Scarlett, and her Big Valley. Hey, Miss Scarlett, look out there through your dyke door.

BETTE: Dutch door! Dutch door!

PRISSY: The Yankees are coming.

BETTE: Really? We must get to Tara, where else? Home—

PRISSY: Oh, don't get dramatic on me, Miss Scarlett. The Yankees are coming. We gotta git outta here!

BETTE: Pack up everything—pack, pack! Pack up Melanie. Roll her down to the oxcart. Pack, pack!

PRISSY: The Yankees are coming! They're gonna plunder and pillage.

BETTE: I'm hep.

PRISSY: Yeah, ya do look a little yellow in the eyes.

BETTE: Prissy! There is no time for camp. Pack, pack. Pack up the curtain rod dress—

PRISSY: Miss Scarlett, the Yankees are coming, and they're gonna rape all you women!

BETTE: Unpack! We're here for the Season!

Charles stopped performing the sketch in his show when another female impersonator stole it, but no one could perform it the way Charles did.

According to what Charles told me, other performers stole his material, including a drag queen who went by the name of Lori Shannon. He had his fifteen minutes of fame when he appeared on the TV show

All in the Family, with Carroll O'Connor, portraying a drag queen named Beverly La Salle. After that, he was the emcee at Finocchio's in San Francisco, and Charles claimed he used all of Charles' material. Charles sent him a notice to cease and desist and Shannon replied, "Material is international." Whatever that meant!

Charles also claimed that Lee Roy Reams, a performer friend, asked him if he could "borrow" a few of his lines for a Hollywood Bowl salute to Jerry Herman on TV. He "borrowed" much more than a few lines, Charles said, and went on using them all in a stage musical he starred in. Most comedians borrow lines from one another, but seldom do they take the whole act!

Charles now "had his act together," but still had no place to perform it. We began a sweep of the area from the San Fernando Valley to Hollywood, Santa Monica, Long Beach, and Laguna, to find a club that would let him stand up and deliver some laughs.

But first he had to pay his rent!

8

The Rent Party

On a bright summer morning, Charles and I were brunching by the pool at Joseph O'Sullivan's snug oasis in the Altadena hills, and the ever-faithful Audrey was at her station in the kitchen brewing Joseph's java fix. The sky was blue, birds were chirping in the weeping willow tree, and all was right with the world—or so we thought.

Suddenly, the gate was flung open, and two official-looking men in dark suits and gray fedoras charged into the yard.

"Where is Joseph O'Sullivan?" They wasted no words as they stormed up to Charles and me.

"He's asleep at the moment," Charles tried to explain.

"Where?"

Audrey heard the loud voices and joined us poolside.

"What is it?" Audrey was frightened.

"We want Joseph O'Sullivan. Where is he? We have a warrant for his arrest." The men were getting impatient.

Audrey was shaken, but she led them into the bedroom and gently shook Joseph awake. Joseph grunted, yawned, and rubbed his eyes. When he saw the men a look of sheer terror spread over his face.

"Audrey! What the—Au-dreee." He sprang from his bed stark naked and locked himself in the bathroom, the two agents charging after him.

"Come out of there and get dressed. We have a warrant for your arrest. You're in this country illegally."

Joseph was finally coaxed out of the bathroom and proceeded to get into his clothes. So Joseph was a citizen of Ireland—an alien! Poor Joseph! After he was fully dressed, he was handcuffed, led through the gate to the agents' car, and driven away. Joseph's white, ashen face peered at us from the window. Audrey broke down and wept. We tried to console her, but she walked to the closet, put on her jacket, and walked out the gate, leaving everything behind. We never saw her again.

Charles stayed on at the apartment, as he had no other place to go. He was still unemployed, and he knew that if he continued to live in Joseph's apartment, he'd have to dig up the rent somehow.

Someone he met at Club La Vie told him he should give a rent party. During the 1920s and during the Great Depression, it had been a popular way to get rent money. Now there's a musical about it on Broadway called *Rent*.

So Charles tossed a rent party. He invited everyone he knew from the Playhouse, the patrons from the Club La Vie, even total strangers, and told them all to invite their friends. Each guest paid five dollars admission, and they had to bring their own beverages and snacks. Charles furnished only the venue.

He had fun decorating the apartment and patio, stringing colorful Japanese paper lanterns and Christmas-tree lights he found in Joseph's closet. There were plenty of candle pads to light and float in the pool, and the hi-fi and records would supply music.

The night was warm with just a breath of a breeze when crowds of guests began to stream through the gate. Charles collected the five dollars from each guest and wrote name tags for identification purposes.

As the evening progressed, couples were dancing on the patio, swarming through the apartment, and gathering around the pool. Alcohol flowed freely, the music grew louder, voices became more strident, and some of the guests removed the candles from the pool and jumped into the water fully clothed. One couple stripped off their clothes and attracted a circle of onlookers when they proceeded to perform their own version of the famous "missionary position." Others had commandeered the king-size bed in Charles' bedroom, threw their clothes and inhibitions to the wind, and enjoyed a no-holds-barred orgy! A very good time was being had by all, and the noise level was loud enough to awaken most of Altadena.

Somewhere around 2 a.m. Charles stopped the music, the revelers began to drift out through the gate to the street, and the party was finally over. Charles counted his loot, much more than he needed to pay the rent. We straightened things up, Charles went to bed, and I stretched out on a pad in a shed just off the patio.

At eight the next morning I was rudely awakened by the shed door being flung open, and when my eyes became accustomed to the bright morning light, a very irate woman was standing over me.

"Who the hell are you?" she demanded. "What are you doing here?"

I told her I was a friend of Joseph O'Sullivan, and that I had spent the night in the shed because the party had ended so early in the morning.

"Where is Joseph?" Her face was flushed with anger.

"He's not here. The Feds arrested him and took him away."

"Oh, for Christ's sake! Not again!"

Charles had heard the ruckus, and he appeared on the patio in his robe.

"What's the problem?" he asked.

"Problem! Problem! I'll tell you what the problem is! The neighbors have been calling me since dawn about your damned party." She vented her rage at Charles. "And who are you?"

"I've been staying with Joseph for a few days."

"Well, your time is up. I want both of you out of here now! Get your shit together and get out!"

"I can pay next month's rent—" Charles began.

"I don't want your rent money, and I don't want either or both of you." She fairly screamed it. "Get out—now!"

We had no choice—after all, she was the landlady—so Charles got his few belongings together, including the rent money, and we drove off in my Nash Rambler.

"Drop me at the Y," he said. "And call me tomorrow."

When I phoned him the next day he was in high spirits.

"I'm gonna do a gig at the Club La Vie. They don't pay anything, but it's a chance to try out the material. Come over at six, we'll grab a bite at the club, and I'll go on later."

Club La Vie was what used to be called an "intimate boîte." It was small, with a bar at the back along the wall to the left as you entered, a few booths and tables, and a plain wall of exposed brick on the right. In the back right-hand corner was a tiny platform under an arch that served as a stage. Close by, at stage right, stood a fountain with a statue of a small naked boy relieving himself in a steady stream from his tiny "spout" into a shell-shaped catch basin. Kitty Kallen's plaintive voice was on the jukebox singing her latest hit, "Little Things Mean a Lot."

We settled into a booth and ordered cheeseburgers, fries, and a couple of draft beers. Charles had obviously been a frequent patron—probably with Joseph O'Sullivan—because a number of men dropped by our booth to greet him. One very good-looking young man named David Bersten was in the group, and he was familiar to Charles and me from our previous visits to the club. David was movie-star handsome—in fact, he resembled the actor Tony Curtis, with his dark hair, worn in the popular DA (duck's ass) style, his long-lashed, deep blue eyes that were almost purple, and a friendly smile that flashed perfect teeth.

"Hi, David," I said. He gave me that smile.

"Charles, how ya doin'?" David was being his usual friendly self, but Charles ignored him completely, and David, confused, walked away.

* * *

I remembered back to one night when Charles had first introduced me to the Club La Vie. On that night he was all keyed up as we approached handsome David Bersten, and Charles made the introductions.

"John, say hello to David. David, this is John; he's helping me with my show." They continued conversing, so I wandered off to get a drink. Soon after, Charles charged up to me, his face distorted by a furious rage.

"Okay, let's go!" And he almost ran to the exit. I turned to see David standing at the bar with a drink in his hand and a look of total bewilderment on his handsome face.

Instead of getting into the car, Charles ran to the rail of the parking lot fence and threw his head down on his folded arms. I thought he'd had too much to drink and was about to vomit.

As I approached him, I heard him moan, and his shoulders were heaving. I put a hand on his shoulder.

"Charles, what—?"

He raised his head and looked at me, tears streaming down his face.

"What in God's name is the matter?" I was deeply concerned, as I had never seen him act this way before.

"David hates me!"

"What are you talking about? David couldn't hate anyone."

"Yes, he does . . . he hates me . . . and I love him . . . and I asked him to come home with me . . . and he refused!"

"But, Charles," I said. "That doesn't mean he hates you. Maybe he has a lover—or maybe you're just not his type. You really haven't known him very long, have you?"

"What difference does that make? I don't have to know him forever to know I want him."

I tried to console him.

"Someday, you'll be a famous star and all these guys will be swarming around your dressing room wanting you to go home with them."

"Oh, it's just like the David I had a crush on in high school—same thing—I wanted him, but he didn't want me!" He proceeded to tell me the whole story of his encounter with David Hartley in the basement of Watertown High School. Ever after that, he seemed to take pleasure in recounting to me all his sexcapades, which he called his "cock tales."

"Evidently you have a thing for guys named David," I said.

"You don't understand! Take me home!" Always a command, never a polite request. He wiped away the tears on his sleeve, and I dropped him off at the YMCA.

* * *

Now it was 9 p.m. at Club La Vie, and Charles was getting ready for his debut. He'd brought along his props and costumes in a suitcase I'd loaned him, and he arranged them on a small table on stage.

After the applause died down, he turned to the statue of the boy in the fountain and "tweaked" his spout.

"Little things mean a lot." He delivered the line deadpan. Kitty Kallen's recording was still fresh in the minds of the audience, and the line got a huge laugh and loud applause.

Charles cut a handsome figure in his dark suit, white shirt, and tie—the same attire Arthur Blake wore on stage. Charles' bright blond mop of hair shone under the lights as he performed his entire repertoire. He donned his wigs and costumes, used his props to create Tallulah, Tallulah's grandmother, Pocahontas Bankhead, Mae West, Katharine Hepburn, Louella Hophead, Eleanor Roosevelt, and his masterpiece, Bette Davis.

The gig was highly successful and very well-received by the mostly gay audience, who stomped their feet and yelled for more. It was a successful beginning, but Charles was hungry for more. He was impatient for stardom, money, and praise for his talent.

The Duncan Sisters had once been acclaimed as international stars known for their musical act titled *Topsy and Eva,* based on two characters from *Uncle Tom's Cabin.* Now they were older women still performing their time-worn routine at various venues in the Los Angeles area, and hoping Twentieth Century-Fox would film their biography starring Ginger Rogers and Kathryn Grayson. They had taken over the main showroom at the Glenwood Country Club in Glendale, California, and in addition to their own performances, they held a Talent Night each weekend where unknowns could do their acts.

Charles made arrangements to appear there on a Saturday night and phoned me to pick him up at the Pasadena Y and drive him over to Glendale.

When we entered the Glenwood showroom, we spotted the famous Hollywood agent Henry Willson sitting alone at a table, his dyed black pompadour and pasty gray face scowling at every passerby. He was famous for discovering Rock Hudson, Tab Hunter, Rory Calhoun, and other young "hunks." We thought his presence was encouraging, although neither of us was a "hunk."

The Duncan Sisters were performing their well-known song "Side by Side," so we took a table, ordered drinks, and watched the show. At intermission, when the applause died down, Charles talked to Vivian Duncan, and she told him to wait at the table until she announced his act.

Other participants in the Talent Night performed their acts, including a frantic chanteuse, perched on a stool clutching her thighs and wailing a torch song, a clumsy juggler who kept dropping his balls, a dog act, and on and on until, finally, Vivian Duncan announced Charles' name. He placed his props and costumes on the top of the grand piano and began his routine.

Suddenly, there was a loud crash in the banquet room above, followed by a band playing loud dance music, the sound of stomping, dancing feet, and raucous crowd noises. It was impossible for Charles to perform with the ruckus thundering overhead.

Charles did persist and finally finished to a smattering of weak applause. It was a total disaster.

"Shag ass outta here!" Charles said to me in a loud stage whisper. He ran to the piano and scooped up his props, I grabbed the suitcase, and we raced out the door, veils and feather boas trailing behind us!

One night soon after, Charles and I encountered what we later referred to as the Malt Shop Gestapo. We had stopped by the Playhouse briefly before deciding to have a malt at the nearby drive-in on Colorado Boulevard. I was driving my Nash Rambler convertible, and we pulled into the drive-in lot and enjoyed our malts as we sat in the car. We noticed a lot of activity and a few police patrol cars moving about the parking lot, but we weren't concerned about it.

However, when we drove off the lot and into the street, a police patrol car with red lights flashing pulled out behind us. I stopped my car and got out to see what the trouble was. The cops told me that my car was a stolen vehicle, even after I showed them my registration slip and my driver's license. They ordered Charles into their car and told me to follow them to the police station in my car.

There they gave my car a thorough search and led Charles and me into the police station. We were put in separate rooms so that we were unable to converse with each other, and they questioned both of us at length. One cop played the part of the "good sympathetic cop"—the other was the "bad, sarcastic, sadistic cop." Finally, after about two hours of harassment and suspense, the two brave crime fighters released us, but not without a warning.

"You'd better have that registration checked," the bad cop snarled. I did, and it was definitely registered in my name, which I knew it would be.

It turned out that the description of the stolen car they claimed was mine was a totally different make, year, model, and color, and was not a convertible. I'm sure those brave guardians of the law were bored and were getting their kicks at our expense!

Charles and I had been through some interesting adventures, but it was just the beginning. What was to follow was a big surprise to me and would rock my so-called prosaic life!

9

Charles Pierce, the Persistent Houseguest

It was December 1953, and I had taken a job as illustrator at Douglas Aircraft Company in El Segundo, California. To be close to work, I moved from my Hollywood apartment to a quaint little studio apartment in Manhattan Beach, two blocks from the ocean. The place was cozy and consisted of one spacious room with a double bed, a large corner window giving a panoramic view of the sea. A small bathroom with a shower stall, toilet, and lavatory, a closet, and a tiny kitchen completed the layout. I had brought along a bookcase, a small table and chairs, and a two-piece sectional couch from my former apartment. It was small, but adequate for my needs, and I liked being close to the beach and my job. I rented a garage across the street for my car.

After graduation from Pasadena Playhouse, I had taken a brief vacation in San Francisco, where I had enjoyed the club and cabaret shows, including Finocchio's, the Beige Room, and the Chi Chi Club. I especially liked the comedy routines of such artists as Harvey Lee, Lynne Carter, and Rae Bourbon. When I returned to Hollywood, I began writing monologues and comedy lines in a notebook, hoping someday I might perform them. One of the monologues about a Hollywood agent was titled "We All Have a Piece of Miss Carruthers' Career," and another was called "Oscar Was Wild." They were all risqué and had a sexy double meaning. Later, I incorporated them and others into a revue called *Of All Things,* which I wrote and performed with five other actors. One of the comedy lines I wrote in my notebook was a parody of Easter at the White House when the First Lady rolled Easter eggs on the White House lawn, but instead of eggs I had the First Lady rolling sailors on the White House lawn. I went on scribbling in my spare time and always placed the notebook in a certain spot in the bookcase.

Before I moved, I gave my new address and phone number to Charles, but I hadn't heard from him since the Duncan Sisters fiasco. I thought he was still at the Pasadena Y, but when I called there I was told that he had checked out.

One Sunday morning I had just finished breakfast when there was a knock at the door. When I opened it, there stood Charles, slightly disheveled, with a scowl on his face. He came in and sat on the couch, and I brought him a cup of hot coffee. He was quiet for a long time, taking sips of the coffee and gazing out the picture window.

"Is something the matter?" I asked.

"Oh, no," he snorted. "Just that I borrowed my cousins' car to drive out here, and the damned thing broke down on the highway, so I left it there and hitched a ride over here."

"Shouldn't you call Triple-A?"

"To hell with it. The Highway Patrol can haul it away."

"What about your cousins? Shouldn't you call them?"

He didn't answer, but he told me he had moved in with his cousins in Tarzana in the San Fernando Valley because he couldn't pay his rent at the Pasadena Y. He'd been living in Tarzana for about three weeks, but the frogs croaking and the hens cackling were driving him nuts.

"Drive me down to Long Beach; there's a coupla gay bars I've heard about. I've brought the props and costumes along in case I get to do the act."

So we drove to Long Beach, but on the way he pointed to a building at the side of the highway.

"Pull in here."

It was a low, barnlike structure set back from the road, facing a large, graveled parking lot. Two small oval windows flashed neon signs advertising "Schlitz" and "Budweiser." A swarm of motorcycles was parked out front.

As soon as we entered and our eyes became accustomed to the gloom inside, we knew we were in the wrong place at the wrong time. We took one look at the grim faces on the crowd of butch lesbians and beat a fast retreat without so much as ordering a beer!

"Wrong bar," Charles croaked.

"Tell me!" I let out a relieved sigh.

In Long Beach we found the Commodore Club and the campy bartender holding camp court behind the bar. Everyone called him

"Frieda," and he put on a wild show, all the while donning ridiculous hats and feather boas and spouting a stream of risqué repartee. We spent very little time there, knowing that with Frieda holding sway there would be no room for Charles to entertain.

The Rendezvous Bar was close by, a huge, high-ceilinged affair, very austere and uninviting. As the room became more crowded, the manager gave Charles permission to do his show, and from the beginning the gay crowd was with him all the way. The audience applauded, stomped their feet, and yelled for more, just as the crowd at Club La Vie had done. His Pocahontas Bankhead and Bette Davis impressions were real winners, and to "do" Bette all he had to do was turn the brim of a white sailor's hat down to form a bucket-shaped head covering, grab a ciggie, and he was "her." Several times after that, Charles returned to the Rendezvous Bar, and he was always welcomed warmly.

Returning later that night to my Manhattan Beach apartment, Charles surprised me.

"I'll have to stay here tonight. It's too far to go all the way back to Tarzana, and without the car, I doubt if my cousins will welcome me with open arms." I had no choice but to agree with him, as I had no intention of driving him out to the Valley at that time of night. The next day was a workday for me and I had to get up early.

The two-piece sectional sofa served as a bed for my uninvited guest, and I collapsed into my own welcoming bed.

Charles was still asleep when I awoke the next morning, and after eating a bite of breakfast and following my usual morning routine, I took off for work.

After work, when I walked into my apartment, there was no Charles. I noticed at once that he had given the place a thorough cleaning, but he had also eaten all the food in the refrigerator! I surmised that he was probably broke and hungry, so I didn't begrudge him the food, and he had cleaned the apartment as a way of repaying me. However, I was disturbed when I found my notebook of material lying on the table, and not in its usual place in the bookcase. Aha, I thought, he's been checking out my stash of comedy lines!

Just when I thought my uninvited house guest had probably hitchhiked back to Tarzana, he returned. He'd been lying around on the beach all day and was beginning to sport a tan.

"Charles! I thought you'd gone back to your cousins'."

"I can't go back there. I know they'll be mad about the car, so I'm gonna have to stay here with you."

I agreed that he could stay until the end of the week, but I couldn't afford to support him, and I was afraid my landlord would charge me double rent if Charles stayed longer than a few days.

We walked down to Pancho's Mexican Bar and Restaurant that overlooked an expanse of ocean and enjoyed a couple of margaritas and two combination plates with warm tortillas and hot salsa. It was fun, but, of course, I paid, because Charles had no job and was now totally broke.

I told him he really should try to get to San Francisco, and I mentioned all the entertainers I'd seen when I'd visited there.

"That's where you belong, Charles, and I've got an idea how we can get the money for your fare. I'm gonna pass the hat every time you do a gig at one of the clubs."

He thought it was a good idea, so we returned to my place and spent the evening writing more lines and laughing our heads off at our own jokes. When I picked up my notebook from the table to return it to the bookcase, Charles looked up from his writing.

"You've got one line in there I have to have. It's perfect for the Eleanor Roosevelt routine."

"Which line is that?" I asked, as if I didn't know!

"The one about rolling sailors on the White House lawn."

"But, Charles, that's my line!"

"Yeah, I know, but I gotta have it." And, of course, there was no way I could stop him from taking it once he had filed it away in that steel-trap mind of his. It became one of the best laughs in his routine.

We kept on writing and laughing all week, and then on Saturday we drove to Santa Monica to a popular bar on the beach called the Tropical Village—TV for short. It was an open-air room with a U-shaped bar, and a small stage raised high above the floor so that the throng below had a clear view of the show. Behind the stage and on the same level was a large hole in the wall, the entrance to what was supposed to be a dressing room. When we arrived, the place was wall-to-wall suntanned bodies in Speedos, some lolling on the window sills, their legs and feet dangling over the sides, swilling their beers, while the jukebox blared Guy Mitchell's "My Heart Cries for You." It was impossible for us to advance through the mass of sandy, sweaty bodies.

We made our way as best we could, Charles holding the suitcase of props and costumes above his head. He had visited the club before, and the owner was expecting him. We climbed up onto the loft-like stage, where I grabbed the suitcase and crawled into the cave of a dressing room. It was gloomy inside, but light enough for me to distinguish one costume or prop from another.

The jukebox was suddenly silent, the owner made a brief announcement, and Charles began his act. There was not a mike, but this voice was loud and clear, and it filled the small space adequately. As he performed his various routines, I passed his props and costumes to him from inside the "cave," and he changed into them in full view of the audience. He slipped into the purloined black, fur-trimmed robe for Pocahontas Bankhead and added and subtracted each bit of attire as needed.

The crowd went berserk when Charles finished his Bette Davis impression, screaming, yelling, and demanding more. As Charles took his final bow, I picked up the bucketlike hat he had used for his Brandon de Wilde routine from *Shane,* leaped off the stage into the crowd below, and forced my way through as I passed the hat.

"Help Charles get to San Francisco!" I yelled above the noisy gathering, holding out the hat as I advanced. By the time I had finished, the hat was a bulging, overflowing mass of bills.

We were so heartened by our success at the TV that the next day we drove to Las Ondas in Laguna Beach, where we had the same response. He appeared at other clubs in Long Beach and the San Fernando Valley, and again at the TV in Santa Monica, and soon Charles' coffers were filling up.

One night, just for fun, we stopped off at the Interlude, a popular club on Sunset Strip, to see and hear Frances Faye playing and singing at the piano while Jack Costanzo beat out a staccato rat-a-tat-tat on his bongo drums. Wild!

Suddenly, Frances stopped the music.

"I am told that Mr. and Mrs. Arthur Miller are in the audience. Will you take a bow, please?"

No response.

Frances repeated her request several times. Still no response.

Finally, way in the back of the room by the swinging doors that led to the kitchen, the Millers stood up and silently walked out. No one would ever recognize the small blonde woman by Arthur Miller's side as the glamorous Marilyn Monroe. She looked very plain and ordinary, and her face was without makeup and was completely expressionless.

Charles had his days and nights free, and he had room and board, also free, at my apartment, so he was able to move around at will and meet a variety of people. He spent most days on the beach getting a tan, and it was there that a fellow beach lounger told him about how men "cruised" the beach after dark near the lifeguard station. The sand in that area was covered by a thick mat of ice plant, a succulent—well-named—that grew profusely and produced spiky, pronglike leaves and large yellow flowers. So the saying, "Going down to the ice plant," meant cruising at the lifeguard station. Charles thought he'd check it out.

One night he came back to my apartment quite late. I'd already gone to bed, but he let himself in with an extra key I'd loaned him. When he turned on the light, I noticed an unmistakable blob of cum on his denim jacket. I pointed to it and wondered what had happened.

"How come?" I asked, no pun intended.

"Oh, I've been down cruising the ice plant."

"The ice plant?" I wasn't aware of the activity that went on down there. I thought he meant there was some sort of ice-making plant at the beach.

"It's a cruising spot by the lifeguard station where the ice plant grows."

"You'd better clean your jacket." I noticed there were patches of sand clinging to it as well.

"I suppose so. I met a guy and we were rolling around on the beach and we got carried away. Then, all of a sudden—wham—he let go, and I must have got in the way. I hadn't noticed till now."

There was very little about Charles that was inhibited. He lived for the moment, and he didn't miss a trick!

Through another acquaintance, Charles was invited to a party at the Laurel Canyon home of Lee Graham, who was a budding Hollywood columnist. Charles was asked to perform, and after he was complimented enthusiastically by the host and groups of others, a close friend of Hollywood gossip columnist Mike Connelly approached Charles. He invited Charles to perform his act at a birthday party the man was tossing for Connelly at Connelly's Hollywood Hills home the following Saturday night.

Mike Connelly was notorious for printing items in his gossip column that were not always accurate. According to movie star Shirley MacLaine, several items he had printed about her were totally false. Miss MacLaine had recently become involved in a contract dispute with producer Hal Wallis, who had her under contract. The star was furious when she read in Connelly's column that she had lost the lawsuit against Wallis, which was not true. She and a witness confronted Connelly at his *Hollywood Reporter* office, and Miss MacLaine proceeded to slap Connelly's face twice.

Hedda Hopper, President John F. Kennedy, and Governor Pat Brown all congratulated her on her act of revenge, and Hollywood scribe James Bacon cautioned her, "You'd better be careful now on dark streets—Connelly may come out of the shadows and hit you with his mesh bag."[1]

Charles was overjoyed to be invited to Mike Connelly's birthday party, and he dashed to my apartment to tell me the news. He invited me because he needed a ride to the affair, and I was happy to oblige. We were both excited and looking forward to our first Hollywood party!

10

A Mahvelous Pahty

If Charles and I expected our first Hollywood party to be an orgy, we were sadly disappointed. After winding our way up into the Hollywood Hills, we came to Mike Connelly's beautiful home high above a sweeping panorama of the colorful and sparkling lights of the city below. It reminded me of the scene in *A Star Is Born* when James Mason turns to Judy Garland and says, "It's all yours, Esther," indicating the Cinemascope view of lights spread out before them.

The living room we entered was spacious and deep-carpeted wall-to-wall. Huge windows offered an unbroken view of the lights below, and contemporary sofas, chairs, and lamps, and a beautiful baby grand piano added to the ambiance.

The other guests were already assembled: Harriet Parsons, Louella's daughter; Harriet's ex-husband, King Kennedy; King's partner, Bill Hendrix; Jane Withers, Franklin Pangborn, Hope Emerson, Mary McCarty, all of the movies, and the birthday boy himself, Mike Connelly, and his male roommate.

Charles had been warned not to perform his Louella Hophead routine because it would be offensive to Harriet, and he complied. He stood at the baby grand with his props and costumes spread out on its top and went through his repertoire.

In a letter to the publication *Classic Images* in April 1998, Charles describes that evening at Mike Connelly's:

> Once at the home of Hollywood columnist Mike Connelly . . . I had been asked to perform . . . my impressions of the stars. . . . Miss [Hope] Emerson laughed so hard at the routine, she slid off her chair and raced for the ladies' room. This was long before June Allyson and her . . . Depends commercial.[1]

It was a real triumph to see an audience of famous Hollywood celebs respond to Charles' act with such overwhelming enthusiasm.

Harriet Parsons, who had had quite a lot to drink, called out in a raucous voice to King Kennedy, who, with his partner Hendrix, was a Hollywood agent.

"Sign him up, King! This kid's terrific." Harriet knew talent when she saw it.

King told Charles to come by his home on a specified day during the coming week and gave Charles the address.

By now, Harriet was quite drunk, but the rest of the guests sat around and talked about—what else?—their pictures and careers. I sat on the floor by Jane Withers and Hope Emerson and enjoyed listening to them recall their various experiences. In 1950, Hope Emerson had been nominated for Best Supporting Actress for her cruel prison matron role in *Caged.* The Oscar went to Josephine Hull for *Harvey,* but Miss Emerson had a tiny gold Oscar dangling from her charm bracelet along with other charms commemorating highlights of her career.

Jane Withers was as vivacious, bouncy, vibrant, and full of life as one would expect, laughing about her experiences with young Shirley Temple, and when she was cast in *Giant* with Rock Hudson, Elizabeth Taylor, and James Dean. Franklin Pangborn, so giddy on screen, was very reserved. He and Hope Emerson were great friends.

We were all invited to another party, and Charles rode there with some of his newfound friends. It was decided that Harriet Parsons would ride with me, so she and I walked outside and along the street to my Nash Rambler. There were no sidewalks, it was dark, and along the side of the street were long piles of earth and a deep trench where new sewer pipes were being installed.

Harriet was deep into her cups by now and was walking on my right, close to the piles of earth. Suddenly, there was no Harriet, just a stream of loud profanity coming from deep inside the ditch.

"Get me outta here, you son-of-a-bitch!"

I reached down into the darkness of the ditch. Harriet grabbed my hand, and I hoisted her to safety. Her stocking was torn and her knee was cut and bleeding, and the profanity never stopped. I got her into the car, and we arrived at the scene of the party.

As soon as we were inside, I led Harriet to the bathroom, where she sat down on the commode lid, and I rolled down the torn stocking. The cut on her knee wasn't deep, but it was still bleeding, so I bathed it with a damp paper towel and peroxide. In the medicine chest I found ointment and gauze bandages, and soon she was ready to join the party. But Harriet was not grateful.

"You son-of-a-bitch! All you wanted was to feel my leg!" That was the thanks I got. Harriet was a real tough cookie. She took no prisoners.

Both parties had been fun, but tame by Hollywood standards—no jumping fully clothed into the swimming pool, or nude orgies. Charles' rent party had been far more outrageous.

On the appointed day, I drove Charles to King Kennedy's home far up into a canyon off Sunset Boulevard. King was away, so his partner, Bill Hendrix, greeted us at the door. Bill got down to business right way and questioned us about Charles' act.

"Who writes your material?"

Charles didn't answer, so I volunteered, "We've been writing it together."

"Well," Bill replied, "for now we'll say that Charles writes his own material, and we'll work something out with you later."

Oh, sure, I thought, and I began to have the feeling of doors being slammed in my face. Charles didn't say a word.

Bill had Charles sign a contract that specified that the King Kennedy Agency represented him, and the meeting ended. Soon after, Charles and I were at my apartment when Bill Hendrix phoned to tell Charles to appear for a gig on the coming weekend at Larry Potter's Supper Club in the San Fernando Valley. I was really excited by the news because Larry Potter's was a very popular spot where celebrities congregated. It would be the break Charles was waiting for. But Charles didn't seem too pleased, though he agreed to appear.

The night of Charles' performance arrived, and Charles had disappeared. I thought it strange that he hadn't made plans for me to drive him out to the Valley. At about eight o'clock, Bill Hendrix phoned me.

"Where the hell is Charles?" he shouted.

"Bill, I don't know. He's not here. In fact, I haven't seen him since yesterday. I thought he was at Larry Potter's."

"No, I'm at Larry Potter's, and Charles isn't. What the hell's going on?"

"Bill, I just don't know. I'll have him call you if he shows up."

In about an hour, Charles appeared at my door.

"Charles! Where have you been? Bill Hendrix just phoned. He's out at Larry Potter's, and he's all shook up because you're not there."

"No, and I won't be there! That place is full of straights, just like the Glenwood Country Club was, and it'll be fiasco time again."

"Then call Bill and tell him you're not coming."

"Fuck it! Take me up to the La Vie, and I'll do a show there."

"Then I'll call Bill," I said.

"No, you stay out of it." So I did.

I drove him to Altadena and watched as he "brought down the house" again. Charles knew instinctively who his audience was and what they wanted, and he gave it to them. In the end, he was right in not appearing at Larry Potter's, but at the time I thought his behavior was unprofessional, and he should have called Bill Hendrix. Of course, King Kennedy dropped Charles from his roster immediately and never contacted him again.

My passing the hat for Charles now gave him enough money to try his luck in San Francisco. I drove him to the bus station, where he bought a one-way ticket and boarded the bus. After about a week he was back at my apartment in Manhattan Beach, completely dejected and broke again. The San Francisco trek had been a disaster. He had gone from club to club trying for an audition, to no avail. His money was gone, so he was forced to hitchhike back to my place, and my sofa.

We started another sweep of the bars, from the TV in Santa Monica, to the Rendezvous in Long Beach, to Las Ondas in Laguna, and every time Charles performed, I'd pass the hat, but this time not for any trips to San Francisco.

One of the clubs we discovered in our swing around the Los Angeles area was a little bar/cabaret on Cahuenga in Hollywood called the Flamingo Club. The front door swung open on a small intimate room with a bar to the left and a cluster of small tables and chairs facing a proscenium stage at the back with a ramp extending into the audience area. As we entered and took a table, the mistress of ceremonies, Beverly Shaw, was introducing a male comedian, Carroll Davis. We ordered drinks and checked Beverly out. She was a slim, shapely woman, probably in her thirties, with shoulder-length naturally auburn hair, bright, deep green eyes, a slash of lipstick, and a few tiny freckles peppered across her pert nose. A very womanly woman— but she was dressed in a man's tuxedo, complete with studded shirt front and black bow tie. I'd never seen that combination before, and I wondered about what kind of place the Flamingo Club was.

Beverly finished the introduction, and out strode Carroll Davis, who, in spite of his feminine-sounding first name, was not effeminate at all. His material was sharp, timely, and very funny. It included a routine where he would tell a joke, get a laugh, and then, in a loud voice, he'd say, "Or," tell another joke, get a laugh, say, "Or," until he came to the final punchline. "This place is beginning to sound like an 'Or' house." That routine was the highlight of his act, and years later he was still doing it at Finocchio's in San Francisco.

Beverly reappeared and introduced the next performer, Lucian, an older drag queen whose act consisted of risqué comments to the men in the front row, saying things like, "I remember you when we were in the navy together. You were a Rear Admiral." Years later Lucian also became a headliner in the Finocchio show.

It was now Beverly's turn to take stage. The lights were lowered, and a spotlight swung to her and picked her out of the gloom. In a husky voice, she began to sing her signature ballad, "Shangri-La," and every lesbian in the crowd that now filled the tables was in love with her. I think some of the men were too—she had an appeal that crossed sexual barriers.

As she moved sensuously along the ramp above the tables, touching the tip of her tongue to her lips and letting her graceful hand slide along her tuxedoed thigh, women close enough reached out to touch her and moaned.

"Oh, Daddy, Daddy. I love you so, Big Daddy!" It was a love feast, almost a religious experience for the lesbians, and Beverly thrilled to it, slinging the mike cord over her shoulder, slinking down the runway. There wasn't a dry pair of women's slacks in the house!

Eventually, Beverly opened her own bar on Ventura Boulevard in the San Fernando Valley, and lesbians flocked in great numbers to see her.

Beverly had a grown son by her ex-husband, and the son often said that he was the only guy he knew who could go into his mother's closet and select a tie!

Charles was getting restless. I could tell he was uncomfortable in the presence of another comedian, so we left. In all the years I was associated with Charles, I seldom heard him say a complimentary word about another entertainer. They were his competition, and he was determined to be the greatest star!

Twice we visited the Club Gala, a unique nightspot perched high above the Sunset Strip that was owned and hosted by a fey entertainer named John Walsh. A long flight of stairs wound up the hill from the street to the intimate stucco building that housed Club Gala. It was frequented mostly by a gay clientele, and by movie notables Marlene Dietrich, Judy Garland, Cole Porter, Janet Gaynor, her husband designer Adrian, and others. The interior was a small, intimate space, candlelit, very much like someone's living room. There was a tiny bar by the entrance, and twin baby grand pianos highlighted the platform stage in front of a cluster of tables. A husband and wife team, Edie and Rack, performed at the keyboards. Years later, singer Bobby Short had a long engagement at the club.

Charles and I weren't impressed with the entertainers we saw at the Club Gala. We watched as British comedienne Queenie Leonard sang her music hall ditties, throwing on a variety of feather boas and hats to enhance her comedy routines. Or we watched Stella Brooks, another impressionist, perform. One of her quick takes consisted of her turning her back to the audience, donning a hat with an upturned brim, and turning back to face the crowd while she raised her hand in a farewell gesture.

"Constance Bennett waving goodbye to the train."

I don't remember how the audience reacted to that, but Charles and I thought it was obscure and inane.

Finally, John Walsh would appear, and, as the pianos tinkled in the background, he'd recite his risqué patter songs, much like Toddy, the character portrayed by Robert Preston in the film *Victor/Victoria,* all the while holding a large undulating pink chiffon scarf to accentuate his recitation.

Charles attempted to audition for John Walsh, as he felt his material would be right for Club Gala, but John Walsh wasn't about to have an act in his club that might overshadow his own. He kept Charles waiting for hours in the hot parking lot and never granted him an audition.

We continued trying out Charles' material at the bars, and it was always interesting to see which lines got the laughs. If they didn't get laughs, we'd rework them until they went over with the audiences. Soon Charles had enough money from his "guest" appearances to try a venture that ultimately changed both our lives.

11

A Naked Moon Dance and the Little Retreat Where Alcoholics Meet

My landlord was a very kind and patient man, and he and his wife—they lived in the apartment above mine—had always been nice to me. One Saturday morning when I was alone—Charles was at the beach sunning himself—my landlord knocked at my door and entered, and we sat down.

"I'll get right to it," he said. "It's about your houseguest. You know, I rented the apartment to just one occupant—you—so I'll have to double your rent if your friend stays on."

I certainly couldn't blame him. He was being absolutely fair, and he had put up with the situation for too long a time. I couldn't afford to pay double rent, and I was content in my little beach retreat, so Charles would have to go.

I assured my landlord that Charles would move out the following day, we shook hands, and he left. But it wasn't going to be easy telling Charles that he'd have to vacate the premises. I hadn't invited him to stay with me—he'd just moved in. Of course, it had been fun working on the material, and we'd had a lot of laughs doing it, but it was time for him to move on.

Charles eventually arrived, tanned and sandy from his day at the beach, and after he had showered and dressed, I gave him the news that he'd have to find other lodgings.

"But I can't!" he shouted. "Where will I go?"

"Charles, I don't know. But you'll have to leave because I can't afford to have my rent doubled if you stay. My landlord said he will do that if you don't leave. You can stay tonight, but you'll have to go tomorrow."

Charles was not pleased by my eviction notice, but early the next morning, he was gone. He rented a room near my place, and after he moved in, he called me from a pay phone. When I dropped by to see him, he was propped up in bed in the most dreadful surroundings. The room was actually a garage with a cement floor and one small unwashed window, and the walls were rough, unpainted boards.

He was very dejected, and I felt sorry for him, but it was time he took charge of his life and stopped depending on others to keep him afloat. With no plans to seek employment and with just the money I'd collected for him at his gigs, his future was grim indeed.

For the next week or so, I didn't hear from Charles, but when he finally did call, he was cheerful and excited.

"I'm staying at Dick Lowery's in West L.A. He wants you to come over for dinner at 6:30, and here's the address."

Dick Lowery had been a fellow student in our class at Pasadena Playhouse, but he had dropped out before graduation. Now he had a well-paying job as a chemist at UCLA, and he and his roommate, Alan, shared a spacious and pleasant apartment.

Dick and Alan were both generous guys, and they loved to cook and entertain, so it was a comfy spot for Charles to crash. He made himself right at home instantly, and his hosts were delighted to have him as their guest.

After dinner, everyone wanted Charles to entertain, which he did, not only by doing his movie ladies, but also by improvising routines that had us all screaming with laughter. Dick Lowery had a wicked sense of humor too, and I think it was he who cowrote the "Scarlett O'Davis/Gone with the Wind" sketch with Charles.

Perhaps Dick Lowery loaned Charles some money, because the next time Charles phoned me, he had rented a small chapel-like building on the side of a hill on Hyperion Boulevard in Los Angeles that was the meeting place for members of Alcoholics Anonymous. A bit odd, I thought, but I met him there that afternoon.

To reach the building, it was necessary to climb a long, winding flight of stairs, not unlike the setup at Club Gala. The small building was perched near the top of the hill, overlooking the street below. We entered through a vestibule and on into the main room. An open beamed ceiling exposed the high gabled roof above. I was sure the place had once been a church when I saw the rows of carved wooden pews arranged in neat rows. The proscenium stage at the far end of the room would be perfect for Charles' act. There were curtains but no scenery on the stage, but I had an idea that would solve that problem.

We drove back to my place and I rounded up several refrigerator cartons. On two flat sheets of the cardboard, I painted signs proclaiming "The Charles Pierce Show" and the dates and times. He would do two matinees only, one on Saturday and one on Sunday, because other organizations had booked the place in the evenings.

For scenery, I opened up two of the large cartons that stood almost six feet high and made them into screens by painting them subdued colors to make a background for Charles and a place for him to hang his props.

The Rambler was loaded with the scenery, the signs, my portable record player and records, and off we sped to the Alcoholics' roost. We nailed the signs up on posts that were in plain sight of the passing traffic and arranged the screens and other equipment backstage.

Dick Lowery and Alan came by early on Saturday to help, operating the lights and curtain and playing the music on cue. I was stationed at the entrance in the vestibule, seated on a rickety chair at an unstable table with a cigar box full of change for a cash register. I charged each person five dollars as they filed in.

It was a full house, which surprised me as Charles hadn't advertised, so it had to be word-of-mouth.

The house lights dimmed, the music swelled, the curtains parted, and Charles entered center stage through the makeshift cardboard screens. The audience went wild, whistling, cheering, stomping their feet, and when they had finally quieted down, Charles began his act. In addition to his Hollywood ladies, Charles did his Brandon de Wilde sketch where he donned a bucket-shaped, brimless felt hat, and while the "Theme from Shane, The Call of the Faraway Hills" played in the background, he gave his plaintive cry.

"Shane! Shane! Come back, Shane! I'm so scared, Shane. There's a huge cloud of dust coming down the road! Shane! Shane! Oh, it's just Elizabeth Taylor walking her elephants."

Elizabeth Taylor's movie *Elephant Walk* was playing in all the theaters at the time, and *Shane* was a big hit, so the audience appreciated the satire immediately.

Charles was pleased with the results of his first experience as an actor-manager, and the box office receipts were most rewarding. He not only had enough money for the rental of the hall, but had made a tidy profit as well.

After securing the premises, we were off to Pasadena. Dick and Alan went home, but Charles and I felt like celebrating. We had dinner at The Clock, a twenty-four-hour eatery on Colorado Boulevard across from Albert Sheetz. Then we drove to Club La Vie for drinks and chit-chat with a gaggle of Charles' fans who had been at his show.

We were told that there was to be a party at Greg Stanton's apartment, and we were all invited. Greg Stanton was a very handsome young man with a blond mane, flawless features, and piercing green eyes. He had been a student at the Playhouse but had dropped out. Years later, he became a producer of Las Vegas extravaganzas.

At the appointed hour, we drove to Greg's place, parked, and went in. The apartment was spacious, with a large living room where we all congregated. The room was jammed. There was plenty of food and drink, and I finally settled cross-legged on the carpet and lost track of Charles.

There was a tap on my shoulder, and when I looked up, there stood David Bersten, the young fellow who had driven Charles to tears that long ago night at Club La Vie. He sat down beside me, and we chatted until someone announced that Greg would now perform his "Naked Moon Dance." David and I snickered at that, as we had no idea what we were about to see.

The crowd gathered in a circle, some sitting on the floor as David and I were doing. The lights dimmed until the room was in semi-darkness. The strains of Ravel's *Bolero* throbbed from the hi-fi as Greg made his entrance, heavily veiled and carrying a single lighted candle, which he placed on the floor in the center of the circle of guests.

As the sensual sounds of *Bolero* filled the room, Greg circled the candle flame, the veils billowing around him. Slowly, he let a veil drift from his body, being careful not to cause a conflagration. After he had discarded all but the last veil, it was obvious to all that he was stark naked beneath it. As the music reached its crescendo, Greg cast off the final veil, revealing his well-muscled, handsome physique, and then, completely nude, he circled the candle one more time. As the music climaxed, he squatted over the flame, somehow snuffed it out with his talented buns without getting singed, threw his arms above his head as a finale, for an instant displayed his naked body, bowed deeply, and ran to the nearby bedroom.

The lights came up, the party continued with loud conversation and dancing, and the drinks flowed on until after midnight when the guests began to leave. David Bersten asked me if I could give him a ride to his place in Laurel Canyon, as his ride had left him at the Club La Vie.

"Sure, David, but I've got to find Charles first. I have to drop him off at Dick Lowery's."

David and I waited outside on the front porch until Charles finally appeared. I don't know where he had been all evening, and I don't know if he had seen the "Naked Moon Dance," but when he saw David with me his face became hard, his eyes narrowed, and he gave me a hateful glare.

"Charles," I said, "are you ready to go? I'm giving David a ride home, and then I'll drop you at Dick's."

Charles' face was a mask of complete hatred.

"You don't have to drop me anywhere!" He ran to my car, threw the door open, dragged his props and costumes out, and yelled over his shoulder as he hurried away. "I have a show to do!"

Well, he didn't have a show to do until the next afternoon, but "stars" love that line and toss it off on many occasions.

"What's the matter with him?" David asked.

"It's too long a story to tell, David," I said. I didn't want to go into the fact that Charles was jealous because I was with David, so I let it go. I drove David to his place, and I was relieved to finally get home.

The next morning, Sunday, Dick Lowery phoned me from the Alcoholics Anonymous theater, and after a brief conversation about Charles' activities, he came to the main reason for his call. "Charles wants to know if you're coming over here to help with the show."

I thought, he's afraid to call me himself after the rotten way he acted last night. "Hell, no, I'm not coming over, now or ever! After the way he treated me last night, he can go to hell!" I slammed down the receiver. I was furious, but I decided I would go over and retrieve my phonograph and other items I had loaned Charles for the show. Charles wasn't there, so after I got my things, I drove to Club La Vie to see if I could find him. Dick had told me that Charles was flying to New York the next day, and I wanted to get my suitcase back, and some money I had loaned him. I thought he might never return.

Charles was seated in a booth at Club La Vie when I walked in. I asked him for my money, but he slouched down in his seat with a mean look on his face. Then he rose, pulled some bills from his pocket, and threw them on the floor at my feet. It reminded me of the scene in *The Letter* when Bette Davis visits her murdered lover's Eurasian wife, played by Gale Sondergaard, and after Bette pays the wife for the incriminating letter, the wife throws the letter on the floor and Bette is forced to kneel to the wife to retrieve the letter.

I lost no time in bending and retrieving my money and driving to Dick Lowery's. Just as I expected, when Alan led me to the bedroom, I found my suitcase on the bed neatly packed with Charles' belongings, ready for his flight to New York the next day. I quickly unpacked the suitcase, piled his things on the bed, grabbed my suitcase, and drove home. It was two years before I saw Charles Pierce again.

Thirty years later in 1983, Charles and I were sitting in his Ford Mustang outside my apartment on California Street in San Francisco.

"Remember that party at Greg Stanton's apartment in Pasadena, and we had a row? What was that all about?"

"Charles, that was so long ago. I don't remember. Let's just let it lie." He remained silent, we said goodnight, and he drove off.

– 12 –

The Big Break and Sex on the Rocks

During the two-year period from 1954 to 1956, when Charles Pierce and I were out of touch with each other, I thought about him a lot. I missed our gabfests and laughing at the material we wrote for his act. But neither of us would make the first move to end our feud.

Dick Lowery phoned me one evening to tell me that Charles had returned from New York and was back living with him and Alan in West Los Angeles. He said Charles was going to open that week at Club La Vie, and he thought I'd like to attend Charles' first professional engagement for which he would be paid. I told Dick that I was glad Charles was finally being recognized for his talent, but that I had no desire to attend, and I did not.

Club La Vie's owners had faith in Charles' ability, so they had leased an empty adjoining building, opened the brick wall that divided the two areas, and built a stage for Charles that faced the tables and bar, so that all patrons had full view of the performing space. Years later, Charles reminisced during an interview, "I was paid $75 a week and my evening meal, which consisted of a hamburger!"[1] All of this activity was reported to me by mutual friends, including Dick Lowery.

Ann Dee, an energetic woman who owned and operated Ann's 440 Club on Broadway in San Francisco, and who had recently discovered Johnny Mathis and Fran Jeffries, heard about "a clever young comedian named Charles Pierce who was packing them in at Club La Vie in Altadena." She lost no time in catching Charles' act and immediately signed him to appear at her San Francisco club. I'd always told Charles that he belonged in San Francisco and that he would have good luck there, and now it was coming true in spite of his earlier disappointment.

Charles opened at Ann's 440 Club in the summer of 1954, which was perfect timing. The City was a tourist mecca because of the beatnik invasion, with their free-love lifestyle and authors such as Jack Kerouac and Allen Ginsberg. In addition, there were the exciting night haunts such as Enrico Banducci's hungry i, Keith Rockwell's Purple Onion, the Bagel Shop, and the old standby, Finocchio's, with its drag revues. The Kingston Trio, Mort Sahl, Bill Cosby, Bob Newhart, and Shelley Berman were all making theatrical history at the hungry i, and Phyllis Diller, and, later, the Smothers Brothers were lighting up the tiny stage at the Purple Onion.

At Ann's 440 Club, Charles joined fellow performers Fran Jeffries, comedians Pat Paulsen and his wife, Joan, and Skip Arnold and his wife, Pat Bond (yes, that Pat Bond who years later had success with her one-woman show as Gertrude Stein). Joan Paulsen's specialty was singing the old 1920s song "Tiptoe Through the Tulips," first very demurely, then, as she gathered momentum, becoming more wildly aggressive, shouting, "Tromping Through the Tulips," eyes blazing crazily, arms and legs flying in all directions. Pat Paulsen did his trademark deadpan schtick. Years later, Pat became a star on *The Smothers Brothers Comedy Hour,* constantly campaigning for President of the United States. After he and Joan divorced, she married Nick Reynolds of the Kingston Trio. The other two members of that group, Dave Guard and Bob Shane, referred to Nick Reynolds as "the runt of the litter" because he was short in stature.

Charles performed his movie star impressions dressed in a tuxedo, and Skip Arnold did a drag character called "Magnolia Calhoun," a dizzy-headed Southern belle. None of the men performed in full drag at Ann's 440 Club.

That year, 1954, the talk of the entertainment business was Mike Todd's soon-to-be-released film spectacular, *Around the World in 80 Days,* starring David Niven and a cast of thousands. The release date was 1955, but it gave Charles and Skip an idea. They wrote and performed a revue at Ann's 440 Club, a satire of the Mike Todd film, called *Around the World in 80 Minutes.* It gave them both a chance to do their various characters as they went "around the world."

The show was a resounding hit, but Charles was not happy being a member of an ensemble cast—he wanted to be the star attraction, so when an offer came from a man named Brownie, who operated the Echo Club in Miami Beach, Florida, Charles jumped at the chance. He purchased a used Hillman Minx convertible, packed up his props, and, with a friend, drove into the Deep South. Charles tells his own story in 1993, when he began his never-completed autobiography:

> I want to tell you how I met Rio Dante, my show partner from 1955 to 1969. Rio's real name was Carol John Watson, and by now I've forgotten why he called himself "Rio"—whether it was after the city or the Grande. He added "Dante" later in keeping with camp horror shows I produced in clubs on Miami Beach. Rio came to the Echo Club almost every night, always dressed elegantly, sitting at the bar with his cigarette holder, a large, ornate ring on his forefinger, and drinking beer out of the bottle. A real character. Arthur Blake, the great impressionist, always referred to Rio as the "Martita Hunt of the Twilight Zone." (Martita was "Miss Havisham" in *Great Expectations,* and had a pointy nose and angular features like Rio.)
>
> My act at the Echo Club in 1954 was performed in a tuxedo, with a box of props. For my impressions of the stars I added a feathered hat for Mae West, a pith helmet with veiling for Kate Hepburn in *The African Queen,* or a turban for "Norma Desmond." I traveled light in those days. The house musician, Bob Teel, accompanied me on the organ. When that season ended in April, I accepted an engagement in New York City and left Miami Beach. In July of 1954, Rio called me in New York from Florida to say that Brownie, the owner of the Echo Club, wanted me back as soon as possible for the 1955-1956 season. Bob Teel was no longer playing at the club, but Rio informed me that he would play for me.
>
> That Rio was a musician was news to me, but I soon learned that he was an accomplished concert pianist. The organ was hauled away and a baby grand was installed in the club. I returned to Miami Beach not only with my impressions act, but also with taped pantomimes I added to my show—a novelty in the 1950s, and a "first" in yet another way—we were the first to use the new stereophonic sound in the act. Rio played for the "live" part of the act; then I started using him in the pantomimes, where he played everything from Count Dracula and Igor the hunchback, to Elaine May's characters, to Mrs. Bates from *Psycho.*
>
> Suddenly, in 1956, Brownie died of a heart attack, and the Echo Club closed.

Charles was lucky, though, because he received a call from Ann Dee in San Francisco wanting him for a return engagement at her 440 Club. Charles left Rio in Miami Beach, and, with a young friend he'd met in Florida named Franklin Townsend, he drove to San Francisco. He and Ann set an opening date for the following week, so Charles left Franklin in San Francisco and drove on to Hollywood.

I had moved from Manhattan Beach to a spacious apartment on Highland Avenue near the Hollywood Bowl. It was an old Italian Baronial-style building where many movie stars, including William Powell, had lived. My apartment was a one-bedroom spread with a huge beamed-ceilinged living room, a large brick-faced fireplace, dining room, kitchen, and bath overlooking a patio below. Directly across from my apartment was my neighbor Stan Read's "digs," reached by a balcony walkway we shared. We could see each other's front doors from our living room windows.

One afternoon I was visiting Stan when I heard footsteps coming up the stairs. From Stan's window I could see the back of a blond-headed man standing at my front door ringing the bell. At first, when I stepped out onto the balcony, I didn't recognize him, but when he turned to face me, he was unmistakably Charles Pierce! It had been two years since we'd seen each other.

It's strange how old friends can forget past differences and slip back into a comfortable mode, even though years have passed. We picked right up where our last conversation had left off, except that we didn't mention our "feud." Over a couple of beers he told me about his engagements at the Club La Vie, Ann's 440, and the Echo Club. Now he was readying himself for his return engagement at Ann's 440, and he asked me to help him sharpen and fluff up his routines. We went over the material, and this time he paid me for my assistance. He had brought along a carton containing a tape recorder and other items that he left with me, with the understanding that I would mail them to him when he returned to Florida. I agreed, and he left.

That June of 1956 I was on vacation, and I decided to drive to San Francisco. After I was settled in my room at the Golden Gate Y, I drove over to Ann's 440 on Broadway to see Charles. He was busy arranging his props for his evening show, and after he was finished, we walked to Upper Grant Avenue, where the annual street fair and art festival was in full swing. The street was roped off, and the crowd was wall-to-wall. The beatnik craze was on with a vengeance, and the street was jammed with long-haired men and women, bearded artists and poets, and grubby dogs and children running rampant. Pottery, painting, stained-glass panels, and racks of colorful and exotic clothing cluttered the area. There were booths where Tarot card readers, dressed in beatnik or gypsy garb, and food sellers, the air around them pungent with intriguing aromas, hawked their wares. The sharp, sweet odor of marijuana wafted over all, and beatnik couples kissed and fondled each other in doorways. Colorful paper lanterns swayed in the evening breeze and burst into light as darkness fell.

"You really have to see the Old Spaghetti Factory," Charles said as we pushed our way inside. What an incredible sight! Chairs and a conglomeration of artifacts and memorabilia hung from the ceiling. Large globular lights lit the room as we drank Anchor Draft beer at the bar. The place was so crowded that we drove to Sausalito, where we had dinner at a little red Victorian restaurant called the Glad Hand, then back to San Francisco.

After I'd seen Charles' show, I stopped by the Purple Onion to see Phyllis Diller, who had been written about in the Los Angeles newspapers and was now a popular new sensation in San Francisco. Tassie Hamilton, a comedienne from Australia, was the opening act, singing English music hall numbers and closing with "Waltzing Matilda."

Charles finished his engagement at Ann's 440, but before he returned to Florida, he came back to Hollywood. Keith Rockwell, who owned the San Francisco Purple Onion, opened a Hollywood version of the club on Sunset Boulevard in a building that had once housed a Dutch restaurant called the Wooden Shoe. The facade was stair-stepped like the houses in Holland. Keith sent Tassie Hamilton and her husband down to Hollywood to manage the new club, and he hired Charles as headliner of the opening show. Tassie would repeat her singing act.

Charles rented a cozy apartment at the Garden Court on Hollywood Boulevard within walking distance of the club and settled in. He auditioned a pretty dark-haired woman named Jackie Altier who sang ballads, and he hired her to share the billing with him in a revue he created titled *Anemic Faces of 1957.* I helped him put the revue together, and I built scenery for the show, consisting of a wooden frame to support several large window shades on which I painted scenes. If Jackie Altier were singing a Parisian song, Charles could unfurl a shade depicting the Eiffel Tower. The show was a hit until, due to poor management and sparse attendance, the place folded.

Charles returned to Miami Beach and got back with Rio, and they opened at the Onyx Room a few blocks from the site of the defunct Echo Club and proceeded to play a year's engagement. Charles wrote to me requesting that I write a comedy monologue for him "on any subject, just so it's funny." It's almost impossible for me to sit down by myself and be funny on paper. I dashed off a three-minute sketch and sent it to him. Back came his reply: "I can't use this shit!"

Charles and Rio were constantly adding new bits to their show. They suspended a swing from the rafters of the ceiling so that Charles could throw on a picture hat and a feather boa and swing out over the audience, lip-synching some soprano's voice trilling a musical comedy number. This was long before he added Jeanette MacDonald to his act singing "San Francisco."

One memorable night, Woolworth heiress Barbara Hutton's cousin, Jimmy Donahue, came into the club roaring drunk, staggered to the piano, snatched up a red feather boa, slung it around his neck, and boarded the swing. He proceeded to swing out high above the customers' heads until one of the suspending ropes snapped, and he hurtled down, crashing onto the tables and sending glasses, lamps, and customers flying. Needless to say, he was hustled out of the club by the burly bouncer.

Jimmy Donahue was a notorious and uninhibited queen who would strip naked at the drop of a jockstrap and dance with wild abandon on top of the bar at any gay saloon he happened to inhabit at the moment. Often he entertained his mother and her friends by getting into full drag and prancing around the room in high heels. Francis Cardinal Spellman was often a guest at these affairs.

Truman Capote enjoyed telling the story of a night in 1946 when Jimmy Donahue and a friend dropped by a gay bar in Manhattan and proceeded to round up a gaggle of servicemen. Jimmy was tossing a party at his mother's posh 5th Avenue apartment while she was away, and commandeered a fleet of taxicabs to whisk the servicemen away to the scene of the party.

During the raucous hijinks, as the booze flowed freely, one of the servicemen passed out on a couch, and the drunken revelers stripped his clothes off. Someone thought it would be a lark to get a razor and shaving cream and shave his pubic area, but they were so drunk that they cut the guy's cock off. The men panicked when the serviceman came to, and blood spurted everywhere. They bundled him into a blanket, then into a car, and dumped him on a bridge on 59th Street. When the police found him he was near death, but they drove him to a hospital, and his life was saved. The mutilated man remembered the name of the bar where he'd met Donahue, and Donahue and his accomplice were tracked down. Mrs. Jessie Donahue, Jimmy's wealthy mother, paid the maimed serviceman $500,000 to prevent him from pressing charges. Nothing about the case was ever reported in the media, and it never went to trial. Mrs. Donahue chartered a plane to fly Jimmy and his buddy off to Mexico for a two-year holiday.

Charles and Rio completed their run at the Onyx Club and accepted an offer to open at another Miami Beach bar called the Red Carpet. It is interesting that Charles was billed with T. C. Jones, another well-known female impersonator, who did many of the same impressions that Charles was famous for. T. C. had had great success on Broadway in Leonard Sillman's revue *New Faces of 1956,* portraying Tallulah Bankhead, Katharine Hepburn, Bette Davis, and Luise Rainer. Short, stocky, and bald as a billiard ball, T. C. was so convincing as a woman that when he removed his wig at the end of a performance, one woman in the audience gasped, "Oh, my, the poor woman is bald."

The following year, 1957, T. C. Jones starred in the revue *Mask and Gown* at the John Golden Theatre in New York. It quickly went on tour and ultimately failed. He and Charles Pierce opened on the same bill at the Red Carpet, which did not delight Charles nor T. C., but they muddled through because they both needed the work.

T. C. Jones was married to former actress Connie Dickson, a quiet, gray-haired woman with pinched features and no glamour whatsoever, always lurking backstage at the ready to respond to T. C.'s orders and whims.

One night, T. C. was in the middle of his Katharine Hepburn routine as "Rosalind" in *As You Like It,* when the light man, who was new to the job, failed to train the spotlight on T. C., who stopped his monologue in mid-sentence. Instant tears streamed down his cheeks as he croaked to Connie, who was crouched behind the curtain.

"Con—nee! Con—nee! They hate me, Connie! I can't go on!" And he proceeded to chew the light man out with some very ornate language. The poor guy finally got the light adjusted, and T. C. dried his crocodile tears and quickly completed Hepburn's speech. Near the end of his career T. C. appeared in a few low-budget films, including *Promises! Promises!* with Jayne Mansfield in 1963. He died at age fifty in 1971.

Charles had all of his days free, and those days in Miami Beach were sunny and perfect for lolling about and getting a tan. Often he would stroll down to the breakwater, which extended out a good distance from shore and consisted of huge boulders where young men gathered to sunbathe in the nude. They called it "The Rocks."

One afternoon Charles was lying on the warm boulders when he noticed a young fellow standing close by, chest-deep in the water and glancing in Charles' direction. Charles slid off his rock like "The Little Mermaid" and swam underwater to where the man was standing. He surfaced for a gasp of air, then went underwater again, pulled the guy's Speedos down, and orally engulfed the man's erect organ. The fellow gasped but didn't resist, so Charles kept coming up for air, then diving under and completing the "job." Charles swam back to his rock and surveyed the scene for more activity.

He soon found it when a young sailor appeared, removed his uniform, stripped naked, and lay on his back on a nearby slab of rock. Charles moved next to the sailor, who was now fully aroused, and began massaging the young man's chest and thighs. The sailor said it felt good, and when Charles began giving him oral sex, the sailor said that that was even better!

In late 1962, Charles and Rio felt it was time to leave Miami Beach and move on. They packed up the drags and props and drove to Central City, Colorado. They were booked for a one-night gig at a dreary club called the Glory Hole! It was named for a famous gold mine in the area—*not* for an infamous aperture in the men's room wall. After an exceptionally dreary audience reception, Charles complained to his cohorts, "And I thought glory holes were supposed to be fun. Colorado should be spelled 'C-O-L-O-N'!" They fled the scene and drove nonstop to Los Angeles, where they were immediately booked into the Statler Hotel's Terrace Room. *Variety* reviewed the show as follows:

> Best comedy turn ever ushered into this spot by Ashton is Charles Pierce and Rio Dante, a record act spliced into three sections of show, doing a Dracula-Vampira satire, a mother-son phone call lampoon, and an artfully tricked marionette bit.

Lines are highly topical, effect electric, well worth $600 weekly act is getting in its first Far West fling.[2]

The Hollywood Reporter had this to say:

> The featured act in the current show spotlights Charles Pierce and Rio Dante who do pantomime to recordings, some their own, a comedy turn that is properly rewarded with laughs and hefty applause.[3]

Later they played the Club Capri, a gay bar in Hollywood. I flew down from San Francisco, where I had moved in 1958, and that's when I first met Rio Dante and Charles' "roommate," Ray.

Charles, in his own words, tells the story best:

> We worked the room at the Club Capri till late March of 1963 when we felt it was time to move again. But where?
>
> Bruce O'Neil, a patron of the Capri, told me he was going to San Francisco for the weekend. I said, "Look around and see if there are any clubs interested in booking Rio and me."
>
> Bruce returned from San Francisco, handed me a card with the words "Gilded Cage" printed on it, and three handwritten words, "Call Uncle Billy," who was one of the managers of the club. When I phoned, Uncle Billy said that the owners, Arthur and Pearl Reeb, were looking for an act and that if we came to San Francisco they would give us an audition. When I told Rio he said, "By all means, let's go!" We closed at the Capri, and with no reason to stay any longer in exotic Hollywood, he and I took off for San Francisco and the Gilded Cage!

"Everybody Came to the Gilded Cage"

Just like Rick's Americaine Bar in the movie *Casablanca,* everyone came to the Gilded Cage, located at 126 Ellis Street, between Powell and Mason in San Francisco. At least, they came in droves when Charles Pierce opened his show there in 1963. As Mae West, he always greeted his audiences with, "Oooh, mmm, hello, boys, hello, girls. Hello, boy-girls, hello, girl-boys. I guess that covers everyone here." Everyone, that is, from stockbrokers to movie stars. They all beat a path to the Gilded Cage! As Charles himself put it, "There never was an ad placed in any newspaper or periodical. How did the nightclub-goers know we were there? There's an old saying, 'Telephone, telegraph, and tell a queen.' Word of mouth did it for six years."

In August 1962, Arthur Reeb and his wife, Pearl, leased the Gilded Cage, bought a liquor license, and, through bankruptcy court, purchased all the furnishings. When they opened, only the front bar area was used and a large room in back stood empty. Business was poor operating as a straight club, but all that changed when they met Billy Morrell, known in the gay community as "Uncle Billy." He convinced the owners to turn the club gay. On Thanksgiving Day 1962, the Gilded Cage went from an unsuccessful straight club to a thriving gay establishment, thanks to Uncle Billy.

Who better to tell the saga of the Gilded Cage than Charles Pierce as he described it in 1993? More from his never-completed autobiography:

* * *

San Francisco in the Sixties! Brunch at the Golden Cask on Haight Street, Jan Jansen singing her bluesy ballads at the Copper Lantern. Yummy go go boys and delicious dinners at the Paper Doll. There was Jackson's, and upstairs, the cabaret called Jackson's Penthouse. Wonderful Gordon's where Harry, the waiter, brought glasses of water and warned, "Don't drink it—fish fuck in it." The Cockettes performed in gender-fuck drag with beards, mustaches, eye shadow, rouged cheeks, lipsticked mouths, flaunting their male genitalia while gowned in outrageous garb. Truman Capote remarked after viewing their performance, "Lack of talent is not enough." And then there was the Gilded Cage.

Let me guide you into the past; the Gilded Cage was a marvelous place to visit. There was nothing quite like it in San Francisco during those happy, carefree days of the Sixties. "I'll meet you at the Cage" was a popular expression. It was a bar, a cocktail lounge, a showroom.

The Cage's impressive feature was an old-fashioned bar, probably left in the building after the 'quake of 1906. The atmosphere was dim, enhanced by turn-of-the-century light fixtures and red, flocked wallpaper. At the end of the bar was a lounge area with about fifteen small tables the size of a steering wheel. Anyone for kneesies? Beyond the tables was a platform with an old upright piano, and a black-draped wall with stationary red side curtains to give a stagey look. Further on was a set of double doors that opened onto a much larger room that was vacant at the time we debuted our show. Later, Arthur transformed the space into a real showroom by building a large proscenium stage for us with real curtains, lights, and another bar. The room held perhaps two hundred people at small tables and chairs arranged cabaret-style.

When Rio and I first opened at the Cage, we did our shows weeknights and Sundays in the front lounge. Our act consisted of the "Moppettes" (or "Living Dolls," as I renamed them after Jim Henson created his "Muppets"), the novelty feature of the show. The dolls were great because they required little performance space.

The "Moppettes" were headless puppets representing various characters from Mae West, to a stripper, to Carol and Julie at Carnegie Hall, to Shirley Temple, to Dracula and Vampira. Even a Singing Nun! Rio and I were dressed in black jumpsuits when we fastened the puppets around our necks with our own heads showing. This left our hands free to manipulate the puppets' arms and legs. We worked on a small table against a black curtain. The effect was amazing as we donned various wigs and headdresses for each character, lip-synching to a prerecorded soundtrack. The dolls opened the shows, then Rio and I performed various pantomimes, such as Mike Nichols and Elaine May routines, and I closed the shows with my live impressions. Because of the intimacy of the room, there was a great deal of kibitzing and camping with the audiences.

One night there was a middle-aged woman sitting down front. I used the word "camp" in a routine and looked down at her and said, "You probably don't know what 'camp' means, do you? It's something incongruous like finding me dressed like this." (I was Bette Davis dressed in a doctor's smock and cap), standing on the corner of Turk and Market selling *Watchtower* and *Awake,* (those religious pamphlets). With that, the woman got up, pulled out copies of *Watchtower* and *Awake* from her purse, and went up and down the bar calling out, "*Watchtower, Awake.* Get your *Watchtower* and *Awake.*" Of course, the bar went up for grabs, and I pretended to faint onstage. Later, of course, I told them that the lady was a friend of mine, Blanche Bennett, up from Los Angeles, and that we had planned the whole charade. Blanche had once worked on stage as a foil for Jimmy Durante, and her timing that night was perfect. The audience went wild.

One year after we opened at the Cage, Rio and I were hired for a five-week engagement in a Las Vegas revue. The money was a big lure, and Arthur graciously gave us time off, so we flew to Vegas and opened at the Frontier Hotel. We performed the Living Dolls and a Frankenstein monster pantomime, but our show was not well received. The audience was as enthusiastic as a room full of tombstones, so when our engagement was over Arthur welcomed us back at the Cage. I was never so glad to see the inside of a nightclub in my life!

Arthur, meanwhile, had built the large stage in the back showroom where, in addition to the tables and chairs, there was a standing room area with gold pillars set in a circle to form the Gilded Cage for which the club was named. It had a waist-high shelf all around on which the customers could place their drinks and watch the show. This area provided the perfect spot to meet someone for a potential love affair, and I've often been told, "We met at the Cage during one of your shows, and we're still together."

Soon after we opened in the new showroom, we acquired a light and sound man named Ray Correia. He and Rio installed lights, sound, and curtains, while I came up with ideas for the pantomimes, live material, and organized the costumes. Ray, with his lover, Ted, arrived in San Francisco from Massachusetts, spotted our show pictures in the display case outside the club, and came to the show every night. At that time, Rio and I would flip a light switch or turn on our tape machine, and go on stage. Ray changed all that when he came to work for us, and though we were delighted to have his help and expertise, we were unable to pay him anything. Ray worked for us several weeks until I learned he was broke and would have to leave us to find a paying job. I induced management to come up with some money for Ray, and he stayed on. We were all happy about that.

When Ray wasn't assisting us with the show, he worked as a cocktail waiter at the Cage. One night, while I was doing my live material, I looked down at Ray busy peddling his drinks, and I noticed he was wearing the largest, flashiest cufflinks Woolworth's sold. He had fashioned the 'links from two huge rhinestone brooches. Off the top of my head I said, "Sabu, what are you doing here in the Gilded Cage hustling drinks?" I was referring to Sabu, the Indian elephant boy in the movies, who always wore huge sparkling jewels on his turbans and fingers. The nickname, Sabu, stuck. Another night I was doing my Turban Ladies routine when, as Maria Montez, I called out to Ray, "Sabu, bring me the Cobra Chool (jewel)! I must have the Cobra Chool!" Ray as Sabu removed one of his huge sparkling cufflinks, came to the stage, bowed, and handed me the "chool." The bit stayed in the show.

During the day when Ray had plenty of free time, he went out "scavenging" and brought back tape recorders, movie projectors, spotlights, curtains, furniture, and a Shakespearean gown he'd "found" in the nearby basement of a theatre company's wardrobe department. He even went to graves in cemeteries and "retrieved" huge floral pieces on easels, which we used during a Mike Nichols and Elaine May pantomime set in a funeral home! I never dared ask where all these "goodies" came from. Ray-Sabu was the perfect Super Go-fer!

A costume shop on Market Street was having a going-out-of-business sale, so we hiked down to see what was available. It was Drag Heaven! Dresses that would "work" for different routines, shawls, flapper gowns, feather boas, fur pieces, a ratty old mink coat perfect for Tallulah, hats, gloves, and shoes of various periods. With this newly acquired wardrobe, our vast Cage repertoire began.

Some of the patrons of the club brought in wardrobe for us too. Franklin Townsend, my young friend who had accompanied me to San Francisco from Florida back when I did shows at Ann's 440 Club, and who was now one of the City's premiere hair stylists, was instrumental in changing my image completely at this time. Before Franklin "made me over," I was still pretty much working in my tuxedo, and just throwing on props as needed. I credit Franklin as the first person to put me into "full glamour drag" and to create a "look" for me. When the Cage held a Sadie Hawkins Day party, Franklin brought me a new dress, shoes, and one of Mary Costa's wigs. (She was, at the time, a famous opera diva, and Franklin did her hair and wigs.) A few weeks later he did me up in a black sequined gown and asked his friend Talven, a clever costume designer, to create another gown for me for our Halloween show. Talven outdid himself by designing a filmy, flowing, floor-length pink chiffon number with—and here was the gimmick—a see-through top with plastic breasts—a tad shocking, but "topless" was just making its debut in the clubs along Broadway in North Beach, and Marlene Dietrich had introduced her famous nude-look gown in Vegas. The Cage wanted to be "current," so we may have had a headstart on Carol Doda!

Working in full drag gave my act a whole new dimension. I could use lines like, "This isn't a wig—my Nair backfired," or "I'm very masculine. I dress this way to counteract it," or "If I were elected President, I could save the taxpayers money by being First Lady as well. My platform will be based on four-inch heels!"

A clever designer named Mr. Black whipped up some gowns for me—literally! Some of them had whips on them! Eventually, I gathered up enough nerve to actually go into a women's dress boutique to buy a gown. My hands were sweating, and I was extremely nervous. I selected a beautiful blue beaded number, but I didn't try it on. I took a chance it would be my size, paid for it, and flew out the door. Fortunately, it did fit, and I still have it in a trunk, but the zipper is rusty, and I wouldn't dare try to get into it. A lot of Baskin-Robbins and dry vodka martinis have gone over the dam since the Fabulous Sixties!

"Through These Portals . . ."

Charles Pierce continues his fabulous saga of life at the Gilded Cage.

* * *

The Gilded Cage became an entertainment mecca for the casts of shows on tour. Usually, the boy "gypsies," hairdressers, and dressers would "discover" our show and dash back to the theatre to spread the word to the stars that the Cage was the place to go after their show. One night Rudolf Nureyev showed up alone. He loved our show and returned the next night with Dame Margot Fonteyn. They, in turn, invited me to their performances at the Opera House. Backstage, after her performance, Dame Margot presented me with a pair of her ballet slippers, which she signed. I had them framed, and they have been on my apartment wall since 1967.

Other celebs who passed through the Cage's portals were Joe Flynn of *McHale's Navy,* who appeared with a sexy young muscle man in a white T-shirt. Flynn, a Hollywood actor, was being very open about his "gayness." Richard Deacon of *The Dick Van Dyke Show* dropped in to "see something gay, I trust." [Other celebrities included] Leslie Uggams with Gale Gordon, who appeared regularly on *The Lucy Show* with Lucille Ball; and even Shari Lewis—without Lamb Chop.

The greatest night at the Gilded Cage was when Angela Lansbury, who was starring in *Mame* at the Curran Theatre, brought her entire company to see our show. My delightful friend, Anne Francine, had replaced Beatrice Arthur in the role of Vera Charles in the national tour of the show. Anne had seen our lounge show a few nights before, thought Angela would enjoy the show, and had organized the party. Anne gave me notice a few days before the group was to come in, so I sent off to Hollywood for the film *'Till the Clouds Roll By,* in which Angela had performed the song "How'd You Like to Spoon with Me?" while sitting on a swing.

The minute Angela and Anne entered the showroom with [Angela's] entire entourage, we played an instrumental recording of the title song "Mame." The audience screamed and applauded so hard that Angela and Anne stood up on chairs, bowing and waving. When the curtain opened on a movie screen with the clip of Angela singing on the swing, she was completely flabbergasted. She told me later it was a great surprise, as she hadn't seen herself in that clip since 1946!

Then came the highlight of the evening when we presented our version, a take-off of *Mame.* I played Angela's role, and Rio was Vera Charles. What blew the audience away was a young boy playing Mame's nephew, Patrick. Nine-year-old John Dennis was dressed as a little sailor who I pulled out of a gift-wrapped box, and he sang "My Best Girl" to Angela. I saw her recently at Bea Arthur's, and she told me that her mouth is still hanging open over that evening at the Gilded Cage. She loved it!

Backstage at the Cage was a marvelous place for dress-up, fun, and laughter. Hermione Gingold camped it up in her distinctive British bleat: "Oh, dear, my eyelashes are on upside down!" Tammy Grimes fingered my falsies, Rudolf Nureyev tried on my large Jeanette Mac-Donald picture hat, or Richard Deacon [wore] my Mae West wig, and [did not want] to give it back!

And I mustn't overlook Boyd Ransome, that handsome, debonair, ex-Hollywood actor turned career-manager for his famous actress wife, Beverly Ashton. Every time Beverly opened in a show in San Francisco, Boyd hung out backstage at the Cage, hoping I would fix him up with a transsexual who might be doing a number in the show. He fancied young boys who had silicone breasts but who still had their male genitalia. I was not a "fixer-upper," so I hadn't introduced anyone to Boyd, but he liked to hang around and shoot the Hollywood gossip breeze, and he did have his charm. Beverly, it seemed, was indifferent or completely oblivious to her husband's sexual preferences, which was strange because her first actor husband was homosexual, and when she found him in bed with another famous male star, she divorced him. Perhaps she was too involved with her fabulous career that spanned movies, Broadway, and TV to notice her husband's peccadillos.

Was the Cage a sort of utopia where everything was warm, people were friendly, and a good time was had by all? One fabulous continuing party with paying guests? Yes! I couldn't wait to go to work each night. If I could put the clock back, I would spin it to the Gilded Cage days! We had pure joy—not a worry in the world.

Some of our pantomimes were classics. I remember Rio dressed as a nun lip-syncing "Climb Ev'ry Mountain," pseudo-seriously, then lifting his habit at the end of the number and roller-skating off stage! He was Lady Rhonda Lay in our sketch satirizing Queen Elizabeth I, the Virgin Queen. (Who ever heard of a virgin queen?) I was Bette Davis in an ornate Elizabethan gown we rented (or Sabu "found," perhaps), and our handsome straight man, Michael Monroe, played dum-dum Lord Essex. Michael joined the show after we'd played the Cage for two solid years, and worked with us on weekends. Tall, dark, and handsome, he was totally uninhibited, and if a number called for him to strip, he gleefully ripped off his clothes to the delight of the audience.

Another uninhibited member of our cast was David Angel. He was a cocktail waiter at the Cage, but when he stripped naked and strapped on a pair of beautiful white-feathered angel wings, he was glorious to behold.

His real name was David Likens, and when he began working at the Cage in 1968, the movie *Barbarella* starring Jane Fonda was playing all over the Bay Area. I took one look at David and decided to cast him as the angel character John Phillip Law had played in *Barbarella* in an effort to spice up our already-popular show. David went for the idea as he enjoyed showing off his handsome looks and smooth, well-muscled naked body.

David was just twenty-four and at the peak of his prime with his perfect movie-star features, long-lashed deep blue eyes, blond hair, straight nose, firm jaw, great smile, and, of course, that six-foot, 150-pound physique rippling with those sculptured muscles!

On the night of David's debut in the show, Debussy's *L'apres-midi d'un Faune* played as the curtains parted revealing a perfectly motionless David caught in a slightly crouched position on a round, carpeted dais, a soft blue light bathing his creamy-white form, clad only in his angel wings and a plastic see-through jockstrap. He was a vision from the portals of ancient Greece.

As the dais began to revolve, David came to life and assumed several other poses; then, as the music swelled, he stepped down from his platform and the apron of the stage, and walked slowly through the audience and disappeared into the darkness.

At first sight of David, the audience gasped. Male nudity was still an unusual sight in San Francisco in the Sixties, in spite of Broadway shows such as *Hair* and *Oh! Calcutta!;* those shows were in New York, and San Francisco audiences had yet to see them.

When David stepped into the audience, the cheering started, and many hands reached out to touch his naked body—and some succeeded. David took it in his stride, loving every minute of his new-found celebrity. I liked to keep the show fresh and very topical, so when the "angel bit" became slightly tarnished, I replaced it with another routine. David shed his wings and see-through jockstrap and went back to peddling his drinks.

Sabu and I did a pantomime of *[Who's Afraid of] Virginia Woolf?,* I as Liz Taylor, he as Richard Burton. I remember I ate a rubber chicken while doing that number!

We did a séance sketch in black light with the table rising and ghosts running around the stage, glowing in the dark. Nine-year-old John Dennis was such a hit in *Mame* that we dressed him in rags to do "Where Is Love?" from *Oliver!* Not a dry eye in the house. He and I did a takeoff on "Indian Love Call" with him as a tiny Mountie in a bright red coat, and I as an Indian maiden.

As a beat-up actress at her dressing table putting on makeup with a paint roller and Brillo pads, and shoving poppers up my nose, I pantomimed Della Reese's "It Was a Very Good Year."

"It Must Be Him" was a smashing number—literally. As I lip-synced Vikki Carr's record, I hurtled around the stage unearthing telephones hidden in every conceivable place, slinging them violently against the walls and smashing them to bits. The audience loved it.

As Marilyn Monroe, I was vamping cowboys Rio and Michael as they played cards, while I carried on as a dance hall girl singing "File My Claim." When the number ended, they got up, locked arms, and waltzed off together.

I pantomimed Barbra Streisand's "Gotta Move" with lots of dry ice billowing across the stage. We did "Put on Your Sunday Clothes" from *Hello, Dolly!* as tramps.

I did a hippie number (the Haight/Ashbury was in full swing at the time) using a lawn mower to cut grass for a joint. By now, Sabu was in the show and one of his best numbers was "Downtown" to the recording by Mrs. Miller.[1] He wore a bright red jersey tube dress stuffed with four large balloons strategically placed, two in front for breasts and two to enlarge his behind, a fright wig, and huge spectacles. Al Jutzi, a superb lighting man, and Sabu built me a huge electric fireworks backdrop that flashed and spun during my Fourth of July number to the song "Irma La Douce."

Two routines became standard hits in our shows: my "live" Bette Davis impression, and, to close the pantomime show, my Jeanette MacDonald number, singing "San Francisco" as I flew out over the audience on a flower-bedecked swing. As I swung higher and higher, tiny electric lights embedded in strings of flowers lit up on the ropes, and bubbles and rose petals floated down from overhead. The routine was not without danger. Glitter from the flowers once became embedded in my eye, and I still have a scar tissue from the operation to remove it. One night a rope suspending the swing broke, but I held onto the rope on the other side, which caused me to spin 'round and 'round. The audience was in hysterics as I kept spinning and mouthing Jeanette's lyrics. Another night I fell off the swing and landed on the front tables, but I kept mouthing to the last note!

To keep the show fresh and give it variety, Rio and I initiated a series of Talent Nights every weekend when anyone could come in and perform as part of the show. Arthur, to hype the innovation, offered a free trip to Las Vegas to anyone who was selected the winner three times in a row. Usually, the acts consisted of drags lip-syncing to records, but two performers, my old friend from Pasadena Playhouse days, John Wallraff, and his partner, Norman Williams, not only won three times in a row, but became a permanent feature act in our show. They did a variety of lip-sync acts, and I named them The Beverly Hill Nellies. They not only did a hillbilly number, but also did routines satirizing the movie *Tom Jones* and *The King and I,* and *My Fairy Lady,* a takeoff on *My Fair Lady.* When John came out as Kate Smith singing "God Bless America," the roof caved in!

Jaye Stevens, who made a lovely drag in the show, especially when he lip-synced "San Francisco (Be Sure to Wear Some Flowers in Your Hair)," dressed in flowing chiffon and actually wearing a crown of real flowers in his long blond locks, was with us for a few weeks.

We were shocked later to learn that he had been murdered, stabbed to death by his sister in Golden Gate Park early one morning. His sister confessed to murdering not only Jaye, but their mother as well. The sister [had] stabbed her to death, hacked her body up, and burned it in the family fireplace. After that, she lay in wait for her older sister to come home from work [and] confronted her at the front door, brandishing an axe and chasing the sister down the street. However, the older sister outran her axe-wielding sibling, and the murderess was apprehended and hauled off to jail.

Before it was known who the murderess was, a memorial service was held for Jaye in Finocchio's showroom on Broadway in North Beach, and I gave a short tribute to him. No one knew at the time that the murdering sister was seated in the audience right next to her mother and older sister! The poor mother had no warning that she would be her daughter's next victim.

The Gilded Cage was always open on Christmas Eve so that a gay man who was alone would have a place to go on that night. We always decorated a beautiful tree with shimmering and twinkling lights, and after we'd performed our Christmas routines we'd invite the audience to join us for champagne and to sing carols with Rio at the piano. There were so many lonely men who got the blues at holiday time, so the Cage was their "home away from home" where, for a few moments, they could forget their troubles and have some Christmas cheer. Many were disowned by their families just because they were gay.

After all those fun years, the Gilded Cage days and nights began to fade. Dance bars and other showrooms in the downtown area were drawing customers away. Arthur hired a pianist, Ronnie Scalare, to play in the intimate front lounge/bar, and our show played in the main back showroom Tuesdays through Sundays. Those fun nights in the front lounge were gone, and the regulars only liked the larger room when we did our full production shows. I asked for a raise, but it was not forthcoming. A door charge would have helped, but management didn't want to chance asking for admission after so many years of customers being able to see the show for just the price of a drink. In addition, Arthur and his wife were headed for divorce, and they decided to close the Cage and go their separate ways.

Closing night was June 1, 1969. It was a gay, gala farewell with four hundred people jammed into a room that seated a couple of hundred with standing room for seventy-five. Rio, Sabu, Michael, and I did our numbers with great emotion, and when I swung out over the room singing "San Francisco" for the last time, flowers were thrown onstage by everyone in the audience. We were standing ankle-deep in carnations as we took our final bows, after bows, after bows. Some in the crowd jumped onstage to pluck flowers from the swing as souvenirs. Then the lights were lowered, the front curtains closed, and our six-year run at the Gilded Cage came to an end.

Dismantling our show was depressing and heart-wrenching for me. It took two full days to remove all of our costumes, props, sound system, the swing, lights, and backdrops. We left a four-foot pile of old costumes and props in the middle of the floor for the janitor to dispose of, and the rest we stored in an empty apartment in the building where Sabu lived. We eventually sold or gave away most of our remaining wardrobe at flea markets, which took weeks.

Though I was saddened to leave behind the Gilded Cage and its memories, I was offered an engagement at the Lazy X Club in Los Angeles, and it was time to move on.

15

Rio Dante,
the Man Who Would Be Dracula

Charles Pierce enjoyed kidding his audiences at the Gilded Cage that Rio Dante would go home after the show and sleep, bat-like, hanging upside down from the rafters of his bedroom! That was because Rio had an uncanny resemblance to Count Dracula, and he enjoyed playing that image up by wearing all-black clothing, a flowing black cape with a high stand-up collar, with his black hair slicked straight back.

Rio may have played up a weird image, but in reality he was a quiet, unassuming man with a sly sense of humor and had a rigid lifestyle. He adhered to his "schedule," as Charles called Rio's way of life, never going to the after-the-show parties, never staying late at the bar, never varying his strict vegetarian diet, and always taking his tonic of a spoonful of honey with garlic and vinegar! His only vices were smoking cigarettes and nursing a bottle of beer.

When Charles first met Rio in Miami Beach, Rio was married and he and his wife June had just returned to Florida after enjoying a luxurious and relaxing Caribbean cruise. Either Rio or his wife had come into an inheritance, and they had decided to live extravagantly until their fortune ran out. Mr. and Mrs. Carol John Watson (Rio's real name) were an elegant couple as they swept into the Echo Club to enjoy Charles' show, but at that time neither Charles nor Rio had an inkling that they would soon be partners in show business and that their relationship would last so long.

Rio and June soon went through their inherited wealth, and June took a job at a local bank to keep them afloat financially. That's when Carol John Watson became Rio Dante and joined Charles' show, performing in the pantomimes and eventually accompanying Charles at the piano.

Years later, when Charles and Rio opened at the Gilded Cage, Rio rented a room next door to the Cage at the Gates Hotel, and Charles took a suite at Hyde Park Suites at the corner of Hyde Street and North Point. Rio didn't have a car at the time so it was convenient for him to live next door to the club. Whenever I'd stop by the Cage before showtime, Rio would be seated at the front bar nursing his bottle of beer, smoking his cigarette in its long holder, and flashing the ever-present ring on the index finger of his right hand. He was always dressed in black to play up his Dracula look, and he had two expressions he used constantly.

"How the hell are you?" He never varied his greeting, and "How does that grab you?" was the other one.

When Rio's wealthy cousin Leola came to visit him from Idaho, she decided to stay on in the City and leased a large, elegant mansion on Camino del Mar at Sea Cliff. She immediately rented out most of the rooms to young male students and to Rio and some of his friends.

Leola was a matronly woman of about sixty-something with graying dark hair, bejeweled eyeglasses, sparkling black eyes, and lots of energy. She loved to entertain in her temporary home, and she often had all of us out to enjoy parties at Halloween, Easter, Thanksgiving, and Christmas. She also tossed tea dances when the students brought their girlfriends, and all of us enjoyed a pleasant afternoon high above the blue Pacific.

Rio reveled in the spaciousness and elegance of Leola's mansion, reliving some of the lifestyle he had once enjoyed with June. He liked to take evening strolls in the fog above the crashing waves on the cliffs that gave the posh enclave its name.

One night, Rio, dressed as always in his signature black with his high-collared black cape draped around him, set out as usual in the dense fog. In the distance the foghorn moaned, and a few night birds rustled in the dense branches of the forest of gnarled old cypress trees.

He had only gone a few hundred feet on the serpentine route of Camino del Mar when he encountered a motorist with his head under the upraised hood of his stalled automobile. Rio approached the man with the intention of helping, perhaps to call the Automobile Club for him.

"May I be of assistance?" Rio asked in his deep somber voice.

The motorist glanced in Rio's direction, saw what he thought was an apparition right out of an empty grave, reared up, smashed his head on the overhanging hood, dropped his wrench and screwdriver, and ran howling down 30th Avenue to Lake Street as if all the banshees in hell were after him.

Rio hadn't meant to terrify the poor man. He ran back to Leola's mansion and phoned the police that a man was running berserk down 30th Avenue toward Lake Street and that he needed assistance with his ailing auto.

Rio's wife, June, stayed on in Florida still working at the bank, and, though the couple communicated by telephone or letter, they never divorced nor saw each other again. I'm sure Rio wasn't gay, maybe asexual, living quietly, never seeming happy or unhappy.

After Leola returned to Idaho, Rio leased a very unique apartment on Haight Street near Market Street, out of the frantic Haight/Ashbury scene of the 1960s. He and two male roommates, and their huge Great Dane named Duke, shared the premises. The apartment reminded me of a 1930s set for an Astaire/Rogers movie musical. There were three units in the building, which was set back from the sidewalk with plantings in front and along the walkway that led to the three entrances. Each unit was two stories and in the Art Deco style. The living room, dining area, and kitchen were on the first floor, with a round swimming pool built into the floor! A stairway with a geometric-patterned railing led to a balcony overlooking the lower level and pool and to the bedrooms and bath. In the ceiling, high above the balcony, was a skylight just large enough to allow a person to slide through.

One morning at about 2 a.m., Rio and his roommates were awakened by two thieves armed with guns who had pried the skylight open and dropped to the balcony. They literally dragged Rio from his bed by the hair of his head, and yanked out tufts of it in doing so. Duke the Great Dane, who was the size of a Shetland pony, was very hospitable to the crooks and allowed them to tie up his masters and loot the place. He probably had a healthy fear of guns.

Rio and his housemates continued to live at the Haight Street apartment after the skylight was made secure, but when the Gilded Cage closed and Rio began his new secretarial job at Time-Life Books, he and and his roommates moved to 22nd Street in the Mission District. Occasionally we would ride together on BART—the

Bay Area Rapid Transit train—that dropped him off on Mission Street and me at my home in Balboa Park. The other passengers always stared at Rio as if they just couldn't believe what they saw. He no longer wore his Dracula cape, but it was his uncanny Bela Lugosi look that seemed to fascinate people.

Our mutual friend Les Natali gave us tickets to see *La Cage aux Folles,* the musical that was playing at the Golden Gate Theatre, and Rio and I attended. Les is a well-known San Francisco entrepreneur who owns and operates the Patio Cafe and the Badlands dance bar in the Castro District, and produced Charles Pierce's fabulous Bimbo's shows.

Before the show, Rio and I had drinks at a nearby bar and reminisced about our old days at the Gilded Cage and about Charles.

"I've never known anyone who was more dedicated to his career than Charles," Rio said. "He lived, ate, and slept that show."

"I know," I replied. "He often told me he'd dreamed a line for one of his impressions, and he'd ask me if I liked it. If I laughed, he put it in the act."

"Anyone who wants to be in show business could learn a lot from that. You have to be totally dedicated to succeed. I enjoyed being in Charles' show, but I really was never fiercely dedicated the way he was."

"Nor was I," I answered. "It was fun while it lasted, but it wasn't my whole life like it was his."

I never saw Rio again after that night. He died suddenly of lung cancer on June 2, 1989. His roommates discovered his body lying on the living room floor, his eyes staring, his mouth agape, and the faithful Duke sprawled by his side.

16

"The Beverly Hill Nellies" and How They Grew

It began to be a habit with me to drop by the Gilded Cage every Friday and Saturday night to catch Charles and Rio's shows, mainly to see how the lines we'd written were going over with the audience.

Over a period of time, I became acquainted with Norman Williams, who also came into the bar on weekends, and we'd joke around and discuss the show. On one particular Saturday night soon after Charles initiated his Talent Nights, I was standing at the bar in the back showroom when Norman came up beside me.

"I want to be in Charles' Talent Night Show." Norman seemed perplexed.

"Well, that's no problem," I said. "All you have to do is work up a pantomime to a record, get a costume, and you're on. I'm sure Charles would be glad to have you try it out."

"Yeah, except I don't want to do it alone. A friend of mine said he'd do it with me, but he chickened out. I was wondering if you would do it with me?"

I didn't realize that Charles had come out of his dressing room and was standing behind me.

"Oh, no, Norman, I don't want to be in Charles' show."

"Go ahead, do it." Charles faced Norman and me at the bar.

"Well," I said, "I guess I could do it. I'd never thought about being in the show." The number Norman had chosen to do didn't appeal to me. "I'll look through my albums and see what I can come up with, and I'll call you tomorrow."

Lucille Ball had recorded the soundtrack of her Broadway musical *Wildcat* and there was a rousing, fun song on it called "What Takes My Fancy." I played it for Norman and he agreed it would be a good number for us to do. Because I was taller than Norman, we decided it would be funnier if I played the Lucille Ball part as a big hillbilly woman, and he would be the little hillbilly man.

Soon our number was blocked, and we began to collect our costumes. Charles loaned me a shaggy blond wig and an old brown velveteen cloche hat. At Goodwill I found a short-sleeved, red-checked man's shirt for a blouse, and I cut a hole in the center of a round, fringed, tan-colored tablecloth for a skirt, which I covered with colorful calico patches. I added a pair of high-topped tennis shoes and two balloons for bazooms, and I was ready!

Norman was dressed in old, faded blue bib overalls, also with patches, a raggedy shirt, and a battered straw hat. We really looked like a couple of clowns from some hillbilly circus. (I never took drag seriously, I always felt I was being a clown.)

Arthur, the owner of the Cage, had told Charles that he would give a prize of a free trip to Las Vegas to any talent act that won three times in a row. Norman and I were all keyed up the night we debuted our act because we wanted to win that trip. After several drag queens had mouthed everything from Streisand to Garland to Dietrich, the audience was ready for a change of pace, and Norman and I were it. We were the last contestants, and Charles' voice announced on the sound system: "And now, John and Norman, the Beverly Hill Nellies!" (Charles had named us that.)

Out we came in our outrageous hillbilly garb. I had painted on a huge red Lucille Ball mouth, and the audience applauded as soon as we made our entrance. The number was rollicking and fast-paced. Norman did a little jig, and I did bellkicks, together we locked arms for a do-si-do, and, for a finale, Norman raced toward me at high speed and leapt into my arms. Thunderous applause, and we won!

The movie *Tom Jones* was in the theaters at the time, so I came up with a spoof of that for our second try for the Las Vegas trip on the next Talent Night. Our soundtrack was a pastiche of *The King and I* song "Hello, Young Lovers," where the voice of "Anna" (Deborah Kerr) sings about "Tom." I played the part of the hag in the woods dressed in rags, and Norman was "Tom Jones" in an authentic period costume he'd rented, blond wig, knee breeches, flowing white shirt, leather jerkin, and silver-buckled shoes. I came on first, mouthing the words about "Tom," then the soundtrack changed to "There Once Was a Man" from *Pajama Game* and the voices of Doris Day and John Raitt. It, too, was a rousing number with lots of wild carryings-on, and we won for the second time! One more winning number and we'd be in Las Vegas—or so we thought.

One Sunday morning Norman invited Charles and me to his apartment for brunch. He had just purchased the record album *Kate Smith at Carnegie Hall,* and after coffee Norman said, "I think John should do Kate Smith singing 'God Bless America.' "

"Oh, I think you should do it, Charles," I said. After all, it was his show, and I wasn't sure how he'd feel about my doing a single number. To my surprise, Charles was all for my doing Kate.

"Get a 1940s drag at Goodwill and come over to my place and we'll work on it." Charles showed me the gestures he wanted me to do, and I went home and rehearsed all week. Then, on the next weekend, Charles put "Kate Smith" in the show. When I made my entrance as Kate Smith, wearing a floor-length 1940s style, blue crepe and lace number and a ratty brown wig Charles gave me, with big red Lucille Ball lips and two huge balloons for breasts, the audience screamed. That number became my signature act, and it was a regular in the Cage show for two years. I added more business as I became more flexible doing the song, such as bending way over backward and then bringing my face up, like the moon rising over the two huge, inflated balloon breasts. One night the entire audience brought small American flags to wave all through the song. To this day, fans come up to me to tell me how much they enjoyed Kate Smith at the Gilded Cage.

Norman captivated audiences when he performed "I'm in Love with Miss Logan," seated on a high stool and dressed like a schoolboy, singing about his crush on his teacher. It became his signature number.

It was at this time that a young man named Garth Brown brought a recording to Charles of Jeanette MacDonald singing "San Francisco." The nostalgia craze hadn't set in yet, so it wasn't easy to find rare recordings, but Garth was a "young old-timer" and had a collection of antique radios, phonographs, and records. At first, Charles wanted me to do the "San Francisco" number, but I knew it would be perfect for him because with his features and his big blue eyes, he resembled Jeanette very much more than I did. When Charles climbed on that swing and trilled "San Francisco," history was made at the Gilded Cage.

When Norman and I performed our takeoff on *The King and I,* it was another hit for us, and we won the contest for the third time. Our dreams of a Las Vegas weekend were shattered when Arthur reneged on his offer, so we had to be content with just the fact that we had won and that the audiences liked us.

For *The King and I* sketch, I entered as "Anna" in a blue-and-white striped outfit with a voluminous hoopskirt and tennis shoes, mouthing "I Whistle a Happy Tune." A gong sounded, and as the back curtains parted to the strains of "The March of the Siamese Children," Norman struck a pose, arms folded across his chest, a pint-sized Yul Brynner in an authentic Siamese "King" costume, complete with jeweled earring and shiny bald pate. I, as "Anna," bowed as he marched around the stage, before we seated ourselves on a large gold hassock and mouthed the lyrics to "I Get Embarrassed" from the musical *Take Me Along*. Suddenly, as my "Anna" character rose and giggled, Norman as the "King" chased her around the stage, caught her, and bent her over his knee, and, as he goosed her royally, she giggled again and screeched, "Oh, that was good, your Majesty!" Blackout.

The next sketch Norman and I performed was *My Fairy Lady*, a takeoff on *My Fair Lady*. Don De Tonque, the maitre d' at the Cage, built us a street sign on a standard on which was emblazoned the name "Enchanted Polk Street." It began with Norman's entrance, with him dressed in a cutaway coat, sleek gray trousers, a gray top hat, spats, and a walking stick. Mouthing a few strains of "On the Street Where You Live," he moved downstage left. The curtains parted to reveal my character posed statuesquely in the black-and-white "Ascot Gavotte" costume, with a folded white parasol in my outstretched hand and my left hand resting akimbo on my left hip, eyes straight ahead. I held the pose briefly as the music from the overture to *My Fair Lady* played, then I walked quickly downstage center and mouthed, "I'm an Ordinary Man," using Rex Harrison's voice while dressed as Audrey Hepburn! All of our numbers were successful, and Charles seemed pleased that we were in his show. He paid me $40 for each weekend—we worked every Friday and Saturday night—and half of that, $20, I gave to Norman. I finally told Charles that Norman and I would have to have a raise because it was costing Norman a lot to rent the expensive costumes he wore, and I was paying for the materials to make my makeshift costumes as well.

"Ask Arthur if you want a raise," Charles told me.

"But, Charles," I said, "you hired us for the show, not Arthur."

He finally came up with a little more money, but I felt it just wasn't worth it to be in his show for so little money, in addition to working at my regular job.

Arthur had told me that if Norman and I worked up our act he would hire us, but when I asked Norman to work with me on it, he said, no, he wanted to stay in Charles' show.

"But, Norman," I said, "we could open for Charles' show. We'd still be in it, and we'd make a lot more money."

"No, I want to stay in Charles' show." And he did. But I told Charles I was leaving the show, and he wasn't pleased. He made me feel like a traitor, but I'd had enough by then. I tried to find another partner, but no one worked out. Norman and I could have been a successful duo like some of the other record acts of the time such as Doodles and Spider, Tony and Eddie, and Maurice and Lamont.

Working with Charles in his show had been fun up to a point, and when Charles was dressed in his male attire he was easier to deal with. When he was in high drag, full face, wig, and Joan Crawford ankle-strap "fuck me" pumps, he could become a six-foot-plus towering inferno, the Bitch Goddess/Control Queen unsurpassed, if he was not amused!

When I first started doing his show, Charles assigned me several quick-change numbers. While the tape recorder spun I had to change costumes quickly and run onstage as different characters. One night the top of my costume got tangled, I heard my cue, and I ran onstage bare-chested with the top of the costume hanging from my waist. I was wearing a silly feathered headdress and my oversized red mouth. The audience came apart, screaming, whistling, and stomping. I finished the number and ran backstage. Instantly, Charles, in full female drag, was glaring at me!

"Just what the hell were you doing out there? Are you trying to ruin my show?" Glare! Glare! The Bitch Goddess was on the loose!

I explained what had happened.

"Well, okay, leave it in—but get a coupla pasties." He knew a good laugh when he heard one, so the number stayed in the show as I had accidentally performed it—but with pasties to protect the innocent!

17

In Love with a "Living Doll"

In 1959, Charles debuted "The Moppettes" at the Echo Club in Miami Beach, Florida. Rio Dante had joined Charles, playing the piano and performing in "The Moppettes" segment of the show. A very clever young man Charles had discovered in Miami Beach created the first "Moppettes." They were beautifully made, and Charles always referred to them as "the original dolls." There was a stripper, a Mae West, a Shirley Temple, and a cute, bare-chested, anatomically correct sailor, complete with an anchor tattoo on his muscular upper arm and tight white bell-bottoms with a flap in front. Later, Charles and I created more "Moppettes" at his Hyde Park Suites suite in San Francisco: two singing nuns, a Dolly Parton, a black-leather–clad dominatrix complete with crotch-high, spike-heeled flagellation boots, and a whip. There was a male masochist doll Charles teamed with the dominatrix, a Dracula, Vampira, a circus clown, a Gay Nineties dancehall girl with red high-button shoes, and a muscular Tarzan wearing only a skimpy loincloth.

Neither Charles nor I could operate a sewing machine, and I guess he didn't want to hire a seamstress, so we used a staple gun to "seam" the tubular arms, legs, and bodies. After these were stuffed with cotton batting, Charles stuffed child-size gloves and attached them to the wrists, and in most cases he used real child-size clothes and shoes. I hand-sewed the "breasts" onto the female figures, and I hand-sewed special high-heeled pumps or boots made out of felt or oilcloth. Other costumes we pieced together out of our imaginations and whatever material was at hand. Mostly, the little creatures were put together with staples, Scotch Tape and Elmer's Glue! We had a lot of fun working on the project, and Charles paid me $25 per puppet plus dinner.

One thing that remains in my mind was Charles' impatience. While I was cutting patterns or sewing "breasts" on, he would be fidgeting and pacing restlessly, every minute or so asking, "Is it ready yet?" If ever there was a man who wanted "instant everything," it was Charles. He hated to wait.

It was at the Hyde Park Suites that we saw the then-unknown Barbra Streisand moseying down Hyde Street toward the bay.

"Look," Charles said. "There goes Babs Streisand moseying down Hyde Street toward the bay."

"Oh, yeah," I replied. "She's doing a gig at the hungry i. Big deal." As it turned out, it was a very big deal indeed. She went on to star in *Funny Girl* on Broadway in 1964, and the rest is history.

Charles had a friend named Ed Wassell who was costume designer on *The Dean Martin Show* on television, so when Ed and his friend, ex-movie star Anne Shirley, flew to San Francisco, he notified Charles of their plans. Charles asked me to drive him to the airport to meet them and to drive them to their hotel. They had flown to San Francisco for the premiere of *Zenda,* which Anne Shirley's husband, Charles Lederer, had written.

On the drive from the airport, Anne was seated up front beside me, and Charles and Ed were in the rear seat. As we passed the Cow Palace off in the distance, Anne told me she had once assisted her friend, Betty Furness, at a convention of refrigerator manufacturers at the Cow Palace. Now married to Charles Lederer, the nephew of movie star Marion Davies, Anne was retired from the screen and the mother of a young son by Lederer.

The night of the *Zenda* premiere, Charles Pierce and I rented tuxedos and escorted Anne Shirley to the Curran Theatre for the performance. Unfortunately, *Zenda* died a fast death that night in spite of star Alfred Drake's efforts, and the show never made it to New York.

One day as I was cutting, stapling, and gluing the "Moppettes," Charles was seated at the table opposite me waiting for me to finish.

"Remember Ray?" Charles asked. "You met him when you came down to L.A. to see our shows at the Statler and Club Capri. He went back to Florida after that. I just got a letter from him. He wants me to send him airfare, and he wants to move back in with me here. What do you think I should do?"

"Charles, I met Ray just that one brief time. You know him better than I do. It's for you to decide." Charles and Ray had lived together in Miami Beach when Ray was discharged from the navy. Charles was thirty-seven years old at the time and Ray was in his early twenties. He was close to six feet tall, with a slim, muscular body, dark hair, blue eyes, and a kind of hangdog manner. Sometimes he followed Charles around like a puppy, and I felt Charles was often unkind to him, with a sort of ambivalent attitude. Their relationship seemed to run hot and cold, and I felt it was doomed from the start. I'm sure Ray looked for love and affection wherever he could find it.

Charles didn't say any more about Ray's coming to San Francisco, and I went on working. It wasn't long after our conversation that Charles moved to a one-bedroom apartment at 241 Francisco Street in the City, and he and Ray shared it for most of the six years Charles was at the Gilded Cage. We three drove to the wine country on Charles' day off, and another time we had a picnic at China Camp in Marin County. Charles and I spread a blanket down on the sand and arranged our food upon it. We'd bought fried chicken, potato salad and green salad, cold beer, veggies, and a big chocolate cake for dessert. Ray had walked up the beach and was wading in the surf. Then he strolled back to the spread-out feast. Without warning, he kicked sand over the entire meal and walked away. Charles didn't say a word, and I didn't either. We dumped the food in a trash can, packed up the blanket, and drove home in deadly silence.

"I think Ray is involved with someone else," Charles confided to me over dinner at The Copper Lantern on Upper Grant Street. "Who do you suppose it could be?"

"I have no idea," I replied. And I didn't. Soon after, Charles learned that the "someone" was the Gilded Cage owner Arthur's estranged wife, Pearl. She and Ray married after her divorce from Arthur.

Sometimes Charles could become the Bitch Goddess even out of drag. We had finished lunch at his apartment after working on "The Moppettes" most of the morning, and Charles and Ray flopped down on the couch in a lovey-dovey embrace. I was sitting in a lounge chair across the room when Charles pulled Ray closer to him in a bear hug and smirked.

"Don't you wish you had a lover?" His glare was indicating to me that he was Queen Triumphant. I knew he was showing his bitchy side, that he had something—or someone—that I didn't have. The last thing I wanted was "a lover." I got up from the chair and opened the door.

"No way, Renée!" I said, walked to my car and drove home.

Another time, I loaned him a rare Carol Burnett record album so that he could record "Ten Cents a Dance" for a pantomime. The number was a hit as he performed it, but at least a year went by, and he hadn't returned my album. When I finally asked for it back, he was immediately haughty and offended.

"Oh, was that yours? I took a bunch of records over to The Sea of Records (a now-defunct store that was located on 10th Street in the City) and traded them in. Guess you'll have to buy yourself another one, won'tcha?"

Years later, Charles and I were walking up Market Street to the Castro when a fellow named Gene passed by and said "hi" to Charles but didn't stop to chat. Gene was a florist and had created beautiful flower arrangements for the piano top when Charles appeared at the Gilded Cage. At the end of the show, Charles always tore the flowers to shreds and showered the audience with them, to the delight of all concerned. As Gene walked past us, Charles ignored him completely, and we continued on our way.

"He doesn't contribute anything to the show," Charles snapped.

"Not now maybe, but he did, Blanche—he did!" I couldn't resist that line. Charles gave me a glower.

Back when Charles was at the height of his success at the Gilded Cage, he suddenly became desperately ill. We had attended a party one night and were relaxing with drinks when he offered his glass to me.

"Here, take a sip, It's really good." I sampled the concoction and handed it back to him.

"What is it?" I asked.

"I dunno—something exotic, for sure."

The next morning Charles was on the phone.

"I've got hepatitis! The doctor says I have to stay in bed for three months, at least. What am I going to do about the show?"

Oh, God, I thought, I drank from his glass! I raced to my doctor and got a shot, and luckily I didn't become ill.

Charles became jaundiced, and a group of his friends took care of him. They worked with Rio in keeping the show going at the Cage until Charles recovered. Finally, after three months, he was back, strong enough to perform again. He tossed a party for all who had come to his aid while he was ill, and when he returned to the Cage, the audiences welcomed him overwhelmingly.

All of "The Moppettes" were a hit with the Gilded Cage audiences, but the one routine that Charles saved for the last and that always brought the house down was the Mae West and the sailor routine. Charles, of course, portrayed Mae West, and Rio the sailor. They lip-synched to Mae West's recording of "A Guy What Takes His Time." The sailor "Moppette" would appear and the two would engage in some sexy banter, after which Mae would saunter over to the sailor and undo his frontal flap, exposing his anatomically correct genitalia. Blackout! The audience would go completely ape, clapping, screaming, and stomping.

One night after the show, a young fellow appeared in Charles' dressing room and expressed to Charles that he was fascinated by the little sailor doll. He kept looking at it and finally asked Charles if he could touch it. Charles didn't like people disturbing his props and costumes, but he allowed the young fellow to take the doll down from its rack and examine it. The frontal flap on the sailor's pants was back in place, ready for the next performance. The young man undid the flap and fondled the doll's private parts. Just as Charles reached out to take possession of the puppet, the man pushed Charles aside and ran toward the entrance to the front bar. Luckily, John, the manager, saw what was happening, blocked the man's path, and retrieved the little sailor. The guy had a crush on a "Living Doll!"

18

In Bed with "Bette Davis"

The night Nikki Rena walked through the entrance to the Gilded Cage for the first time, all conversation stopped. Even Jack the bartender, who was thoroughly jaded from all the unusual sights he'd seen, stopped in mid-martini mixing to drop his jaw in utter amazement.

In all my days and nights at the Cage I had never beheld a vision like Nikki Rena. She was simply "drop-dead gorgeous," to coin a well-worn phrase. Tall, slim, just under six feet tall, with flawless, lightly tanned porcelain-smooth skin, her honey-blonde hair shorn à la Ingrid Bergman's in *For Whom the Bell Tolls*—a rowdy short-cropped mop of unruly curls, an ivory-colored man's silk shirt open to her waist that barely covered her tiny breasts. No bra for Nikki! I never saw her in a dress—always a silk shirt and perfectly man-tailored gabardine or sharkskin front-pleated slacks that hugged her sculptured derriere lovingly and clung to her long, shapely legs. Her perfect "buns" were those of a teenage boy. In fact, at first glance you'd almost think she was a young boy, except for the gold bangle she wore on one ankle and the slim sling pumps on her perfect feet. She never wore a speck of makeup—with that flawless complexion she didn't need it, and no mascara had ever soiled those outrageously long eyelashes. Her slender fingers were beautifully cared for, but completely sans polish, and except for her anklet, she wore no jewelry. That would be gilding the lily, and Nikki needed no gilding!

Of course, she was a model—you knew she had to be with looks like that. She had done her time on the catwalks from New York to Beverly Hills, and even a brief stint in Paris. In Beverly Hills she met Bobker Shani, a filthy-rich entrepreneur who whisked her to San Francisco to share his lavish penthouse atop the Hotel St. Claire on Nob Hill. His famous and very popular Le Chateau Bistro occupied the skyroom, commanding a spectacular panoramic view of the City and the bay. It was crammed nightly with San Francisco's richest and most important—the Richly Beautiful and the Beautifully Rich.

Nikki and Bobker were a striking couple with her perfect blondeness and his dark, brooding, mustachioed guise. However, they seldom appeared together, mostly because Nikki was a free spirit going her own way, and Bobker was a workaholic, making and counting his money. In addition, he had a humiliating secret—he was totally impotent, so he was content to allow Nikki to have her countless affairs and assignations, as long as she allowed him to watch! He usually lurked behind the draperies with his bulging eyes fixed on Nikki's sexual activities.

The clientele at the Cage was mostly gay men—maybe a lesbian or two, but that was very seldom. I don't think there was a man in the place, gay or straight, who didn't secretly lust after Nikki Rena. She had an androgynous appeal for both sexes, and she was well aware of it. But Nikki always left the club alone. If she had made an assignation she would rendezvous later—never leave the club with someone she'd met. She'd call a cab and disappear into the night.

Yes, Nikki was a woman of mystery and that was a great part of her appeal. In addition to that and her stunning good looks, she possessed a rowdy sense of humor and a unique accent. No one seemed to know what her place of origin was—Yugoslavia, Russia, Finland, Iceland, maybe even Transylvania! It didn't matter, the accent was the icing on the cake, and some of the gay boys loved to tease her by imitating her speech. She'd throw back her lovely head and roar with laughter at that.

Nikki would tell anyone who'd listen all about her sexual conquests, and she was never without an audience. Men gathered around her, eager for her company, even when she was completely silent. But that was very seldom.

She loved to tell about the time she was seated at the front bar of the Cage and a famous actress's ex-husband came in and sat next to her. She could tell right off that he was tipsy, and he proceeded to belt down a few more. He tried to engage Nikki in conversation, but she knew he was on the prowl, and she wasn't buying his aggressive overtures.

All of a sudden, he slid off his barstool onto the floor with his face close to Nikki's leg. Without warning, he grabbed her leg and bit it—HARD! Nikki screamed, and Jack the bartender stretched himself across the bar to see what was going on.

"What the—" Jack leaped over the bar and went into action.

"Jack-ee, theese fool, 'ee eez bite ma leg. Blood is coming out!" Nikki was in shock.

Sure enough, her leg was bleeding from the wound. Her attacker straightened up and started for the door, but Jack was quick and apprehended him. The police were called, and after their arrival, they took Nikki to a hospital and her attacker to jail. Nikki agreed to a large financial settlement out of court and the biter was fined.

"Theeze men—they vant to eat me. Thaz okay, but no biting, pleeze!" Nikki hadn't lost her sense of humor.

Because Charles enjoyed being surrounded by beautiful people of both sexes, he allowed Nikki to come backstage either before or after the shows. She'd straddle a chair Dietrich-style, legs wide apart, her beautiful head resting on her folded arms on its back, and watch Charles perform miracles at his dressing table. She definitely had a "thing" for him.

"Ooh, Chahles, dahling. You are sooo beautiful," she cooed. "One night soon we make lahve, no?"

"That's right, we make lahve, no!" Charles would respond.

Some women did have a fascination with Charles, but, of course, his preference was "men only" when it came to sex. However, he enjoyed the company of women and several became lifelong friends.

One night Nikki appeared backstage after the show with a bottle of Dom Perignon tucked into an ice-filled bucket, three champagne flutes, and a very handsome young man in tow.

"Chahles, dahling, say 'hello' to ma frien' Tonio. We modeled together in New Yawk. 'Ee's so beautiful, no?"

"He's so beautiful, yes!" Charles was smitten with Tonio instantly, and the three chatted and sipped their champagne. Charles couldn't take his eyes off Tonio's tall, slender figure, dark curly hair, and deep-blue, long-lashed eyes.

"Chahles, I bring Tonio for you. You see how much I lahve you? I know you don' vant to make lahve weeth Nikki, so I bring Tonio. You like?"

"I like and I lahve!" Charles retorted.

Tonio looked embarrassed, but he was interested in Charles too. He had seen Charles perform many times and particularly enjoyed his Bette Davis impression.

Nikki finished her drink, said goodnight, and left, leaving Charles and Tonio together in the dressing room. Charles rose from his chair and took Tonio into his arms, pressing his lips to the boy's unresisting mouth.

"Let's go to my place," Charles suggested. "My roommate just moved out." In a matter of minutes they were in Charles' apartment.

The two men walked down the hall to the bedroom and disrobed. Charles' heart was throbbing wildly as his gaze swept over Tonio's beautifully tanned, muscular body, and his now-erect organ. They embraced and kissed lingeringly, then climbed into the big double bed and propped themselves up on pillows.

"Cigarette?" Charles offered, then placed two of them between his lips, lit them, and handed one to Tonio. It was a scene right out of Bette Davis's *Now, Voyager.*

They smoked for awhile, then Tonio turned to Charles.

"Charles, do Bette Davis."

Charles was completely flabbergasted! In all his days and nights of cruising, he had never had a request like this—especially in bed.

"Oh, no!" Charles bellowed, "I never do women in bed! Now, put that cigarette out—I'll do you instead!"

And that's just what he did do!

19

Chicken-in-the-Nude, Cock Tales, and Other Assorted Orgies

Charles Pierce was a horny guy, and a lot of the time he was on the "prowl" for sexual assignations. He didn't miss a trick with those roving Bette Davis eyes! I remember watching him operate at the Gilded Cage bar after the show, when he'd come out front for a drink and to check the action. If he spotted a likely young fellow who looked available, he'd take his drink in hand, walk over, and start his pitch.

"Where's your lover tonight?"

If the fellow said he didn't have a lover, Charles moved in, and usually succeeded in taking the guy home. If the fellow had a lover, Charles moved on. That opening line, "Where's your lover tonight?" let Charles know how far to pursue his target.

Charles delighted in telling me all about his "sexcapades," or "Cock Tales," as he called them. For a long time he'd been reluctant to explain the big white bandage that covered a cut over his left eye that long-ago night when I'd met him and Bernie Wiesen at the Golden Carp bar. Now it could be told, and he gave me all the juicy details.

He had stopped at Nardi's bar in Pasadena late one night, just before last call. He saw a lone sailor sitting at the bar, so he struck up a conversation with him, and when the bar closed they walked back to Charles' room at the Green Hotel. The old hostelry had once been one of Pasadena's upscale gathering places, but now it was seedy and in disrepair.

Charles and the sailor stripped, climbed into the double bed, and had rowdy sex. When Charles awoke the following morning, the sailor was fully dressed and helping himself to Charles' wallet and wristwatch that were lying on the dresser top. Charles sprang from the bed, stark naked, and attempted to retrieve his possessions, but the sailor was quick as he struck Charles above his left eye, a sharp-edged ring on the sailor's finger cutting a deep gash in Charles' forehead. Blood spurted everywhere as Charles fell to the floor, his face and eye drenched in gore. The sailor stripped a valuable ring from Charles' finger and ran down the hall, with Charles, still totally nude, yelling and in hot pursuit. The sailor thief escaped. Heads popped out of rooms, and some of the "Little Old Ladies of Pasadena" gasped to see a naked man—perhaps their first glimpse of one—running and screaming down the hall.

*　*　*

When Charles was my "houseguest" at my Manhattan Beach apartment, one Saturday I had to work overtime and was unable to drive him to Laguna Beach. He decided to hitchhike instead, and arrived at the Las Ondas bar close to six o'clock in the evening. The place hadn't filled up, so Charles wasn't about to do his act. He was nursing a beer and listening to Judy Garland on the jukebox when Floyd, a giddy old codger and habitué of the bar, approached him. He had become a fan of Charles after seeing him perform there.

"Charles! Are you on tonight?" Floyd was always "up" and camping.

"Not enough crowd yet. It has to be packed to go over."

"Listen, dear, I want you to come to dinner tonight at Chez Floyd—my place, darling. Finger-lickin' fried chicken just for you!"

"Lead me to it. I'm starved." At the moment, Charles was grateful for any hand that offered a sandwich, so off they drove in Floyd's old Studebaker convertible up into the hills above the beach.

When they arrived, Floyd led Charles into the living room of his modest cottage and served drinks. Soft music was drifting from the hi-fi and the smell of frying chicken was wafting from the kitchen.

After chit-chatting for a brief moment, Floyd wriggled his way to the bedroom and returned bearing two Japanese Hapi coats—short, belted, thigh-length cotton robes, emblazoned with bamboo designs and Japanese script.

The table was set for three, and Charles wondered if the person who was frying the chicken would be the third person.

"Now," Floyd instructed, like the control queen that he was, "slip out of your clothes—yes, shoes, socks, everything, dear, and don this gay apparel. That's right, now finish your drink and we'll have din-

din." Floyd had stripped quickly and was wearing his brief kimono. Charles, too, had stripped and slipped into a Hapi coat identical to Floyd's. If Charles hadn't been so broke and famished, he might have resisted Floyd's directions, but the heady smell of the dinner being prepared had him hooked.

"Now, we will remove our robes and be seated. You're allowed to drape your napkin over your lap. That's the rule if you want to eat— that's the queen's command!"

Charles and Floyd seated themselves at the table as the queen "commanded," when out of the kitchen came a handsome young hunk, stark naked and carrying a large tray laden with plates heaped with fried chicken, mashed potatoes and gravy, cranberry sauce, and green peas. He set a plate at each guest's place, joined Charles and Floyd at the table, and passed the dinner rolls.

"This is Toby, my roommate. He's a helluva cock—I mean, cook— among other things." Floyd gave Charles a knowing wink, and then all three fell to, enjoying every mouthful of the delicious meal.

Charles had not been impervious to Toby's masculine charms, so when Floyd excused himself to go to the bathroom, Charles slid off his chair and under the table and proceeded to enjoy Toby's endowment for oral dessert. Toby loved every minute of it, but just as he climaxed, his chair slipped on the waxed floor and fell back, the front of the seat clipping Charles under the chin and knocking him out cold! Toby was lying on the floor entangled in his chair and spouting like Moby Dick, when Floyd walked back into the room.

When Charles came to, he was lying on the couch covered with a Hapi coat, and Floyd was playing "Nurse Ratched," applying cold compresses to Charles' chin and forehead. Toby was mopping the floor and rearranging the furniture.

"Mercy! Mercy! *Quel tragedie!*" quoth Floyd, and he continued daubing at Charles' injured anatomy.

* * *

While Charles was still a guest at the Algonquin Hotel in Pasadena, he was riding down Colorado Boulevard with a friend when they spotted a young, sturdy, handsome marine, dressed in his uniform, hitchhiking streetside. Charles' friend pulled to the curb and called out to the serviceman.

"Hey, Mac, wanna ride?"

The marine climbed into the car as Charles slid over to make room.

"We're going to a bar. Wanna come along?"

"Sure." The marine introduced himself as Steve, and he was eager for adventure. They drove to Club La Vie in Altadena, Charles' hangout. The friend dropped Charles and Steve off, and, as he drove away, they entered the bar and ordered drinks. Later, Charles gave me all the details of what followed.

Club La Vie was packed with patrons, and after a few drinks, the marine was getting restless.

"Have you got a place? It's too crowded in here." Steve unbuttoned his shirt collar and loosened his tie.

"Sure, we can go to my hotel. It's just down the hill. We can walk." Charles was getting excited at the thought of what was about to transpire.

When they reached the hotel, they entered Charles' room.

"How about a shower? I really got hot and sweaty standing on the street." Steve was getting aroused and it showed. Charles didn't hesitate. He and Steve stripped off their clothes and were soon lathering each other's bodies under the hot, stinging spray. The sensuous strokes of the marine's strong hands moving over his body caused Charles to abandon himself to a voluptuous sex drive he couldn't control. Once he had heard it said that a cock had a mind of its own, and he wasn't going to try to change it now!

The two men dried themselves and walked back to the large double bed in the one room that served as living room and bedroom combined. There was no kitchen.

After many months of rigorous training, Steve's body was hard and muscled, deeply and completely tanned from hours in the hot Camp Pendleton sun. His features were rugged, with a strong jaw, dark eyes, and short-cropped dark hair. Charles thought he might be Latin or Cherokee. He had a curly mat of chest hair that tapered down to a narrow strip on his flat belly to his dark pubic area. There it became a curly mass surrounding his now-erect shaft.

Steve sprawled on his back on the bed, legs wide apart, and Charles lost no time going for the prize. He allowed his tongue to linger on the marine's chest and nipples, then glide down his belly to the inside of his muscled thighs. Steve raised his legs, allowing Charles' tongue to explore his deep cavity, then lick his way up to the waiting shaft.

"Use your tongue! More! More! Oh, God, you're driving me nuts!" Charles was going nuts, too, and his body was shaking. He knew the marine was "rough trade" and was here only to be sexually satisfied, but he didn't care.

After being robbed and beaten by the sailor at the Green Hotel, one would expect Charles to be cautious about inviting another disaster. However, Steve was not belligerent, and he was grateful for the relief. After he climaxed and rested for awhile, he pulled Charles to his feet.

"Got KY or Vaseline?"

"In the drawer—there." Charles pointed to the bedside table.

Charles lay on his back on the bed, his legs raised high as Steve hovered above him. Charles was so excited he almost came, but he held back while the marine prepared himself, letting his fully erect shaft enter deep within its target.

"Oh, yeah! Don't stop! Fuck me! Fuck me!" Charles clutched Steve's hard buns and pulled him deeper into him, one finger exploring the marine's rear cavity. Steve's body bucked from the unexpected but welcome invasion into his body, his fully erect member sliding in and out of the writhing, panting form that engulfed him.

Charles whimpered as the unrelenting pounding became more intense. Steve was grunting, and both bodies were drenched in sweat.

"Oh, God! Don't stop! Don't stop!" Charles cried out. "I'm coming, don't stop!" And he surrendered to the release. Just then, Steve, unable to hold back any longer, burst inside the warmth that held him.

They lay together for a short time, and then the marine dressed hurriedly and was gone. It had been a release and a relief, but when it was over Charles wondered why he always felt unfulfilled and wanted something more.

* * *

Every Saturday night after the Gilded Cage closed, someone would toss an impromptu bash, and the entire cast of Charles' show was automatically invited. It might be in a penthouse high atop Nob Hill, a hippie pad in the Haight, a walk-up in the Panhandle, or a sleazy basement apartment in the Tenderloin. The word spread quickly, and when Charles, Sabu, and I entered the parking lot, there were eager groups gathered there wanting a ride to the party or asking where the bash was to be.

There's an old showbiz adage that cautions, "You can't take the audience home with you," and that's very true, of course. However, Charles did the next best thing by going home with some of the members of his audience!

Many times Charles' live-in lover Ray would ask Charles for a ride to the party.

"No, you can't go with me! Find another ride!" So I would take Ray and as many others as I could cram into my tiny Karmann Ghia. I couldn't bear the shattered look on Ray's face at being rejected by the man who professed to love him.

Norman, my record act partner, never attended the parties, instead always going home to the apartment on Haight Street that he shared with his lover Zane. I think Norman was afraid not to be there when Zane came home from his bartending at The Huddle, a gay bar on Polk Street.

One night, when Norman and I were rehearsing at his apartment, Zane walked in and scowled at what we were doing, then went into the bedroom and closed the door. A few minutes later Zane called to Norman to come to the bedroom, and when Norman returned, he was visibly agitated.

"John, you'll have to leave now—Zane wants a blow job." So I left, but I thought that Norman had to do exactly what Zane wanted or else. It wasn't long after that that Zane left Norman for a guy he'd met at The Huddle, leaving Norman with a stack of bills Zane had charged to Norman's credit card.

At first, the parties were rather tame. Each guest brought a six-pack, a bottle of champagne, or whatever he or she wanted to drink. (Yes, there were girls at these affairs!) The host usually provided potato chips, dip, and other snacks, and the main activities were kissing, hugging, dancing to records, or just gossiping about the show or show business. Mostly, the conversation centered on Charles. It wasn't a matter of "Enough about me—let's talk about you." No, it was Charles saying, "Enough about you—now let's talk about me."

This was the time when the hippie explosion invaded Golden Gate Park and the Haight/Ashbury. The streets were so crowded that the Muni buses had to detour around all the madness, and tourists were everywhere, gawking at the "freaks."

Soon the Saturday night after-the-show bashes became more orgiastic. The hippies were preaching free love and "Let it all hang out!" and drugs were the order of the day. I remember parties where the host would warn Charles and me that "The punch is laced with LSD," or "The brownies are loaded with marijuana," and I'm grateful that he did, because neither Charles nor I dabbled in drugs or large quantities of alcohol.

I remember, too, seeing groups of young people, both girls and guys, sitting cross-legged in a circle, so heavily stoned that they could barely speak, and others standing and weaving, glassy-eyed, completely "out of it."

Nudity was "in," and two of our Cage members, Sabu and Michael Monroe, were usually the first to climb onto a table, toss their togs into the air, and bump and grind to the wild beat of the record player, flaunting their genitalia with gay abandon! One time, Sabu began stripping on a large, food-laden table, and, after he was completely naked, his foot slipped on a smear of mayonnaise, and his bare buns landed squarely in a big round bowl of potato chips. Not too appetizing! He pried himself loose and continued his prancing among the paper plates and plastic cutlery.

On another occasion, Michael Monroe stripped naked and lay on his back on the wall-to-wall in front of the fireplace. Instantly, a group of girls and guys descended onto him like a swarm of ravenous locusts, ravaging every inch of his body. Michael enjoyed it so much that it became his specialty at every party.

Two gay boys who were lovers decided to strip at one of the parties, but they didn't stop there. They proceeded to perform various sex acts, completely oblivious to the other guests looking on.

Sometimes the floor was so strewn with bodies, clothed and unclothed, nude and semi-nude, that it was necessary to step carefully over them like Scarlett O'Hara at the Atlanta train station wending her way among the wounded!

Maybe it was because I was older than most of the others and not doing drugs that I tired quickly of these affairs. It was like watching a boring porno flick over and over. Charles seemed to enjoy all the action and, of course, he loved the adoration of his fans, who constantly told him how much they loved his show. One night while the orgy was in full swing, I walked out the door and drove home. Ah, the old ennui! Many of those young people destroyed their lives and lost their lives at an early age. Some moved to New York and became habitués of the notorious Studio 54. Because of the excesses they were involved in, many died while in their twenties from drug overdoses or AIDS. I can still see their young glowing faces, pictures of health, feeling that they were "living it up" while throwing their youthful lives away!

Baby Charles Pierce before The Baths

Young Charles as a swashbuckler

Charles' mother Jessie Hickman Pierce

Charles' father Gerald Sloat Pierce

Charles at age 13 with his mother

Off to see Manhattan

Charles Pierce's family home in Watertown, New York

Charles revisits radio station WWNY, Watertown 1949

Pasadena Playhouse, Pasadena, California

Charles, left, and the author, right, pictured in the Playhouse yearbook 1948

Charles and Rio pose with local fauna, Miami Beach, Florida, 1955

Charles, his friend Ray, and the author, Hollywood 1963

The Gilded Cage, San Francisco, California

Rio Dante, left, and Charles perform "The Moppettes"

Michael Monroe, Sabu, Rio, and Charles in "the cage" at the Gilded Cage

Charles as "Kate Hepburn" at the Gilded Cage

Charles parts the curtains at the Gilded Cage

Michael Monroe and Charles as "Essex" and "The Virgin Queen"

Charles and Rio as "Mame" and "Vera Charles" at the Gilded Cage

Charles and Norman ogle the author making up as "Kate Smith"

"The Beverly Hill Nellies," Norman and the author perform *Tom Jones*

Charles as "Mae West"

Charles as "Jeanette MacDonald" on the famous swing and as himself

The author and Charles toast film star Anne Shirley

Rio Dante, the author, Charles, and Angela Lansbury at the Plush Room

The program cover for Charles' Male Actress portrayal of "Margo Channing"
1974

Charles and his mother do London

Charles takes New York and New York loves it!

The author, Joan Edgar, and Charles in his Hotel York suite (1992)

Charles, the author, and Bea Arthur at the Plush Room, Hotel York

Charles onstage in the Venetian Room, Hotel Fairmont, San Francisco. The author and Les Natali are at right

Charles Pierce and his Farewell Performance poster in the lobby of the Pasadena Playhouse

20

Chez Sabu and La Ballet de Marijuana

Sabu, Charles' Super Go-fer, loved entertaining in the basement apartment on Ellis Street that he shared with his lover Ted. The ceiling was low and strung with exposed plumbing pipes along its surface. Sabu would fill the place with total strangers, the cast members of the Gilded Cage shows, and any visiting celebs he could round up. He was a talented chef, cooking up a storm—usually preparing spicy Portuguese concoctions larded with sausages and garlic.

One weekend, Ted took a trip to Lake Tahoe and brought back a large container of snow, so Sabu threw an instant bash, and the crowd amused themselves with an impromptu snowball fight right in the apartment! A chilly good time was had by all!

In July of 1967, Rudolf Nureyev came to a party at Sabu's and danced with a go-go boy till dawn. At the same party, Fran Jeffries, the gorgeous songstress/actress, got giddy on wine and chinned herself on the overhead plumbing pipes. Sabu and Michael Monroe danced naked for the crowd.

Fran had just finished her role in a remake of Cecil B. DeMille's *The Buccaneer,* which starred Yul Brynner. Later, she appeared in *The Pink Panther* and *Sex and the Single Girl.* Fran regaled the crowd with "cock tales" about which male Hollywood stars had the biggest "chachoonas," as she called their appendages. She was an authority on the subject, saying that the most outstanding were those of Frank Sinatra, Milton Berle, Forrest Tucker, Dick Haymes, whom she later married, and Yul Brynner himself. Marilyn Monroe said that Sinatra's was a twelve-incher, but he "was no Joe DiMaggio!"

Before he left, Nureyev invited Charles, Sabu, and some of the other Cage cohorts to attend a performance of his ballet *Paradise Lost* the following evening at the Opera House. He would "comp" them in for the ballet he and Margot Fonteyn would perform, and Charles agreed to attend. Norman and I were not invited, I remember, and as it turned out, I'm glad we weren't.

After the performance that evening of July 11, 1967, Charles, Sabu, and the members of Charles' entourage went backstage to congratulate Nureyev and Fonteyn. While they were conversing, a long-haired hippie couple, a young man and woman, approached them and invited them to a party at their "pad" in the Haight. The two ballet stars and Charles thought it would be a blast and readily agreed to attend. The hippies slipped Margot the address, 42 Belvedere Street, and left.

It was after midnight when Charles, Fonteyn, Nureyev, and their group arrived, and the party was in full swing. The music coming from the hi-fi was blasting so loudly it could be heard blocks away, smoke clouded the room, and cheap red wine was flowing from a gallon jug.

Charles noticed at once that his rival Michael Greer was in attendance, and they greeted each other though there was a strong rivalry between them. They both did impressions of Bette Davis in their shows. Later, Michael appeared in several successful films, *The Rose* and *Fortune and Men's Eyes* among them, much to Charles' chagrin.

The noise level heightened as the room grew smokier, though no marijuana was being "toked." It was 3:30 a.m. and some of the neighbors were getting angrier by the minute because of the loud music. According to the *San Francisco Chronicle*'s account of the event, Maria Detrick, who lived in the apartment below, said, "It was incredibly noisy—like at least twelve people were stomping around and rock records were playing, and someone was beating the bongos. I banged on the ceiling but the noise kept up, and I couldn't sleep."[1] She said a nicely dressed couple had rented the flat, located one-half block from Haight Street, and then about 3,000 people moved in.

Someone in the vicinity finally called the police, and when the hippie hostess heard footsteps coming up the stairs, she jumped to her feet from where she had been squatting cross-legged on the bare wooden floor and looked out the front door. The police were coming up the stairs, and she panicked.

"The fuzz! The fuzz!" she screamed, and all the guests scrambled as the police pounded on the front door.

"Run to the roof!" Michael Greer yelled. "Follow me!" And they did. The entire crowd swarmed up the narrow stairway and came out

onto the flat graveled roof, huddling together like sitting ducks waiting to be shot. But not Charles!

"Come with me," he said, and already he had leaped the low para-
pet that separated the apartment house from the building next door.

"Come on! Hurry up!" But Michael Greer calmed them down and
told them that they'd be safe where they were. Bad mistake!

Charles decided it was every man for himself and ran quickly
down the stairway of the adjoining apartment house and onto the
sidewalk, escaping the long arm of the law.

When Patrolman Arthur Fobbs and another policeman arrived,
they heard loud noises coming from the apartment above and then a
scream. The street entrance door was open and they heard the sound
of a lot of feet running. They went upstairs and pounded on the door
to the apartment. On entering, they saw a crowd of people trying to
squeeze through the back door. Inside a medicine chest in the bathroom they found twelve marijuana cigarettes, two suspicious white
capsules, a pipe commonly used to smoke marijuana, and a porno
film but no projector.

The policemen climbed the stairs to the roof and found most of the
partygoers lurking in the shadows, huddled together and shivering in
the fog. They had no idea they had two world-famous ballet stars in
custody. Using flashlights, the police found Dame Margot Fonteyn,
wrapped in a magnificent white mink coat, crouched near a roof para-
pet. Shaggy-haired Rudi Nureyev, the "fey Russian genius," was discovered lying flat on the graveled rooftop by a picket fence, dressed
in a red satin-lined pea jacket, mod pants, zippered boots, and a multi-
colored shirt. He muttered to the arresting policemen, "You pay a lot
to see me perform."

Eighteen people were arrested—but not Charles Pierce! After his
flight down the stairs, he was just in time to join the crowd that had
gathered on the sidewalk to watch Nureyev, Michael Greer, Sabu, the
hippie hosts, and all the others except Dame Margot loaded into the
paddy wagon. Margot Fonteyn had the dubious honor of being driven
to the Hall of Justice in a patrol car. They were all booked for disor-
derly conduct and for being in a place where marijuana was kept. Bail
was set at $330 each. Nureyev indulged in some sarcastic remarks,
prancing and posturing before the TV cameras and even blowing into
them to fog the lens.

On the morning of July 12, 1967, the *San Francisco Chronicle* headlines screamed in huge black type, "DANCERS' HIPPIE SPREE," and in smaller type, "Margot, Rudi Freed—the Great Ballet Bust— Dancers' Rooftop Arrest—Charges Dropped." After contemplation among the police and the DA's office, it was reported that "no complaints will be filed." Royal Ballet manager V. H. Clark bailed the two stars out, and they left the Hall of Justice. Rudi was annoyed. "You're all children," he said to reporters.[2]

Dame Margot kept her composure and was vaguely amused. "In England they don't allow the press into the jail," she stated. She denied any smoking of marijuana had taken place at the party. "As if we could smoke marijuana," she scoffed. "We don't even smoke cigarettes."

In London, *The Evening News* headlined: "MARGOT, NUREYEV IN PARTY RAID" and the *London Evening Standard* reported: "DRUGS PARTY; FONTEYN AND NUREYEV HELD."

When reporters knocked at Fonteyn's St. Francis Hotel room door she called out, "I'm not talking to anyone," and Nureyev refused even to acknowledge the reporters' knock at his door two floors above.

Meanwhile, Charles Pierce, snug in his apartment and watching the images of Rudolf Nureyev making rude faces on his TV screen, lost no time in phoning Herb Caen at the *San Francisco Chronicle* to give him the "scoop du jour" of the year—a full account of the bizarre event. Caen never forgot that favor and always gave Charles plugs in his column whenever Charles appeared in San Francisco.

Because Charles had been quick-witted and fleet of foot, he had evaded arrest, but he had a problem. Sabu and others who were invaluable to staging his show were locked away in jail, and he panicked, wondering how he was going to get his show on the road that night. He needn't have worried. Arthur, the owner of the Gilded Cage, came to the rescue with all the bail money.

In September 1988, during his engagement at the San Francisco Fairmont Hotel's Venetian Room, Charles gave an interview to David Perry for the *Bay Area Reporter.* David sets the scene:

> Lingering over brunch at the Waterfront Restaurant, Pierce holds forth in the expected fashion, along with longtime confidante John Wallraff. This is the man who once almost got arrested with Rudolf Nureyev and Dame Margot Fonteyn. (In Charles' own words):

"Do you really want to hear about that?—Well, we had been to the Opera House (in San Francisco) to see Rudi and Margot dance. As we were coming out, some hippie person came up and invited us to a party. Well, Margot took down the address, and we all went, much to my surprise. Of course, this was 1967, and people did things like that.—Oh, it was quite a night. All these queens were in the back of the police van singing *There Is Nothing Like a Dame* to Margot, and when I got down to the police station, Rudi was doing his Bette Davis impression, camping, 'What a dump!' for the cameras. The Queen of England even called Margot to find out what hippies were like. Oh, yes, it was a big story!"3

– 21 –

"Mother Didn't Tell Me
There'd Be Nights Like These!"

In the nearly fifty years Charles Pierce performed his act, there were only six times that he had difficulties with his audiences. There were always occasional hecklers, but Charles knew how to handle them. At these other performances, circumstances made things difficult for him and were beyond his control.

The first of these was the fiasco at the Glenwood Country Club in Glendale, California, when Charles had appeared on the Duncan Sisters' Talent Night and the banquet crowd upstairs had been so noisy that they drowned out Charles' voice, and he had to give up.

Another embarrassing experience was the time he flew to Hawaii to perform at the Hawaiian Village on the notorious island of Molokai, the location of the leper colony. Charles joked later that as the plane circled overhead he was afraid its wings might fall off. It was no joking matter, though, when he gave his performance and the audience sat stony-faced, not understanding one line of the show!

The worst of all the disasters was the night of the day President John F. Kennedy was assassinated, November 22, 1963. Charles phoned me from the Gilded Cage. "Can you believe? I have to perform tonight?"

"Charles!" I was shocked. "I can't believe it. It's unthinkable that the Cage would demand that you give a show after such a horrible tragedy."

"Well, they told me I have to. You coming?"

"Sure, I'll be there, but I'm not in the mood for laughs."

"Neither am I. It's gonna be hell trying to be funny, but I have no choice."

When I entered the back showroom that night at the Gilded Cage, there were four people including me sitting in the audience, and no

more arrived after Charles began his routine. Watching Charles struggling up there to entertain four grim-faced onlookers was so painful I
wanted to leave. No one was laughing, and it was a grotesque spectacle that should not have been happening. There was no response from
the minuscule group, and that was certainly understandable. Finally,
Charles spoke directly to us:

"Okay, you try being funny on a night like this!" And he walked
offstage. Later, I went to the men's room and found a five-dollar bill
under the urinal! A memorable evening!

Charles really bombed when he was on hiatus from the Gilded
Cage and opened for the Smothers Brothers at The Purple Onion. He
was still working in a tuxedo and with his array of props atop the
grand piano. But Charles' routines didn't click with the Onion crowd,
nor were the Smothers Brothers pleased at having him on their bill.
Their aloof manner toward him prompted him to lick his wounds and
hightail it back to the Cage where he belonged.

In 1974, a friend of Charles who called himself Ed West—real
name Ed Maglin—took over the management of the old Italian Village nightclub at 901 Columbus Avenue in San Francisco. He hired
Charles and Steve Silver's *Beach Blanket Babylon* as the grand opening acts after renaming the spot Olympus. He added a few Grecian
columns and a crew of young waiters dressed in brief chitons.

On Halloween night, October 31, 1974, Olympus had its Pre-
Grand Opening by presenting a Halloween Best Costume Contest to
be judged by Charles. After that, *Beach Blanket Babylon* would perform, and Charles would be the closing act. The gala Grand Opening
of Olympus would be on November 1st.

The late John L. Wasserman, in his *San Francisco Chronicle* column "On the Town" dated November 4, 1974, covered the Halloween
event as follows:

> We headed for Olympus, the new club-theatre located on the
> premises of the old Italian Village. Olympus was to have its gala
> opening the next night, with Charles Pierce and *Beach Blanket
> Babylon,* but no self-respecting club-to-be could keep its doors
> shut on this Night of Nights (Halloween).
>
> We were escorted to a front table by a toga-clad lovely named
> Bill. The joint was packed: gays, straights, and decline-to-state.
> Charles Pierce swept out as Bette Davis. Claude Sacha, late of

French Dressing, swept out as Bette Midler. And Lori Shannon, real name unknown (actually, Don McLean), swept out as Lori Shannon, a mammoth chap in platinum wig, double chin, double eyelashes, and double ankles. The three locked arms and danced across the stage singing obscene lyrics to the tune of *Tea for Two.*

The costume parade paraded and after a momentary lull Charles Pierce surveyed the scene.

"Any more people coming out? I mean costume-wise?"[1]

After the costumes had been judged, *Beach Blanket Babylon* took to the stage. The applause was deafening, stomping feet thundered, and whistling and cheering shattered the air. This was the early version of the show that starred Nancy Bleiweiss, Mary-Cleere Haran, Tony Michaels, John Noles, Roberta "Bug" Bleiweiss, and Steve Silver himself. Nancy did her Glinda the Good Witch number from *The Wizard of Oz* and a Carmen Miranda take-off, Mary-Cleere Haran was Rita Hayworth singing "Put the Blame on Mame," and Steve Silver and "Bug" Bleiweiss were dancing Christmas trees. There were many other songs and sketches, such as Tony Michaels in a huge cowboy hat doing a western song with Nancy, and a group of surfer boys in Speedos going through their paces clutching their surfboards. The whole thing ended with the entire cast singing "San Francisco" and "Happy Trails." The screaming, stomping, whistling, and applauding broke out again with endless standing ovations. How could any act follow such hysteria? Charles tried, but . . .

When the audience finally calmed down, and after a short intermission, Charles was introduced, and he strode out onstage. But it was impossible for him to follow the cult-madness the audience had exhibited during the preceding show. He tried everything in his repertoire, but it just didn't go over. It wasn't the right decision to book both shows on the same bill. Olympus went belly-up soon after.

One of the most dramatic evenings Charles endured was on the night of April 18, 1980, when the Lesbian Chorus walked out of his show en masse at the Castro Theatre. They called him racist, sexist, classist, and women-hating!

It all began when Charles agreed to headline a midnight show at the Castro Theatre as a fundraiser to retire Harry Britt's campaign debt. The bill would also include organist-comic David Kelsey and the newly formed Lesbian Chorus, numbering sixty or so singers, who were seated in the audience awaiting their turn to perform.

Charles was in the midst of his world-famous Bette Davis impression, and several times he had chided the lesbian group to loosen up, laugh, and enjoy the show. They were having none of that, thank you! Then Charles told his well-worn joke: "Why do they have a cock on a weather vane? Because it would look like hell to have a cunt up there. The wind would blow through it and give off erroneous weather reports."

The outraged lesbians stood up and stomped out of the theater to the accompaniment of thunderous applause, shouts, and boos. Charles didn't miss a beat, and in his best and loudest Bette Davis voice thundered after the group that "In all my twenty-five years doing this material I've never had a reaction like this!" He immediately picked up where he'd left off, switching to his Tallulah Bankhead routine.

"Really, dahlings, am I the only lesbian in history with a sense of humor? You can betcher bippy on that!" And he gave out with a boozy-baritone roar of laughter that brought the house down.

Other acts followed Charles, then he reappeared triumphant as Jeanette MacDonald, mouthing "San Francisco" sans swing, and the crowd went wild as he flung long-stemmed chrysanthemums into the audience.

The *Bay Area Reporter* covered the event with an article by Paul Lorch under a headline that screamed, "Charles Pierce Quakes the Castro." Excerpts from the article follow:

> Comments of patrons as they left the theatre were not favorable to Lesbian Chorus behavior. Said one Pierce fan, "The dykes were a part of the show, and should have seen it through, regardless." Commented another, "I'm glad they didn't come back—who needs them? They're only a bunch of amateurs anyway."
>
> One outraged Charles Pierce fan summed it up: "Charles Pierce has been around for 25 years, as star for every one of them. Who is this Lesbian Chorus anyway? A year from now they'll be fragmented into six warring quartets. In two years they'll have voted themselves out of existence and Pierce will still be knocking them dead."[2]

Charles was also quoted in the article:

> "What caused it all?" he mused. "I sensed that the Lesbian Chorus was slightly jarred by my appearance—as a glamorous woman on stage in sequined gown and jewelry. Was I, a man, too much of an illusionary woman for the Lesbian Chorus? For over 25 years," continued Pierce, "I've been sending up everybody and everything—that is until last night when my satire, based on the human condition, confused and aggravated the Chorus as a group.
>
> Should I have been reading Keats or Shelley, or would they have me plunking a guitar in a folk dress with long stringy hair? No, my following wouldn't have been there if I changed to appease some group. They know over the years the content. That's why they came," Pierce concluded.

David Kelsey was also criticized for his material, called sexist, and for his costumes, which were considered by some as antiwomen. The *B.A.R.* article continues with one such remark: "The way he (Kelsey) was dressed in a frumpy drag for this first set—as an old bag lady/ (with) a stringy red wig covered with a brown cloche hat."

The Lesbian Chorus finally performed their four songs on the sidewalk in front of the Castro Theatre, and on April 24, 1980, they published in the *B.A.R.* a list of their demands, which included:

> 1. A demand for a public apology from Supervisor Harry Britt and an explanation of why Charles Pierce's show was allowed to be performed.
>
> 2. That some of the proceeds of the concert be used to educate young white gay males about racism, sexism, classism, and women-hating.
>
> 3. That the Lesbian Chorus receive $100 for the concert (even though they walked out!), and that they objected to Charles Pierce's material, such as lines like, "Liz Taylor has more chins than you can find in a Chinese phone book."[3]

In spite of it all, Charles did continue to "knock 'em dead" as his fans predicted. And as for the Lesbian Chorus? Where are they now?

- 22 -

Death in the Dressing Room

When the Gilded Cage closed in 1969, Charles Pierce flew to New York City. Katharine Hepburn was auditioning actors for her upcoming musical *Coco,* and Charles Pierce wanted the part of "Sebastian Baye," Coco's assistant. For his audition Charles chose the Cole Porter song "Farewell, Amanda," which Porter had composed for the Tracy-Hepburn film *Adam's Rib.* Charles was not a singer—although he had a fine speaking voice—but he figured if Katharine Hepburn could sing in a musical so could he.

On the day of his audition the stage was bare except for one dingy work light on a standard, and out front the rows of seats were in utter darkness. Charles stood on the gloomy stage and read "Sebastian Baye's" sides, then handed his sheet music to the piano player. When he had finished his song, there was dead silence in the huge dark cave of the auditorium. Then, from the pitch-blackness out front, came the unmistakable, quavering croak of La Hepburn herself: "How very, very tactful."

Charles left the stage and flew back to California. Rene Auberjonois got the part and won a Tony to boot! Charles finally met Miss Hepburn after a performance of *Coco* at the Dorothy Chandler Pavilion in Los Angeles. He went backstage with a friend who knew Hepburn, but she was vague and disinterested when they were introduced. She was annoyed because she felt the room was hot and stuffy and demanded that something be done about it.

Years later, Katharine Hepburn and Dorothy Loudon appeared in *West Side Waltz* at the Curran Theatre in San Francisco, and Charles and I were "comped in" by Miss Loudon. After the show we went backstage to see Dorothy Loudon, Charles walking on ahead and disappearing into Loudon's dressing room. Suddenly, Hepburn appeared, dressed in a gray slack suit, and gave me a haughty, arrogant glare as if to say, "Who the hell are you and what are you doing on my turf?" I hightailed it to Loudon's dressing room!

Even before his last performance at the Gilded Cage, Charles had his next gig lined up, only this time he would be doing it without Rio Dante. Rio decided to stay in San Francisco and secured a secretarial position with Time-Life Books. So it was on to new horizons for Charles, this time at a club on Ventura Boulevard called the Lazy X in San Fernando Valley.

The Lazy X was a western-themed watering hole that had once been owned by a cowboy actor who had done a few B westerns and then disappeared from the Hollywood scene. The place had stood empty for several years with its scaling paint, dilapidated neon sign, and shabby knotty-pine paneled interior. The decor consisted of steer horns, plastic cacti, and well-worn Naugahyde-covered banquettes. In spite of its rundown condition, the place had a certain charm and intimacy that included a long mahogany bar with stools backed with a huge mirror, several round-topped tables and chairs, and a small stage in one back corner. Through a door at the side of the stage was a small kitchen, restrooms, and a tiny dressing room with metal lockers, a clothes rack, and a makeup table. The place needed a lot of help.

That help came in the person of Jon Dee, a steady patron of the Gilded Cage and a good friend to Charles and Rio. Jon's parents were morticians, and when his father died suddenly, Jon inherited a large sum of money and proceeded to buy the Lazy X, refurbish it, and hire Charles for his opening act.

Charles was relieved to have a play date lined up, but leaving his beloved Gilded Cage had not been easy and performing without his trustworthy partner Rio Dante would not be pleasant. He took a deep breath, packed his drags, Living Dolls, Sabu, and his other worldly goods, and off he went to the Lazy X and new adventures.

Charles had many loyal fans in the Los Angeles area even though he had been away for several years. When the word spread that he was appearing at the Lazy X, the little club was jammed on opening night. Jon Dee had done wonders with the place. Gone were the steer horns and plastic decorations. The room was freshly painted, the banquettes and chairs reupholstered. Sabu had done a masterful job rigging the lights, and he had managed to construct a handsome pro-scenium and curtains to frame the stage. Now the club had the look of a sparkling jewel box. He even had "Jeanette MacDonald's" swing secured from the beamed ceiling just as it had been at the Gilded Cage.

Without Rio to accompany him at the piano and to perform with him in the show, Charles had to rearrange his routines. He and Sabu did the Living Dolls together, Sabu performed the numbers Rio had done, and Charles recreated his Hollywood Ladies impressions and finished with Jeanette swinging out over the tables trilling "San Francisco."

Because the Talent Nights at the Gilded Cage had been so successful, Charles decided to revive them at the Lazy X. Every Friday and Saturday night a stream of drag queens with dreams of stardom appeared on the tiny stage, lip-synching Barbra Streisand, Judy Garland, and other recordings. Among the group was one outstanding performer, a young petite Filipino lad who went by the name of Raven, and who was not only drop-dead gorgeous in drag, but also very professional in the way he put over a song. He wore his dark hair long and straight, doe-eyes tilted and beautifully shadowed, his slender figure enhanced by a padded bra that gave the illusion of cleavage. In a dazzling black sequined gown he was a vision to behold as he appeared in the spotlight holding the mike and mouthing an old Lena Horne recording of "It's All Right with Me." Charles was so impressed with Raven that he added him to the show every Friday and Saturday nights.

Soon Raven had an enthusiastic following, which didn't bother Charles in the least. He was happy to have any talent that brought a crowd to the club. But Raven wasn't satisfied with being just a weekend "star." He wanted to become a full-fledged female, complete with breasts and the removal of his male genitalia. He didn't have the money for such an operation, but it was his number-one dream.

One night as Charles looked out over the audience, he spotted his once-frequent acquaintance from the Gilded Cage days, Boyd Ransome, the ex-movie actor husband of Beverly Ashton, the dazzling Broadway and film star. Boyd, a handsome Englishman with rugged features and a perfect profile, came backstage to Charles' dressing room at intermission. After they had brought each other up to date on all the news, Boyd moved closer to Charles and kept his voice low and confidential.

"What's with Raven?" he asked.

"What d'ya wanna know—exactly?" Knowing Boyd, Charles was sure what the answer would be.

"Are those tits real?" Boyd was intrigued.

"No, he pads his bra to get the effect of cleavage, but he wants to get silicone implants and a complete sex-change operation."

"Wow!" Boyd enthused, "That kid really turns me on! Could I meet him?"

"He'll be back for the late show. You can meet him then."

"I want him to be in drag when I meet him. Not as a guy—as a girl."

"Okay," Charles soothed, "go back to the bar and I'll arrange everything later. I've gotta make a change."

Boyd not only met Raven, he became completely infatuated with the boy, and it led to a brief love affair. It might have lasted longer if Boyd had not financed the silicone breast implants as part of Raven's transformation. Raven was ecstatic that part of his dream was coming true, and soon he was off to Tijuana, Mexico, to have the silicone enhancements.

Boyd Ransome had one kinky hangup. He wanted Raven to have womanly breasts but to retain his male genitalia, so when Raven returned from Mexico with new breasts, he was half-man and half-woman, just the way Boyd wanted him to be!

Raven continued performing at the Lazy X and seeing Boyd on a regular basis. Boyd came to the club every weekend when Raven was on, and they appeared to be a happy couple. Boyd described to Charles all the details of their intimate moments that first night he and Raven were together. When Boyd finally met Raven after the late show at the Lazy X, the couple drove to Raven's tiny North Hollywood apartment in Boyd's convertible. Raven had stayed in full drag at Boyd's insistence, but because it was raining he had thrown a well-worn trench coat over his shoulders. Once inside, Boyd looked the apartment over closely. He was used to his own lavish Bel Air mansion with his wife Beverly and their two young sons. This was new to him, the shabbiness, the sagging sofa that became a fold-out bed at night, the minuscule kitchen and even tinier bathroom. But his heart raced in spite of his surroundings—he had what he wanted—he was with Raven! This beautiful boy-woman made the blood race to his penis, which was now swelling in his tight white trousers.

Raven had slipped out of the wet trench coat and into a very dry vodka martini, another of which he placed on the battered coffee table for Boyd. Then the two men made themselves comfortable, sitting side by side on the lumpy sofa. Martinis were not Boyd's favorite cocktail, but he was willing to drink paint thinner just to be near this fabulous creature.

"Salud," Raven said as he raised his glass and smiled his most beguiling smile, all bright red lips and a flash of perfect white teeth. By now, Boyd's erection was in full bloom, and Raven's dark eyes drifted to it.

"Mmm," he purred. "So beautiful." His slender manicured hand, with its flame-tipped fingers, reached down and stroked Boyd's amazing manhood through the tight white fabric. Even before they'd finished their drinks, they were in each other's arms, kissing hungrily and craving each other's body.

Boyd unzipped the back of Raven's gown, and the glittering ebony-black garment fell off his shoulders and down to his waist. Raven rose and stepped out of the gown, his bikini panties clinging to his throbbing tumescence.

"Ooh, Boyd," Raven crooned as he unzipped Boyd's trousers, allowing Boyd's generous manhood to escape its bounds. "You are a beautiful man." Raven slipped Boyd's trousers down to his ankles—he was wearing no underwear—knelt between his lover's spread legs, and quickly engulfed the throbbing organ with his eager mouth. Boyd thought about Beverly and how she had always refused him oral sex, even though he willingly satisfied her craving to receive that satisfaction. Well, he had found what he craved with Raven, the boy-woman he desired—everything about him—everything he was doing to him now. Screw Beverly!

When Raven had finished, Boyd fell back on the sofa, and immediately the boy was covering Boyd's face and mouth with sensuous kisses. He couldn't get enough of this handsome man—the man of his dreams! The man who could make all his dreams come true. A man who could change his sordid surroundings and lifestyle to a world of luxury and glamour!

How different his life could be now from the days of shabbiness and poverty when he and his mother had shared this apartment and had only each other. His mother, Lita Torres, was a seventeen-year-old girl when she and her mother came to Los Angeles from the Philippines, where Lita had danced in nightclubs and cabarets. The young girl was so beautiful and graceful as a dancer that she was soon performing in nightspots in Hollywood and along the Sunset Strip.

One rainy night when she and her mother were returning home from a club date, their taxi skidded on the wet pavement and crashed into a huge tourist bus. The taxi driver and Lita's mother were killed, and Lita was terribly injured, her right leg badly crushed. The doctors feared they'd have to amputate. The leg was saved, but after many operations and months in a cast, Lita was left with a limp that ruined her dancing career, but gave her a sexy undulating walk.

Lita had to find another means of livelihood and soon began to frequent sleazy bars. Eventually she drifted into prostitution. Men were drawn to Lita's ravishing face, petite figure, and swelling breasts, and she had no problem luring a steady stream of johns to her shabby abode. If one of them commented on her slight limp, she threw back in her accented English, "I don' leemp een bed!"

One day she discovered she was pregnant and had no idea who the father was. She knew she would have the baby because she couldn't afford an abortion, and her Catholic religion forbade such action.

Her beautiful baby son, whom she named Emilio after her father, was born in June, a Gemini child and a delight from his first day on earth. He enriched her squalid life, but he was also a responsibility, so she was forced to continue her degrading profession.

Young Emilio grew to be a handsome teenager and soon found part-time work in the stockroom of a large downtown department store. Lita, who was ill with heart trouble and complications from her accident, was unable to continue her "career," so her son was now the sole breadwinner.

Emilio wanted more from life than being a stock clerk, so when he heard about the Lazy X Talent Night from some gay friends at work he decided to try.

Lita grew more and more frail each day, and one evening when Emilio came home from work he discovered his mother's body slumped on the bathroom floor. She had succumbed to a massive heart attack while trying to get her medication from the medicine chest.

Now Emilio was alone in the world, but he wasn't defeated. He still had his menial job to keep him afloat, and his mother's raven-black sequined gown hanging in her closet. Raven! That's what I'll call myself, he mused, and, with the gown and his makeup case in tow, he set out for the Lazy X, and, he hoped, a new adventure.

Raven ended his reverie and turned to face Boyd on the couch beside him. Boyd looked into Raven's dark eyes.

"You're so far away. What are you thinking?"

"Only of you," the boy replied. "Only of how much I love you and how knowing you has changed my life."

"You've changed mine, too." Boyd meant every word. He'd finally found the one he'd been searching for.

"Come here, let me hold you." And they fell into an all-consuming embrace. Boyd released the boy and knelt over him for a moment, then allowed his lips to caress Raven's smooth, young, naked body. The padded brassiere was still in place with its illusion of deep cleavage, but that was the only garment Raven wore.

Boyd's hot open mouth continued its path down Raven's taut belly and thighs, then to the silky nest and vibrant shaft that awaited his eager attention. Raven gasped as Boyd engulfed his manhood, then sighed and let his pink tongue moisten his full lips.

"Oh, Boyd, my lover. Oh, oh!" he whispered hoarsely. Boyd had stripped and was kneeling between Raven's upraised legs. He found lubricant nearby and gently entered the half-sobbing boy.

"Do what you want, Boyd! Anything you want!"

Boyd withdrew and took Raven in his open mouth, then entered him again. Boyd's insistent thrusting grew more intense, but just before he climaxed, he dropped his mouth to Raven, who could hold back no longer, and, as Boyd withdrew, they burst together in a shuddering climax.

The relationship might have continued if Raven hadn't become terribly ill very suddenly. One night as he was "singing" his number, he stumbled and collapsed onstage. Boyd rushed to him and drove him to the emergency room of a nearby hospital. The boy had a ferocious fever and lay in a coma for a week, then passed away. The silicone in the breast implants was highly toxic. It was illegal in the U.S., but not in Mexico. Boyd was devastated, and nothing anyone could say consoled him. He had lost his soulmate—the one he truly loved. For the rest of Charles' time at the Lazy X, Boyd never returned to see the shows. For him, the club was haunted with sad memories of a beautiful vision named Raven. It was years later in London when

Charles appeared at the Fortune Theatre that Boyd Ransome re-entered Charles' life.

More high drama was to unfold while Charles played on at the little club on Ventura Boulevard. Over the weeks and months he discovered that some of his male fans had developed crushes on him. He did look glamorous in his full-face high drag, with his long, shapely Betty Grable legs exposed in a sequined sheath slit to the hip. One fellow in particular was a steady patron, and he began to loiter in Charles' dressing room between and after the shows. His name was Jared Lange and he seemed pleasant enough at first, but as time went by he became weird. He'd stand very close to Charles and watch silently as Charles applied his makeup and wig, and often zipped up the back of Charles' gown for him.

Jared was in his twenties and very handsome—blond, blue-eyed—a real California surfer type with a healthy tan and a fine, sturdy build, so it was flattering to Charles that Jared hung around. Normally, Charles would not have let anyone other than Sabu or Sam, the stage manager, spend so much time with him while he was getting ready to go on.

On one particularly warm summer night, Charles was sitting at his dressing table when suddenly Jared was standing at his elbow. Though startled, as he hadn't seen the young man enter, Charles continued to apply his false eyelashes and touch up his eye shadow and blusher.

"Charles . . ."

"Oh, Jared, you startled me."

"Charles . . ."

"Yes, Jared, what is it?" Then, in his best Bette Davis voice, "Cat gotcher tongue?"

"Don't jerk me around—I'm serious!"

"Yes, I can see that. What's the matter?"

"You don't care about me. You're playing games with me and I can't stand it anymore."

Charles was alarmed and turned from the dressing table to face the young man.

"Jared, why are you so upset? I haven't been playing games with you."

"Yes, you have. You don't really love me—not the way I love you."

"But, Jared, we're just friends—not lovers."

"No, but we should be. I want you to love me the way I love you."

"Jared, I like you very much, but I'm not in love with you."

"There, you see, you are toying with me. Why can't you say you love me? I can't stand the way you treat me. Don't you have any feelings at all?"

"Jared, I'm going to have to ask you to leave now. I have a show to do and . . ."

"Come with me now! Now! If you don't come with me I'll kill myself right here. I will! I mean it!"

"Jared!"

In an instant, Jared pulled a pistol from his jacket pocket, brandished it wildly, then held it to his temple as tears streamed down his face.

"Goodbye, Charles. I love you."

Charles was terrified and frozen to the spot. Just then, Sabu entered the room and saw the gun at Jared's head. What happened next will never be known.

"It was chaos for one split second—the blast of a gun and Jared lay dead in a pool of blood on the dressing room floor," Charles said later. He had been horrified and petrified, but Sabu was calm as a clam and ordered Sam, the stage manager, to help him remove the body. Meanwhile, the bartender, hearing the gunshot, called the police, who arrived moments later to discover Sabu and Sam carrying the dead body into the parking lot. So much mystery surrounds this incident! Why did Sabu and Sam remove the body from the death scene, and where were they taking it? Why didn't the police arrest them for doing that, and why was no one ever arrested? Did Sabu scuffle with Jared before the gun was fired? All very strange, and Charles never, ever again spoke of the incident under any circumstances!

– 23 –

Gold Street and Touched by an Angel—Of Death!

In 1970 Charles Pierce opened his show at Gold Street, a Gold Rush-themed bar and restaurant on alleylike Gold Street in North Beach in San Francisco, and stayed there four years. The room was not designed to be a showroom. There was no stage, so it was necessary to reconstruct the area somewhat so that the show could go on.

An antique bar lined the wall to the right side of the entrance, the small kitchen was straight ahead, and the main space to the left was spacious with a square of parquet flooring for dancing. Along the front wall to the left of the entrance was a beautiful carpeted staircase with a handcarved walnut banister that led to a balcony overlooking the dance floor. The upstairs area consisted of the business office, a storeroom for liquor and provisions, and one small cubbyhole Charles dusted off for his dressing room.

The decor at Gold Street was inspired by the Gold Rush days of '49. The walls were covered with ornate deep-red flocked wallpaper and dark walnut paneling, and suspended high above the dance floor hung an old period crystal chandelier.

The staircase was perfect for Charles' initial entrance each night. A spotlight and other theatrical lighting had been installed, and the dance floor had been converted into a cabaret area with a large platform stage against the left-hand wall and a group of small round-top tables with chairs to seat the audience. A grand piano was on the stage for Rio Dante to tinkle when Charles did his monologues, and Sabu had hung the swing from the rafters for the "San Francisco" number. With a few changes the room had been transformed into an intimate and practical cabaret.

Each night at show time when Charles was announced, the spotlight swung to the top of the staircase and Charles appeared, gorgeously gowned in one of his magnificent bejeweled creations, makeup, wig, and jewelry flawlessly in place, pausing for a moment, then descending seductively to the room below to cheers, whistles, stomping of feet, and thunderous applause. Often the audience included celebrities such as Bette Midler and Paul Lynde.

One fateful night when Paul Lynde was in town with a male companion, a tragedy happened when they returned to their Sir Francis Drake Hotel room. Both men had been drinking heavily, and when they entered their room, Lynde's companion walked to a window, climbed out, and clung to the windowsill many stories above the busy street below. Paul tried to coax him back into the room to no avail, and when he reached out to pull the man in, Lynde's unfortunate friend lost his grip and fell to his death. An investigation concluded that it was an accident, but it left Paul Lynde shaken and bereft.

As an added attraction, Charles had introduced a young comic named Glenn Elliott to the Gold Street show. In addition to performing to records, Elliott did a hilarious live routine when he removed his false teeth, donned a shabby smock and cap and "became" Moms Mabley. He had appeared in Charles' fabulous Bimbo's shows. George Buchanan and his puppets also appeared with Charles at Gold Street.

One night Charles charged out of his dressing room, rushing to be on cue at the top of the stairs, when he collided with a young waiter and a glass of red wine the waiter had on his tray. The scarlet liquid spewed all the way down the front of Charles' white satin gown. Instead of becoming a screaming prima donna and perhaps causing the poor guy to be fired, Charles apologized to the young man, flew to his dressing room, slithered into another gown, and was poised in place when the spotlight hit him. It's no wonder Charles was truly loved, not only by his fans, but by the crews who worked at the clubs where he performed.

At the time Charles was at Gold Street, I had taken a job there as an assistant cook, helping our friend chef Jim Tate. I was between drafting jobs, and I'd had experience as a cook while I was in the navy, so I poached eggs Benedict for the brunch crowd that frequented Gold Street and made sandwiches for lunch. No dinner was served, just cocktails and hors d'oeuvres for the evening patrons and at show time.

On the day I reported for my kitchen duties, I was surprised to see David Likens, the former naked "angel" of the Gilded Cage days, tending bar at Gold Street. It had been three years since we had worked together at the Cage. He was very reserved when I greeted him, and he ignored my attempt at conversation. He had always been reticent, so I reported to the kitchen and began my routine. Still, I wondered where he'd been and what he'd been doing since I saw him last. When I eventually found out the truth, I was deeply shocked!

Charles finally closed his show at Gold Street and moved on to other engagements. He also acquired the services of a Hollywood agent named Budd Haas, who secured bookings for Charles in more famous venues in New York City, London, the Fairmont Hotel in Dallas, Texas, and eventually the Venetian Room in the Fairmont Hotel in San Francisco.

One day early in 1977, Budd Haas dropped by Charles' Toluca Lake condo. Over Charles' favorite vodka martinis, Budd bombarded him with a battery of proposed bookings and a film offer.

"Listen Chaz, ol' buddy—have I got a script for you!" he gushed excitedly. "You're gonna love it!"

"Oh, yeah?" Then, becoming instant Bette Davis, Charles scoffed, "I bet it's a doozy."

"It is that, and more. You'll play "Robin Turner," a gay Toronto hairdresser who wants to be a nightclub performer doing movie star impressions. What could be more perfect? It's like it was written especially for you, babe."

"A hairdresser! Ugh! What other exciting characters are there?"

"Well, there's a fruit fly-fag hag who works in the beauty shop with you."

"The plot thickens—like shit! Who wrote this crap, the janitor? I wouldn't fly to Toronto to play the life story of *Lana* Turner!"

"Look Chaz, you were born to play 'Robin Turner,' the hairdresser. I can get you a terrific deal. You'll fly to Toronto, all expenses paid, luxury hotel suite, jacuzzi, room service included. What more do you want?"

"I vant to be alone." This time Charles became a world-weary Garbo.

"This could be the turning point of your career. You'll get star billing."

"I always get star billing! Toronto? Never! It's the Frozen North. You represent Craig Russell; let him do it. No way, José!"

Craig Russell was a rival of Charles in that he also performed many of the impressions that Charles was famous for. He had come to Hollywood when he was president of Mae West's Fan Club and met her, and she let him try on one of her gowns. He was very petite, and, after appearing as Tallulah Bankhead at a Halloween party, he worked up an act and appeared in Las Vegas, and eventually on Broadway. His reviews were glowing for his one-man show, *A Man and His Women,* and Budd Haas signed him up posthaste. He was a big hit in Berlin, Germany, and Sydney, Australia.

The film Charles turned down was titled *Outrageous!* Craig Russell starred in it, and the picture was a big hit. In 1987 a sequel was made called *Too Outrageous!,* but it bombed. Poor Craig became addicted to drugs and died soon after.

Another time Budd Haas called Charles with a deal for a two-week engagement in Australia. "I can get you $18,000 and all the perks. Now or never."

"Then it'll have to be never. Do you know how long it takes to fly down there? Sorry, dahling," Charles rasped in his Tallulah baritone, "I don't go Down—Under! It's not my month for kangaroos and aborigines. Call Tassie Hamilton. She'll love going home to her outhouse in the Outback, warbling 'Waltzing Matilda' all the way. They can roast her and a shrimp on the barbie while they're at it!"

"Okay, then, I can get you a gig at a little club in Hayward . . ."

"Hayward! Hayward! Are you brain dead? You've gotta be kidding! Hayward! That's where they'll insert the tube if they ever give California an enema!"

In spite of it all, Haas did arrange a bevy of TV appearances for Charles—guest spots on *Wonder Woman, Love, American Style, Starsky and Hutch, Fame, Laverne and Shirley, Madame's Place* with Wayland Flowers and Madame, *Designing Women, Chico and the Man,* and talk shows hosted by Dick Cavett and Merv Griffin. He was offered the starring role in a musical called *Tallulah's Party* but he rejected it, and it opened at the Martin R. Kaufman Theatre in New York with Tovah Feldshuh in the starring part. Charles was outraged that a woman would play Tallulah and fired a note off to Liz Smith, the syndicated gossip columnist: "Don't you think there should be a Broadway show called *Only a Man Can Play Tallulah?*" And Liz Smith printed it in her column. If Charles knew that Kathleen Turner is currently performing her one-woman show *Tallulah,* he'd be livid!

An engagement Charles did accept was a highlight of his career. It was his one-man triumph at the Dorothy Chandler Pavilion in the Los Angeles Music Center. That now-famous *Evening at Dottie's Place* on April 6, 1982, wowed the critics, and the capacity audience gave Charles no less than ten standing ovations. The show was filmed and is available on VHS cassette.

After Charles left Gold Street, David Likens stayed on as bartender, and I returned to drafting. Friends at the restaurant told me that David had disappeared suddenly and his whereabouts were unknown. He'd always been a loner, and it seemed that he had very few friends, but on the job he had always been polite and a dependable worker. I'd heard he'd moved to Los Angeles just before his name hit the headlines in San Francisco. He had been arrested for the torture-murders of several young men he'd picked up as hitchhikers and taken to a dungeon in his apartment, where he bound, tortured, and murdered them, then dumped their bodies in the undergrowth down the peninsula from San Francisco.

Likens' roommate returned to the apartment late one night to find the mutilated body of a young man strung up in the dungeon, bound and gagged, his nude body dripping blood. Its entire surface had been slashed with countless razor cuts. Either the victim had been strangled or he had died of fright. David Likens, his killer, had vanished.

The roommate was terrified as he had no idea David had been engaged in such gruesome activities, and he called the police. Soon after Likens was apprehended and jailed, he was discovered dead, hanging in his cell with a noose around his neck. It was never known whether he had committed suicide or been murdered. It was so sad and shocking to remember those nights at the Gilded Cage when handsome David Likens, with so much potential, shone in the spotlight, a glorious angel with his feathered wings, and then, tragically, threw it all away to become the Angel of Death!

* * *

A certain group of straight and married men were sexually attracted to Charles. Somehow they found their way to his shows, and as they watched him impersonate his females, they had fantasies about what it would be like to have sex with him. Kinky, they hoped! Not the "normal" variety they enjoyed at home with their wives. They wanted something wilder and far-out. Some found it with prostitutes, and some found it with female impersonators.

While Charles was appearing at Gold Street, a married guy named Matt began hanging around Charles' dressing room, watching him remove his drags and makeup. He'd make small talk and ask Charles a lot of questions about the show.

At first, Charles didn't know Matt was married and he tried his usual "Where's your lover tonight?" routine. Matt confessed that he was a married man, but he wondered if Charles would meet him for lunch the next day. Charles was instantly attracted to the handsome six-footer with striking features, big masculine hands, and tousled dark hair. Matt worked in the Financial District, and he always wore a well-tailored three-piece suit and sleek Italian leather shoes. He had a dazzling smile that lighted up his flirty gray eyes, and Charles thought Matt's wife was a very lucky lady.

The next afternoon, Charles met Matt at a little boîte off Montgomery Street, and, after several martinis and a satisfying lunch, Matt invited Charles to his office in a nearby highrise. When they entered, the rooms were deserted and the staff was out to lunch, so the two men had the space to themselves. Matt immediately locked the door, drew the heavy drapes, and removed his jacket and vest. Facing Charles, he unbuckled his belt as he rested his buttocks on the edge of the desk, and let his slacks fall to the floor. He was wearing only his shirt and tie and his gray jersey bikini shorts. Immediately, Charles was on his knees, his open mouth caressing the jersey-covered bulge that was growing larger in Matt's shorts. Before Charles could accomplish his mission, Matt pushed him away and pulled his pants up. He buckled his belt, threw on his jacket and told Charles to leave.

"I'll call you . . . ," was all he said. Charles went out the door, and, riding down in the elevator, he wondered what had caused Matt to panic so abruptly and shove him away.

Several weeks passed, and one night after the show Charles encountered Matt at the Gold Street bar and joined him.

"Long time, no see," Charles cracked.

"Yeah, I know—I've been on vacation with the family." Embarrassed, Matt looked down at the floor.

"Where'd ya go?"

"Sequoia. We camped out."

"We?"

"My wife and the kids—my two boys."

"Fun."

"She's away for a week—she's off to L. A.—to see her folks. I was wondering if you'd like to come over to the house tonight? We'll have to be quiet 'cuz the kids are asleep in the front bedroom."

Charles was shocked that this guy would invite him to his house, maybe to have sex, with his kids so close by.

"That's too weird—let's go to my place." Charles was curious to see what Matt had in mind—and what was inside that bikini-covered bulge. He'd give the guy another chance.

When they entered Charles' suite, they went directly to the bedroom and Matt sprawled on his back on the bed. This time he abandoned himself to Charles and allowed himself to be completely undressed without any resistance. Charles couldn't wait to explore Matt's naked, sexy, well-buffed body, and was immediately drawn to the long-awaited sight of the erect male organ that was at last all his to enjoy. Matt groaned as Charles' mouth engulfed him, but soon he changed positions and raised his long legs above him.

"Fuck me! C'mon, fuck me good!" Charles didn't wait for a second invitation. He quickly stripped and reached for lubricant, preparing Matt and himself for what was to come. Somehow it was a thrill to enter this guy who couldn't get this satisfaction at home.

"Oh, God, give it to me! Oh, God, don't stop! I'm cumming—I'm cum—" Matt cried out hoarsely.

When it was over, both men were exhausted and lay on the bed panting. There was no display of affection between them. Although Charles tried to kiss Matt on the lips, he turned his face away.

"No, I'm Not the Girl
in the Fishbowl at Bimbo's"

When columnist Herb Caen of the *San Francisco Chronicle* heard that Charles Pierce was opening at Bimbo's 365 Club on Columbus Avenue, he phoned Charles immediately. The glamorous Las Vegas-style nightspot was world renowned for, among other things, being the home of the "The Girl in the Fishbowl." It was an illusion that patrons of the club viewed as they entered the foyer—a tiny, scantily clad young woman appearing to be swimming in a small fishbowl. The illusion was created by the woman going through swimming motions against a black background in another part of the building and then projecting that image into the fishbowl upstairs. It was a good gimmick that caused interest in the club.

With Herb Caen on the line, Charles couldn't resist making a crack before the columnist had a chance to say a word.

"No, I'm Not the Girl in the Fishbowl at Bimbo's!" Charles chortled. "That should make a clever 'scoop du jour' for your column." Caen agreed, and it appeared the next morning in the *San Francisco Chronicle*. Charles' first show at Bimbo's was in June 1971, and again in July of that year. Les Natali, a good friend to Charles and me, produced both shows and both were sellouts.

At the June opening, several acts preceded Charles on the bill. There was Brian Avery singing the Academy Award-winning song "For All We Know," Glenn Elliott doing his schtick as toothless Moms Mabley, another singer, lovely Eileen Gallagher, a vivacious tap dancer named Wendy Lynn, and others. A short intermission, then a drumroll, and the orchestra struck up the medley of Charles' overture, themes from Bette Davis's films. The lights came up full on the closed curtains, and a voice on the sound system announced: "Ladies and gentlemen, Les Natali presents—CHARLES PIERCE!"

The curtains parted to reveal a stage billowing with clouds of dry ice that swirled around the figure of Charles Pierce poised atop a stairway upstage center. He swept down the stairs in a resplendent red-sequined gown, sparking necklace, and blond wig, flourishing a huge pink ostrich-feather fan. He launched immediately into his familiar zingers:

> These aren't my tits—they're my balls. My Living Athletic Supporter went up on me. I'm a man dressed as a woman for financial reasons only.

He segued into two of his zany, improbable TV commercials:

> Hi, I'm Peg Bracken. I wrote *The I Cook to Hate Book*. When unexpected guests drop by my house I don't serve them chipped beef on toast. Hell no! I serve them shit on a shingle.
>   That Mrs. Olsen is so crazy about Folger's coffee that when she dies she's going to have her body freeze-dried. Neighbor women are always coming into her kitchen: "Oh, Mrs. Olsen, my husband Tom says my coffee tastes like panther piss."
>   "Now Nancy—relax. Tom must be a camp."

As Mae West, he did a few vintage bits:

> *(Fluffing up his feather boa)* Two thousand Sausalito chickens died for this. Ooh, mmm. I sauntered into a bar dressed in my form-fitting, gold lamé toreador pants.
>   The bartender said, "How do you get into those?"
>   "Oh," I said. "You might start by buying me a drink."

Then Mae was out West "where men are men and the sheep know it":

> One time I was out West. I was a lady sheriff and I had four hundred men in my posse. Another time, I was riding a stagecoach with Liberace. He had just made a Hollywood picture called *I Married a Woman*—a science fiction horror film. Jesse James came riding up to rob the coach. He said, "Pass what you've got out the window."
>   I said, "Hold it, J. J.—what I've got is too big to pass out any window."

Then he pleased me. He said, "What I've got is too big to pass in any window." I genuflected. Then Jesse said, "I'm gonna rob all the women and rape all the men."

I said, "Tush, tush. Just a minute, Jesse, you've got that backwards—rob all the women, rape all the men?"

Liberace spoke up from the back of the coach, "Shut up, Mae. Let Jesse rob the coach the way she wants to."

In a flash, Charles became Tallulah Bankhead staggering around the stage clutching a drink:

> I love this drink—vodka, orange juice, and tomato juice. I call it a Screw Mary. I'm no longer with you, dahlings. I'm in the Big Rummage Sale in the Sky. When I arrived at the Pearly Gates, there stood a handsome sailor and a sexy marine. Saint Peter said, "Look, dahlings, if you think dirty thoughts your wings will crumple and fall off." I walked past the sailor and his wings crumpled and fell off. As he bent over to pick them up, the marine's wings crumpled and fell off. I was at the wrong gate!

Tallulah spied her old arch rival, Bette Davis, and they began their famous bitch fight:

TALLULAH: Oh, look, there's the only reject from the Sexual Freedom League, Bette Davis. Bette dahling, if you ever become a mother, may I have one of the puppies?

BETTE: Oh, there you are, Tallulah. You've outgrown your skin. How sweet. You know, LSD is a mind-expanding drug. You really ought to try it.

TALLULAH: I didn't think you'd take offense at my little joke. After all, I didn't take offense at the joke your father and mother made.

BETTE: Really, Tallulah, you ought to cultivate your voice. Someone should shove some fertilizer down your throat. Then your voice would be perfect for calling hogs.

TALLULAH: And here you are.

BETTE: I caught your act in Vegas. Fortunately, penicillin cures everything.

TALLULAH: You know, Bette, your tongue will dig your grave, and your funeral will be a cheap one.

BETTE: Why?

TALLULAH: Because there are only two handles on a garbage can.

In an instant, with just a quick change of a vintage hat and fur piece, he became Eleanor Roosevelt:

> My day has been a busy one! I just returned from abroad—well, if Franklin can have a mistress, so can I. Reporters asked me what I thought about the Greek position. I said I hadn't tried that one.
>
> Easter morning, Bess Truman and I were rolling sailors on the White House lawn—Adlai Stevenson dropped by to invite me to become a member of a very secret society. I agreed, and we went to Camp David—and David camped right back! At the initiation, Adlai and I had to strip naked and leap over a blazing campfire. He was blackballed, and I was deferred. They voted me Ms. Singed Fringe.
>
> In Arizona, I saw a royal Indian woman stringing her beads by the edge of the Grand Canyon—she was a rim queen.
>
> Franklin! Come out of the water, dear, you'll catch your death of polio!

Charles eliminated the sketch from his show when a female fan of Mrs. Roosevelt complained.

Then, with another lightning change, he became a gossip columnist, Louella Hophead:

> Hello, from Hollywood. This is Louella Hophead with gossip about all your favorite Hollywood har—starlets. My first hot flash. I've been expecting it all day. I went to a fabulous Hollywood party. Everyone was there: Mae West and her sister, June; June West, one month hotter; Doris Day and *her* sister, Doo Dah, Doo Dah Day; The Ria Sisters, Pyah, Dyah, and Gonna. All those fab stars with their fab names: Steve McQueen is well-named, and Natalie Wood—and did! Who starts these vicious, malicious rumors? Listen to this: Barbra Streisand phoned me from the cystic fribrosis ward at Cedars of Lez—Lebanon Hospital. She's having plastic surgery and she wants me to come over and help her pick her nose. Marlon Brando is trying to strengthen his masculine image—and well he should after those homosexual movies he's been making. He's had his entire body

covered with leather. Now he can recuperate and hand-tool himself at the same time. This is Louella Hophead bidding you good night from Hollywood!

It's true that Charles seldom changed his material, and the audiences, as he said many times, could recite the lines along with him if they chose to do so. They loved the vintage routines and looked forward to them like kiddies wanting to hear their favorite bedtime stories.

It was backstage after one of Charles' performances at Bimbo's that I met Tallulah Bankhead's older sister, Eugenia. She was not at all as flamboyant as her notorious sister, but both were petite women. Eugenia was quiet, beautiful, gracious with her Southern charm, and beautifully gowned in a soft gray shimmering floor-length sheath. She told Charles that he had captured the essence of her outrageous sibling.

Charles had removed his makeup and was relaxing in his dressing gown in a lounge chair. I hadn't seen him for several months and now, seeing him there au naturel, I was shocked by his appearance. He was only forty-five, but he looked frail and haggard.

"Why, he's an old man!" I thought to myself, as I noticed the many facial wrinkles and a wattle under his sagging double chin. "Time for some nips and tucks!" He'd always joked onstage that when he removed his makeup, his head was the size of a garbanzo bean. That was a joke, but it wasn't the size of his head that needed fluffing up, it was his face!

He must have been well aware of his aging appearance because he phoned me a few weeks later after the Bimbo's show closed to tell me that his face was swathed in bandages, and that he'd had a face-lift (the first of three) administered by the Bay Area's foremost plastic surgeon. When the bandages finally were removed, it was as though Charles Pierce, Male Actress, was reborn! He looked terrific! At least ten years younger.

"Charles, now you have spit curls *back* of your ears!" I teased.

He was not amused. As the years progressed, those "lifts" kept him looking "younger than springtime."

In 1973, Charles had just completed a guest appearance on *The Merv Griffin Show,* doing his Bette Davis impression, when his mother phoned from Watertown that Charles' father, Gerald, had passed away. Charles flew home immediately to give his mother comfort and support and to arrange for the funeral. He made the mistake of taking Sabu with him. Because there was not direct airline service to Watertown, they flew to Syracuse, and Charles rented a car for the drive to his mother's home.

Sabu had been drinking heavily, and he was disheveled and unshaven and appeared rather menacing. When they arrived, Charles' mother, Jessie, took one look at Sabu and became instant Barbara Stanwyck.

"Oh, no, Charles! Oh, no, not in my house! You'll have to make other arrangements." Her lips were frozen to her teeth exactly as Charles' were when he performed his impression of the actress.

Charles drove Sabu to a local motel, booked a room for him, and drove back home. At about two in the morning, after Charles and his mother had retired, the female proprietor of the motel was on the phone screaming hysterically.

"You've gotta get that maniac outta my motel . . ."

"Why? What's he done?"

"He's gone completely nuts! He's smashed the window, tore the rugs up, and destroyed all the furniture. The place is a shambles. You better get over here before he sets fire to the place!" She slammed the receiver down.

When Charles arrived, Sabu was passed out on the floor of his room surrounded by several empty bottles of blackberry brandy, his favorite alcoholic beverage.

"He was screaming that there were little green men attacking him," the proprietor explained. She had called the police, who soon arrived and took Sabu off to jail to sober up. Dealing with his father's death was traumatic enough, but now Charles had the added burden of coping with Sabu's catastrophe. Charles gave the motel owner a check to cover all the damage, and Sabu remained in his jail cell until it was time for Charles to return to Los Angeles.

Enduring the sad ordeal of Gerald's funeral was particularly difficult for Charles. He had always yearned for a closer bond with his father, and now he was dead and there was no chance for that. His father had been away from home so much because of his occupation that he seemed almost like a stranger to Charles, and often when he was home the poor man was ill with the severe attacks of asthma that eventually caused his death.

Charles knew that his father was a loving and understanding man in spite of his quiet and withdrawn nature, and he knew that deep down his father loved him. Now Charles stood with his mother at graveside, surrounded by family members and friends, completely overwhelmed with grief and a tremendous surge of loss and yearning.

The City Cabaret and Disco—
The Times They Were A-Changin'

In 1978, the City Cabaret and Disco on Montgomery Street and Broadway in North Beach was a magnet for young, beautiful, and not-so-young-and-beautiful people who danced the night away in the upstairs disco with its swirling psychedelic lights, mirrored, glittering globe spinning above, and its pulsating disco beat.

In those last wild times before the AIDS plague struck, many straight girls discovered that gay boys were fun to be with, and in most cases they were better dancers than their straight, macho boyfriends. The girls could abandon themselves, "boogie-ing up a storm" with gay boys with their tight-fitting jeans, flashy shirts, bare midriffs, and buffed bods, bumping and grinding their denim-upholstered buns as the music throbbed. The girls could "have fun," as Cyndi Lauper's song declared, and they didn't need to have sex when the night ended, although some, the "fag hags" or "fruit flies," were attracted sexually to the gay men.

Just as in the days when Rudolph Valentino set women's hearts aflutter with his dark, smooth, "patent leather" hair and Latin charm, the macho guys who called Rudy a sissy and a "pink powder puff" soon learned that to impress the ladies you had to be a "sheik," and they began slicking their hair back and taking tango lessons. And it worked!

Now, in the late 1970s, the macho crowd was beginning to ape the gay boys, wearing gold earrings, applying blusher and eye shadow, wearing cologne, having their hair "styled" at beauty salons, and stuffing their gym-buffed bods into tight jeans that displayed their sculptured buns and bulging baskets to full advantage. And they added the gay jargon to their repertoire: "hunk," "buns," "come out of the closet," "camp up a storm," and they bleached their hair. But the straight girls were still enchanted by the gay boys, and some found it fashionable to take a gay man home to dinner to meet Mom and Dad. The girls didn't have to worry about date rape, although some of the guys were bisexual and actually had consensual sex with their female friends. In general, though, the girls enjoyed talking "girl talk" with the gay crowd, while their macho guys had one thing on their minds, and it wasn't "girl talk!" Even Madonna was inspired by the black drag queens of New York City when she introduced her *Vogue* recording and video. Those queens had been "vogue-ing" long before Miss M hit town!

On December 27, 1978, Charles Pierce returned to The City cabaret, his fourth engagement there after his unprecedented two-week run as opening act for Ann-Margret's lavish Las Vegas revue at Caesar's Palace in October. When he performed in the Ann-Margret show, he opened with his "Living Dolls," but this time he had a new gimmick. He wore his Bette Davis *All About Eve* gown, but over it he draped a solid black robe to conceal it while he worked the "Dolls." At the very end of that sequence he performed with a Bette Davis puppet, then total blackout. The robe and the doll stage were whisked off and when the lights came up, there stood Charles as a life-size Bette Davis! He went through all of his Hollywood ladies, then he was off, and Ann-Margret was on.

Charles loathed working in Las Vegas, and while he was there he wrote me a short note on the back of a brochure from the hotel:

> Dear John,
>   I have no paper in the room—how chic!
>   Thanks for the telegram. *Loved it!*
>   Many technical problems on the dolls—bad lighting they couldn't correct until last night, and mike-ing the talking dolls. Better now, but *puleeze*—these audiences SUCK! Give me mine back! Doubt if I'd want to return in December ('78) unless they *get with it!*
>   More later,
>   C

It was during his stay in Vegas that he dropped by Jim Bailey's dressing room while Jim was making up for his Judy Garland impression. Charles told me the following exchange happened between them:

CHARLES: Hi, Jim.

JIM: *(Shushing him)* Please—Judy's here!

Charles never played Las Vegas again, and instead chose to open at The City cabaret. There he performed his Las Vegas show in the downstairs showroom while upstairs in the disco the beat went on— and on. His mother, Jessie, temporarily overcame her fear of flying and was present in the audience on opening night. She never would have risked the flight if a friend hadn't accompanied her. I had spoken to Jessie many times on the phone, and I knew she'd be a vivacious blonde lady with the same sparkling wit as her famous son. Charles introduced her from the stage, and she stood up and bowed graciously to thunderous applause. When I met her later backstage, it was if I'd known her forever. She was just as I'd imagined her to be, and I could see where Charles got his good looks, blue eyes, and sense of humor. Jessie once made up a line for Charles that he used in his act for years afterward: "Liberace's commode is shaped like a piano, and when you flush it, the water gurgles up and plays 'Ebb Tide.' Seagulls circle and bomb from above."

One night the notorious Divine was in the audience. He was famous for his performances in the films of John Waters, in which he appeared in outlandish drag. In one scene in the successful Waters film *Pink Flamingos,* Divine actually devoured poodle droppings. When Charles opened the show, he looked down, saw Divine, introduced him, and declared, "Lips that touch poodle shit will never touch mine!" After the audience stopped shrieking, Charles went on with the show.

Lee Hartgrave, the renowned San Francisco Bay Area drama critic, reviewed Charles Pierce's City cabaret show on KQED radio:

> Charles Pierce is breaking all records at The City showroom. He has lots of new material this time around, even the jokes sound new. Seeing Pierce has become a San Francisco pastime, which means that it shouldn't be missed. . . . It's the next best thing to sharing a cigarette with Bette Davis.

The AIDS plague struck in the 1980s and gay men across the country died in droves. It was a mystery illness, and suddenly everyone was terrified of gay people. No more taking them home to meet the family or dancing with them till dawn in the gay discos. Charles lost so many friends and associates when the disease broke out, including Herman George, his clever and talented costume designer, and Ken Dickmann, who had been in the shows at the Gilded Cage and went on to be a writer and affiliate of Filmex in Hollywood. So many talented young men lost.

The lights finally went out at The City cabaret and disco. No more nights of frenzied dancing under the glitter globe. A gray, desolate pall fell over the gay community, and its members were now pariahs to be shunned and feared.

Charles packed his drags and headed East, where he faced the New York critics for the first time. The *New York Post*'s Curt Davis praised Charles at Les Mouches, in a review dated November 1, 1979:

> You go to Les Mouches—and are bewitched by Charles Pierce .... The impressions [are] awesomely right in hair and costume .... Most of all you praise the wit, the class, the lack of sleaze. Charles Pierce is an actor, and the fact that he portrays women does not lessen his abilities.[1]

In *Women's Wear Daily,* November 16, 1979, Howard Kissel in his "Night Life" column had this to say about Charles at Les Mouches: "... when Pierce does (Bette) Davis' monologue on the meaning of being a woman in *All About Eve,* he shows he can be as touching as he is hilarious."[2]

An item from *Variety* by Lee dated November 7, 1979, reports:

> ... he admits that his Carol Channing at times sounds like Jack Benny ... one liners that would rival those of many comics. ... In between costume changes which are many and extravagantly tacky ... Pierce plays Joan of Arc at the stake thanking Heaven for her smoke alarm. ... The fun is nearly non-stop.[3]

Then it was back to Los Angeles and his only meeting with the real Miss Bette Davis!

26

The Backlot—
And the Real Miss Bette Davis

Studio One's Backlot was a favorite nightspot for Hollywood celebrities, and when Charles debuted there in December 1979 the word soon spread that his show was a "must see." A stream of Hollywood luminaries flocked into the club to see the show, including Bea Arthur, Alice Ghostley, Thomas Tryon, Robert Wagner and Natalie Wood, Richard Deacon, Dom DeLuise, Debbie Reynolds, and Charles Nelson Reilly.

Sabu had returned with Charles to Los Angeles from Watertown and had recovered at the Salvation Army's Alcoholics Rehabilitation Center. Now he was back, assisting Charles with preparations for the Backlot show.

Without Rio to play piano for him, Charles had to find a replacement. One night he wandered into a little bar in Los Angeles called the Toy Tiger, and as he listened to the young man playing the piano and singing a set of old show tunes, he became more and more impressed with the young man's talent.

According to what Charles told me later, the following transpired:

At break time, Charles attempted to introduce himself to the young man.

"Oh, I know you. You're Charles Pierce! I know all about you, and I love your show. I'm Michael Feinstein."

"Well, Michael Feinstein," Charles replied, "I must congratulate you on your talent. How do you know those old, old tunes?"

Michael related that he had been working for Ira Gershwin, cataloging all of Ira's sheet music and recordings, and because of that he had met Rosemary Clooney, Mrs. Oscar Levant, and other celebrities.

"How would you like to play for me at the Backlot?" Charles made Michael an offer he couldn't refuse, so he accompanied Charles at the

piano for the run of the show. Michael's career took a definite up-
swing later. One night Liza Minnelli heard him perform, and, as they
say, the rest is history. Michael Feinstein is now recognized as a
world-famous performer, appearing in concerts and clubs, and recording a number of albums.

Before Charles Pierce completed his engagement at the Backlot,
he finally met his idol, the real Miss Bette Davis. As long as he had
been doing his famous impression of her, he had never come face to
face with the star, and he had no idea what her reaction would be. He
remembered watching Ralph Edwards' *This Is Your Life, Bette Davis*
on television. After Edwards had greeted Bette and brought out her
friends and relations, he introduced Barbara Heller, who was well-
known in the local nightclubs for her impression of the star. Heller
performed her version of Davis's scene from *The Letter,* where Bette
Davis shoots her lover to death on the veranda steps of a rubber plan-
tation. Heller sashayed her hips, twirled her arms, and puffed on a
cigarette, and when she had finished twitching and twirling and being
introduced to Miss Davis, she took a seat behind Bette's sofa.

There was a long silence. Davis said absolutely nothing. She was
not amused, and Edwards had to fill the silence with mindless banter
until the next guest was introduced.

Charles tells in his own words what happened during his first and
only meeting with Bette Davis in an interview he gave to David Perry
for the *Bay Area Reporter:*

> "I met Bette Davis just once—. It was at the opening of
> Geraldine Page [actually it was Geraldine Fitzgerald who had
> been in *Dark Victory* with Davis and was now performing folk
> songs in cabarets] at Studio One's Backlot in L.A. during the
> late 70s. Miss Davis was there surrounded by people like Kirk
> Douglas, Olivia de Havilland, and Gregory Peck. Right before
> the show started, I was brought over and introduced to her. Her
> one remark was, 'Arthur Blake (the famous female impression-
> ist) was the first one to do me.'
> "Well," says Pierce, "where do you go from there?"

What really happened was quite different from what Charles said
in the above interview, according to what he confided to me later:

BETTE: *(Leering at Charles after introduction)* Oh, yes, I've heard
you do me. *(She takes a deep drag on her cigarette, then exhales a*

cloud of smoke.) You know, Arthur Blake did me. *(Her tone implies that Blake is the impressionist she regards above all others.)*

CHARLES: Yes, I know. *(Not missing a beat)* He once did me on the backseat of his Hupmobile! *(Turns on his heel and exits.)*

BETTE: *(Speechless, mouth agape)*

Quick curtain
The End

Bette Davis wasn't the only movie star Charles encountered during his engagement at the Backlot. One afternoon, he and a friend named Gary visited the famous Hollywood Ranch Market on Beverly Boulevard, and as they were seated in Charles' car ready to drive off, a young fellow drove up beside them and leaned his head out of his car window.

"Wanna go to a party?"

"Sure, where?"

"Follow me."

They did, and after winding along the serpentine road that led up a Beverly Hills canyon, they followed their leader onto a parking space outside the gates to a rambling hilltop mansion.

"Wow!" Charles thought. "What do we have here?" It was none other than the fabulous Spanish-style home of famous movie idol Rock Hudson. Charles and his two companions entered the house and surveyed the premises. Two sections of the building bordered a large flagstoned patio, the focus of which was a large rectangular swimming pool, overlooking a panorama of Beverly Hills. At each corner of the pool stood an antique lion statue, and, at the far end, a colonnade of iron pillars. Leading to the house from the patio an old Chinese elm spread its branches over an expanse of green lawn that sloped down to the canyon below.

An exuberant party was in full swing in and around the swimming pool. A bevy of scantily-clad young men in Speedos were frolicking poolside, and Rock himself, drink in hand, was reclining on a chaise nearby, enjoying the ribald spectacle that swirled around him.

Charles and Gary sampled the refreshments and sat by the pool watching the boys playfully pulling at each others' Speedos and laughing as they played "grab ass." Before they left, Charles and Gary were given the "Grand Tour" of Rock Hudson's manse. The fellow who had invited them led them into the spacious downstairs living room. Charles was surprised at how few rooms there were. This was a movie star's home, and he expected it to be on a grander scale.

In addition to the living room, the first floor included a den, a kitchen, and a guest room that had access to the patio. A master bedroom and another guest room were on the second floor. Standing in the living room, the men admired a beautiful Italianate Renaissance fireplace, velvet-covered couches, wing chairs, many flower arrangements, potted plants, and a grand piano.

The den was done in a rugged, masculine style with white plaster walls, wood paneling, and shelves of heavy planks that held an elaborate collection of books and records.

The master bedroom on the second floor contained a huge canopied four-poster bed, a concealed TV set, a fireplace, and a collection of nautical prints and ship's hardware. Charles was impressed with the shower in the master bathroom, which had a clear glass wall overlooking the view of the canyon below.

At sunset, the view of the city lights sparkled below and Charles and his friend said their "thank yous" and drove back down the hill.

Another time, Charles was invited to the beautiful Art Deco home of the "women's director" George Cukor. Mr. Cukor (or Miss Cukor, as he was known to his intimate friends) was in Europe, so Joey the caretaker, who knew Charles, invited him for a drink and to see the house. William Haines, the famous interior designer and ex-movie star, had done a magnificent job decorating Cukor's abode. Painted white, nestled into a hill, and surrounded by lush gardens, it had a feeling of openness with its floor-to-ceiling windows.

Charles and Joey sat in French Regency armchairs under a crystal chandelier in the stunning Oval Room, their drinks resting on top of a huge oak coffee table. Haines had covered the walls with smooth, tan suede, and a tall bouquet of calla lilies graced the top of a black lacquered commode.

After a tour of the house, they walked onto the white-bricked terrace to a shaded walk that led past pools, pergolas, and Italian statues, ivy clad, called "The Seasons." Joey pointed to a small guest cottage nestled and almost hidden in foliage.

"That's where Spencer Tracy and Katharine Hepburn stayed when they were having their secret love affair."

"How nice—for them." Charles became instant Bette Davis.

They continued along the curving pathway until Joey stopped by a stone bench. He was very quiet before he spoke.

"Here. Here's the spot—right here—where George Cukor sat Vivien Leigh down on this bench, and then, as he took her hand, he told her the exciting news: 'You've got the part, darling. You're going to be Scarlett O'Hara!'"

"There ought to be a shrine," Charles said. "And what did Vivien do—shit?"

27

An Evening at "Dottie's Place"

The year is 1982. The scene is the fabulous Dorothy Chandler Pavilion in downtown Los Angeles, and backstage everything is in readiness for this groundbreaking night of nights. What a triumph for Charles Pierce to tread the boards where so many greats had trod before him: Katharine Hepburn in *Coco,* Robert Preston in *Mack and Mabel*—not to mention that this theater had been the scene of many Academy Award shows!

Now the sellout crowd is seated, and the huge auditorium is abuzz. Onstage, Michael Biagi has alerted the Crystal Palace Ragtime Orchestra for the downbeat and overture, then for the music that will bring Charles onstage. In a tiny booth at stage right, crammed with costumes, wigs, and props, Herman George, Charles' dresser and costume designer, is at the ready to assist Charles with his lightning transformations.

In the dressing room off stage left, Charles is seated at his makeup table touching up his blusher and false eyelashes. Franklin Townsend, his advisor and hairdresser, is teasing and combing wigs and arranging them on head stands:

FRANKLIN: Now, Charles, you must remember when you make your entrance that you're at the Dorothy Chandler Pavilion and not one of those seedy little nightspots you used to play in.

CHARLES: *(Doing his lips)* Mmmmmm—

FRANKLIN: You can't use a lot of profanity, and especially, you must avoid the "F" word!

CHARLES: *(Standing and checking himself out in the floor-length mirror)* Mmmmmm—

FRANKLIN: Remember, you can't be your naughty self tonight—not at Dottie's Place.

CHARLES: Mmmmmmm—

The orchestra is playing Charles' entrance music, and he strides onstage in his golden sequined gown, blond wig, and extravagant white swansdown wrap, unfurling an enormous red feather boa which he holds aloft and lets it trail in his wake. He grabs the handheld mike and storms down centerstage to the very brink of the apron.

"My hairperson has been lecturing me backstage. He says that because I'm here in the Dorothy Chandler Pavilion that I must watch my language, and not be the naughty girl I usually am. *(Big pause)* Well, fuck him!" The audience goes berserk!

Riding high on the riotous applause, Charles begins his routine:

"I'm wearing street makeup—asphalt and tile. Your Valley Girl is here—Death Valley Girl, really, and for sure. *(Indicates his super-lengthy boa)* Listen, if I had anything this long I wouldn't have to be a female impersonator."

After a quick change, he's back as Mae West:

"Oh, mmm. I was strollin' through a cow pasture when a bull chased me. I was tired so I ran. An old rube farmer called out, 'Hey, Lady, what's the matter? Can't ya take it?' I said, 'Sure, I can take it, but what would I do with a calf in a three-room apartment.' "

He dashes to the changing booth and returns instantly as Katharine Hepburn.

"*Lion in Winter,* Pussy in Summer—I work when I can. *Suddenly, Last Summer.* I had a gay son in that film. Sebastian. How gay was Sebastian, you might query? He had his entire body tattooed as a Gucci bag. That's pretty damned gay!

"We had a house in New Orleans—everybody did. And it had an elevator. One day there were two young men already in the elevator when I stepped in. 'Going down?' I asked, and they were."

He builds up a momentum and quickly goes through his repertoire of memorable ladies of the silver screen, from Marilyn Monroe to Joan Crawford to Barbara Stanwyck.

"Where in the Big Valley in 1865 would you find an all-leather slack suit? She (Stanwyck) lost her ranch because she couldn't keep her calves together."

The Crystal Palace Ragtime Orchestra plays a little jazzy intermission music so that Charles, who has been sweating profusely under the hot lights, can take a break.

After the intermission, Michael Biagi gives the orchestra direction for the downbeat and the dramatic strains of "Would It Be Wrong?," the theme from *Now, Voyager*, fill the theater. Clouds of cigarette smoke billow up from the orchestra pit, the hand of "Bette Davis" reaches up, clutching a smoking cigarette, and "Bette," as only Charles can "do" her, emerges from the depths and takes stage. "She" struts, strides, fusses, and twirls.

"Remember when we all wanted to look like Liz Taylor—and now we do? She used to be so pretty. Pretty, pretty, pretty fat! I saw her at Macy's shopping for stretch jewelry."

For variety, he does a different version of *What Ever Happened to Baby Jane?*:

BETTE: Look at her! Blanche Hudson, Miss Pepsi-Cola, all scrunched down in her wheelchair. Blanche, lift the tea cozy on yer plate and eatcher din-din.

BLANCHE: Why, Jane, it's an old dead bird.

BETTE: Yeah, what did ya expect it to be—alive and kickin'? I basted it with Pepsi.

BLANCHE: Oh, Jane, you're so unkind to me. You never compliment me.

BETTE: Bullshit, Blanche! Compliment 'cha? I'd rather sew a red sequin on a rat's ass. If yer lookin' for sympathy ya'll find it in the dictionary between shit and suicide. I did something nice fer ya once. Remember the time I pushed ya all the way to San Francisco in yer wheelchair on Highway 5—before it was open? And I took ya to Lombard Street, that crookedy little tourist street on Telegraph Hill, and I pushed ya down, yer spike-heeled wedgies diggin' all the way down. Yer lips did a circle 'round Coit Tower. Ya remember what happened next, Miss Showbiz?

BLANCHE: Why yes, a big seagull circled overhead and did doo-doo all over my head and down my dress. I said, "Quick, run for the toilet paper!"

BETTE: Are ya nuts? By the time I got back, that bird's ass would be halfway across the Pacific!

Charles finished the routine with his famous closing lines, with the audience chiming in:

BLANCHE: Oh, Jane, you wouldn't be so cruel to me if I wasn't a cripple in a wheelchair.
BETTE: But ya are, Blanche. Ya are!

Quick-change time again and Charles is back as "Celine Kendall," a pretty drag created by him from the depths of his fertile imagination. Dazzling in another stunning gown and a stylish auburn wig, he tosses off a string of risqué bon mots, then goes into his version of the song from *Woman of the Year,* "I'm One of the Boys Who Is One of the Girls," and segues into "Illusions," Marlene Dietrich's torcher from the film *A Foreign Affair,* but with Charles' special lyrics. As he slowly climbs a stairway upstage center, he sings:

"It's been an illusion, strictly entre nous. Such a lovely illusion, all for laughs, all for you!" Curtain. Bows. Thunderous applause!

28

Charles Pierce Takes New York— And New York Loves It!

By now, in 1982, Charles Pierce had played just about every important nightclub in the United States, including Molokai, Hawaii. He had triumphed in London, England, and had turned down offers to appear in Australia and Edinburgh, Scotland. In New York City he had entertained at the Village Gate, The Ballroom, Grand Finale, and Les Mouches. On the East Side he had knocked 'em dead at posh Freddy's, where an array of celebrities flocked to see him. There were Lucille Ball, Claudette Colbert, Paulette Goddard, Debbie Reynolds, Dorothy Loudon, Ingrid Bergman, and gossip columnist Liz Smith, who told him, "Darling, this is cabaret. You can say anything you like." Not that he needed her permission!

Years before, Charles and I had written a sketch based on the film *For Whom the Bell Tolls,* which, of course, starred Ingrid Bergman and Gary Cooper. In the routine, during the famous sleeping-bag scene, "Roberto" (Gary Cooper) gets his zipper stuck and other calamities. "Maria" (Ingrid Bergman) does a lot of moaning, calling out, "Roberto, Roberto," and so forth. At the time we wrote it we had no idea that someday Charles would meet Miss Bergman in the flesh. During one of his performances at Freddy's, Charles revived the old sketch, and Bergman herself was in the audience. After the show, she appeared in Charles' dressing room and sat down beside him at his makeup table, watching him cold cream his face. She was not amused.

"You vant to learn to do impression uf me—come to my apartment. I show you how to imitate me." She rose without saying another word and swept out. Charles didn't take her up on her offer.

When, in May of 1982, Charles opened at Freddy's at 308 East 49th Street in Manhattan's East Side, he was the absolute toast of the town. "He turned them away in droves," as one critic wrote. Columnist Liz Smith became an instant fan and constantly plugged the show in her syndicated column:

> Freddy's has talked Mr. Chuck [Pierce] into staying around through the July 4th weekend . . . it's still the best show in New York City . . . Charles, one of the best actors of our time . . . a great talent!"[1]

Curt Davis wrote, "Making the first two annual visits to Freddy's . . . Charles Pierce is at his peak . . . I defy you to laugh any more anywhere else in town."[2]

A short uncredited item states:

> Charles Pierce . . . at the wonderful Freddy's on 49th Street . . . [celebrities] just keep cramming in there . . . Everybody loves Charles' gowns, his makeup, his impressions, his chatter. Everybody likes best [his impression of] Admiral Bull Halsey in drag saying, "It takes a man to wear a dress like this."[3]

Another item, also uncredited, said:

> If Lon Chaney was The Man with a Thousand Faces, this star [Pierce] is The Man with Two Thousand Boobies. Pierce is our numero uno, unequaled female impersonator. When his time arrives, he should be placed in the Smithsonian.[4]

Rex Reed added his praise: "I marvel at Pierce's cleverness and timing."[5]

In "Key, This Week in New York," a short item lauded Charles' show:

> The laughter is non-stop in the most hilarious and ingenious one-man show ever in New York. The amazing Mr. Pierce transforms himself into a galaxy of cinema's grandest dames. It's all done with spectacular professionalism, sensational satire, and sheer brilliance. Go catch him in the act . . . and you'll be a fan for life![6]

Chip Orton in his "Nightcrawling" column enthused:

> . . . I have heard one reaction over and over from people in Pierce's audiences at Freddy's, "I'm exhausted from laughing!"

And you, dear reader, will be exhausted too, should you . . . make reservations at this gem of a club . . . this consummate actor . . . is nothing short of genius . . . Don't miss this act.[7]

Charles wrote me from the Shelburne Murray Hotel at 303 Lexington Avenue when all the above hysteria was at its height:

Monday
June 14, 1982

Dear John,
The sun is *out* for the first time in 2 weeks! Here's a "C. P. update"—as if you really needed one—but wanted you to see my "artwork." [A collage of all his reviews of his shows at Freddy's, and a few photos.] I cut, glued, and kept saying to myself, "Now, John would have done it this way!" [I used to design brochures for him.]

Liz [Smith] really keeps the show going with her plugs—and here's Debbie [Reynolds'] picture—different pose than the *S. F. Examiner.* That picture was released U.P. and ended up all over the country.

I'm interested in a dancer in *A Chorus Line*—terrific—named Michael!! Only he's "non-gay"—I'm *told* that, but I want to find out for myself!

I've been held over twice [at Freddy's]—now till July 4th, then to L.A., then maybe the Plush Room in August.

C

P. S. Alice Faye was in and so very nice.
Another P. S. 8 weeks! I'm ready to be on my way. I feel I live here!

29

"The Tush Room at the Hotel Yuck"

When, in 1982, Charles Pierce performed at the Plush Room at the Hotel York on Sutter Street in San Francisco, he immediately christened the establishment "The Tush Room at the Hotel Yuck." Actually, he loved the room at first sight, and it became his favorite venue—his home away from home. He always occupied a suite in the hotel on the sixth floor when he had an engagement there. Long before the building housed the Hotel York, it was known as the Empire Hotel, and it became famous when film director Alfred Hitchcock used the hotel as a location for Kim Novak's character in *Vertigo*.

The Plush Room is entered through double doors off the hotel's spacious lobby. It is intimate, with a grand piano situated on a low platform stage sans curtains, Naugahyde banquettes against the walls, and small round tables with chairs set up to make a cozy cabaret ambience. A large, lighted, rectangular stained-glass panel highlights the low ceiling, and a small dressing room is located off stage left. Les Natali, Steve Silver, and other friends always gifted Charles with beautiful flower arrangements for the grand piano top, adding to the elegance of the room.

Many celebrities came through the portals of the Plush Room to see Charles' show whenever they were in The City. Lauren Bacall came by when she was starring in her musical *Woman of the Year,* and after the show she and Charles huddled in a banquette near the entrance to the room. I wonder if they compared notes on the role of "Margo Channing" in *Applause*? Angela Lansbury, still a fan from the Gilded Cage days, brought her husband, Peter Shaw, and a female friend to the show when she was starring in *Sweeney Todd* at the Orpheum Theatre. She and her party were charming and gracious, and we had pictures taken with her. Before he became famous, Michael Feinstein came to see Charles at the Plush Room, and soon he would be appearing there in his popular one-man musical show.

Shirley MacLaine didn't come to Charles' show—instead, we went to see her when her fabulous show opened at the Circle Star Theatre in Redwood City. Through the publicity woman for the theater, who was a friend of Charles, he, Sabu, and I drove down the peninsula to enjoy a matinee of Shirley's performance. Before the show, we had lunch in the theater dining room. Then we were seated in the vast auditorium, which featured a theater-in-the-round style stage. Before the show began, Shirley MacLaine appeared onstage and announced, "We have a celebrity in our audience this afternoon. Please welcome Mr. Charles Pierce." There was a long pause. Finally, I nudged Charles.

"Charles, stand up! It's for you!" Dazed, he finally stood up. Then the show began.

We were invited backstage after the show to meet Ms. MacLaine, but first we encountered Fred Travalena, the clever comic who opened the show, and we talked with him until Shirley appeared.

Introductions were made by the publicity woman. Then Charles, indicating me, said to Ms. MacLaine, "He knows all about you."

"I first saw you in *Artists and Models*," I told her. "I thought you deserved someone better to end up with than Jerry Lewis." Shirley threw back her head and roared with laughter, then took me by the shoulders and kissed me full on the mouth! A very sweet lady and a flawless performer.

* * *

Now it's showtime at the Plush Room. The house is packed. Backstage, Charles is at his dressing table adjusting his false eyelashes and lipstick. Standing before the full-length mirror, he checks his pantyhose and girdle before slipping into his sequined gown and blonde wig. It's precisely nine p.m. He's always punctual—never keeps his audience waiting.

The house lights dim. A single spotlight swings across the stage to pick out the petite figure of auburn-haired Joan Edgar seated at the baby grand, resplendent in her man's tuxedo, playing the overture, a medley of showtunes and selections from Bette Davis' films, including "Would It Be Wrong?," the theme from *Now, Voyager,* "They're Either Too Young or Too Old" from *Thank Your Lucky Stars,* and others.

From backstage a male voice announces over the sound system, "And now, ladies and gentlemen, the star of our show, Male Actress, the Master and Mistress of Disguise—MR. CHARLES PIERCE!"

He makes a dazzling entrance in full face, high drag, and heels, blond wig flipped and teased, shimmering silver-sequined gown slashed to the hip, one long shapely leg boldly exposed, and that viper tongue—the Fastest Tongue in the West (and points, East, North, and South) at the ready! He's "Celine Kendall," his glamorous made-up character, tossing off some rapid-fire repartee:

> It takes a man to wear a dress like this. In high school, I didn't go to my vocational guidance teacher and say, "I want to be a female impersonator." No, he came to me. "Charles, I've seen you in the halls. You're a female impersonator."

He chatters on and on, then disappears into the wings, keeping us amused with racy quips over the sound system until his parade of "Legendary Ladies of the Silver Screen" begins. It might be a shaky Katharine Hepburn croaking her way through a scene from *The African Queen:*

> *The African Queen*—nobody you'd know. Why, I haven't seen Johnny Mathis in ages!

Suddenly, she's Eleanor of Aquitaine from *The Lion in Winter* in the year 1132:

> In those days no one was gay. They were glum. We didn't have gay bars—just glum bars—imagine going to your first glum bar! Everything was gray and glum. *(Katharine segues into the present.)* The calla lilies are in bloom again. Strange, I planted marijuana.

Next she takes us to the shores of "Golden Pond":

> Here we are, Henry Fonda and I, "On Goldie Hawn"—oh, I mean "On Golden Pond." Henry, you old poop, stop calling the loon and playing suck-face in the berry patch.

(The lights dim and Charles goes dramatic as Hepburn doing "Always Mademoiselle" from Coco.*)* He gets a rousing, standing ovation for displaying his true acting ability.

Occasionally, there's a heckler in the audience, but Charles takes it in stride. If it is a male, he'll answer back, "You have a high voice for a lesbian." A redneck type bellows out, "Marilyn Monroe had a cuter ass than you." Charles doesn't miss a beat:

"Oh, and did she also have a cuter cock and balls?"

Back to the show, and this time he's Mae West, six feet tall in heels, sashaying from the wings, hand on hip, patting his coiffure, an illusion in gold lamé, trailing a bright red feather boa. A tiny Tweetie Bird is nestled in the top-knot of his long, blond wig, which he explains is the "sacred burial ground for Tweetie Bird."

> Oh, mmm, I didn't know what to wear so I wore everything. In this outfit with all the horse hair, foam rubber, and whalebone, I don't know if I'm a great star or a five-piece room group at Levitz warehouse. Come up and see me for an occasional piece in the living room sometime—I'm talkin' about a sectional.
>
> Oh, I met a handsome croupier in Las Vegas. He said, "Mae, I'd like to lay ya ten ta one." I said, "That's an odd hour, but I'll be there." Oh, I feel like a million tonight, but I'll take 'em three at a time.

In rapid succession comes a frozen-lipped Barbara Stanwyck on the deck of the sinking *Titanic:*

> Oh, no, I can't go down. I've never gone down before, and I'm not going down now! Oh, no!

An undulating and mincing Marilyn Monroe cooing breathlessly:

> I was eight before I was seven. Arthur Miller wanted me to read Walt Whitman, and I said, "Oooh, I just love his chocolates." Joe DiMaggio had terrible dandruff. My girlfriend said, "Give him Head and Shoulders." I said, "How do I give him shoulders?"

And then come the Turban Ladies. Charles, from backstage, as he changes into his next costume, explains on the sound system why they wore turbans:

They wore turbans because their hairdressers threw a hissy fit and told them, "Do it yourself! I'm going to the beach!"

Norma Desmond from *Sunset Boulevard* leads the pack with her insane eyes, garb, and acres of jangling beads:

Norma Desmond! Back with you—all you wonderful people out there in the dark. Do you have some popcorn for me? An old, used Eskimo Pie? Oh, I forgot, people who come to see me can't chew. The only part of my body that hasn't wrinkled—my teeth! Mr. DeMille, I'm ready for my closeup!

Charles quickly becomes a heavily accented Maria Montez:

Where is my twin sister? She is my brother. Sabu, bring me the Cobra Chool.

Next, Charles becomes the old gypsy woman Maria Ouspenskya croaking to the Wolf Man:

You are strange, my son. The way you walk—in heels—no fault of your own. When the moon is full you will change—into drag. You will shave and go from Wolf Man to Wolf Woman—the wolves will love it.

Joan Edgar plays on and Charles disappears into the wings. He returns as Marlene Dietrich, a scarlet beret atop her blonde pageboy bob. She seats herself on the piano top with a long cigarette holder rammed inside her cheek:

I'm going to do some numbers from some of my pictures. Some of them are in the audience tonight. *(Sings)* "Falling in Love Again." That's a song I did during the war. I won't say which one, but Grant took Richmond—and Richmond loved it! *(Sings again)* "There is a story the gypsies like to hear—that when your love wears golden earrings, he's a little queer." *(To a young guy sitting in the front row)* Are you in show business? No? Then get your feet off my stage! Your jeans are so tight I can tell your religion. *(Sings again)* "Falling in Love Again."

There's more to come, and now he's Lucille Ball:

Ricky, the Mertzes want a four-way!

A fat-lipped, cooing Joan Crawford, brandishing a wire coat hanger, calls to her beloved daughter Christina:

Christina. Christina, darling. It's time for your bath. Mommie Dearest has had the water boiling for three days. *(Leans toward audience)* These lips could dismantle a tractor—and have.

Another Joan, Joan Collins:

What do I put behind my ears to attract men? My legs!

Now it's Tallulah-time *(she enters through the audience clutching a vodka bottle):*

Oh, God, dahlings. I've just been on a drunk—and he loved it. Is this an Alcoholics Anonymous meeting? No? Then give me a drink! *(She seats herself spread-legged on the piano top and addresses the front row)* Ever been this close to an open grave, dahlings? *(she exits laughing uproariously)*

At last, the moment we've all been waiting for. Out she strides, hips swinging, arms twirling, bug-eyes glaring, skirt and nostrils flaring, spewing jets of smoke to the ceiling from the cigarette clutched in her twitching hand. It's gonna be a bumpy ride! It's Bette Davis as only Charles Pierce can do her, and the crowd goes berserk, standing, applauding, stomping, cheering! This is their favorite, and they can't get enough:

Oh, then you know who I am? *(Leering)* Good! I've never been so relaxed *(twitch, twitch)*. I just took a Valium—a really big Valium—it was *that* big! I'm going to do a scene from all of my pictures. We may be here till Shelley Winters becomes anorexic! How do you have sex with Shelley Winters? Roll her in flour and look for a wet spot.

I need a drink! *(Calls to waiter)* Herbert! Hustle yer tight little buns over here and bring me a drink! Post haste! *(Herbert appears with a drink on a tray)* Oh, there you are, Herbert. What have you brought me this time? I know it's not a Tom Collins, and it can't be a Joan Collins because it has a cherry. I don't have mine—I ate it, but I still have the box it came in. *(Shrieks)* What is this shit? *(Picks lemon twists from glass)* Barbra Streisand's old nail clippings! Yuck! *(Tosses them over her shoulder)* Herbert, you never laugh—you're the Great Stone Face. Try as I will, I can't break you up! *(Holding the cherry she has taken from the glass, she gulps it down. Herbert still doesn't break up and leaves.)*

I'll never forget my pictures, and I won't let you forget them either. Remember the scene from Now, Voyager? "Oh, Jerry, why ask for the stars when you can moon me?" My favorite line from all my movies was from *Cabin in the Cotton:* "I'd love ta moon ya, but I jest washed ma hay-ya."

And let's not forget my stinkers—*Beyond the Forest.* I was Rosa Moline stuck in a little town called Kansas City, New Mexico— what a dump! The tide went out one day and never came back. The Avon lady didn't ring your doorbell—she tinkled on your lawn. The only female impersonator in town was a real woman—Debbie Reynolds. I was Rosa Moline—a nine o'clock woman in a five o'clock town waiting for twelve o'clock—with five o'clock shadow. Creeping and crawling up the railroad tracks with peritonitis—a Greek I met in a bar. Not bad.

Then there was the time I was driving Tallulah Bankhead to Palm Springs. She said, "Bette, dahling, you really must stop the car. I have to wee." So I stopped the car and Tallulah went behind a large cactus and let go. It was a flood, like *The Rains of Ranchipur.* The desert suddenly bloomed. A small lake formed. Swans floated by. Dolphins played, and Esther Williams came out of retirement. The natives began building an ark. But before Tallulah finished, a rattlesnake bit her—right in her own private Bermuda Triangle. She screamed, "Bette, burn rubber and get a doctor! You've got to save me! Godspeed!" I cruised leisurely into town, had lunch—a smorgasbord—saw a movie—*Gandhi*—twice, had a fingerwave and a manicure, and finally found a doctor. The doctor said, "Take a knife, cut the wound, and suck the poison out." I became Barbara Stanwyck instantly, "Oh, no, my lips are stuck to my teeth." I drove back, stopped at McDonald's for a really Big Mac, had the car lubed, and finally made it back to Tallulah. Tallulah was all ears, "What did the doctor say, dahling?" I inhaled—deeply. "The doctor says you're gonna die!"

BLACKOUT

Charles returns, taking bow after bow. The applause is thunderous and continues for at least twenty minutes. Another triumph for Charles Pierce at The "Tush" Room!

One Sunday at noon, Charles phoned me from his suite at the York Hotel. "Bill and Wil are picking me up and we're driving to Guerneville to check out a gig I might do at The Woods. If you want to go along, be here at 2 p.m."

Bill and Wil were a couple—longtime lovers—and had been waiters at the Gilded Cage. The Woods was a very attractive and popular bar and restaurant close by the Russian River. I drove right over and met Charles in the lobby with two young men he had invited to come with us. Bill and Wil arrived in their new luxury van, and soon we were on our way.

Bill was at the wheel, Wil sat next to him, and I was seated in a deep, leather-upholstered swivel chair which was secured to the van's floor right behind the driver's seat. Charles and the two boys were away in the back, sprawled on a plush, carpeted area. We all had soft drinks, and we were having a merry time—especially Charles and his two handsome companions!

I swung my chair around to speak to Charles and was confronted by a surprising scene. Both young men had their jeans and shorts pulled down to their ankles, and Charles was busy servicing both of them orally! When he had finished, the boys pulled their pants up, and they all went on talking and sipping their drinks. Other than that, the trip was uneventful, and Charles decided not to do the gig at The Woods.

Not long after this episode, Charles joined me at the York Hotel bar one night after his show. He said he had something serious to tell me, and we took our drinks to a secluded table in a back corner of the bar. He was very quiet, and I could tell he was deeply troubled. After a long pause, he told me he was being sued by a young man who claimed that Charles had molested him back in the 1960s when the man was a nine-year-old boy! What a shock!

"Do you remember the boy I used to baby-sit?" Charles asked.

"Of course," I said.

"Well, he's the one who's bringing suit against me on molestation charges! He's no longer a little boy—he's twenty-three."

"Charles," I said in disbelief, "that's ridiculous. You were always so good to that kid."

"I used to baby-sit him when his mother had a hot date."

"Charles, I know you, and you'd never molest a child. I'll go to court and testify to your good character."

"No, I can't have you go to court. I'll have to pay him to keep it out of the papers. I'd be finished if it ever came out."

Then Charles told me about a previous incident he was involved in in New York City, when one day he happened to meet the young man on the street. Now in his early twenties, he had ambitions to be a dancer. He was living with another struggling young dancer named Eddie, and they both had hopes of eventually performing in a Broadway show.

Charles hadn't seen the young man for several years, and, at first, they were glad to see each other. When Charles asked him to join him for lunch, the mood turned ugly.

"Charles, I can't. I'd like to, but Eddie's waiting for me. I've gotta get home."

"Oh, Eddie! Eddie! Eddie! Are you still letting that creep screw the hell outta you? You must be a masochist. Jesus, you've got lousy taste in men!"

"I wish you wouldn't talk that way about Eddie. I happen to love him." He was deeply hurt.

"Love! You call that love? What do you know about love? It's just plain lust! Are you coming with me or not?" Charles, the control queen, was in high dudgeon.

"No, I'm not! And you can go to hell!" He started to move away, but Charles was quick and slapped him across the face—hard! Tears streamed down the young man's face. He gave Charles a look that was close to hatred, then he turned and hurried away.

"Charles, don't you see why he's suing you? It's because you slapped him! I'm sure some shyster lawyer came up with this molestation charge to get a larger settlement, when probably all the kid wanted was to sue you for assault." I was sure my theory was correct.

"Yeah, you could be right at that. I shouldn't have hit him—the little bastard!"

"I suppose when the lawyer discovered that you were once the kid's baby-sitter, he got greedy. I can't imagine why he waited twenty years to sue you. I think you should fight it." I was adamant.

"No, I'll pay him off and forget it." One quick slap in the face and Charles was slapped with the suit! He did settle out of court for $50,000.

"We could have had a luxury trip to Europe for what that son-of-a-bitch cost me!" Charles seemed philosophical about it all and just filed the incident away.

The Venetian Room—
"Top o' the World, Ma!"

There was one venue in San Francisco that Charles hadn't played—the Fairmont Hotel's Venetian Room on Nob Hill. Russ Alley, who had been Talent Coordinator at the Plush Room, later became employed in the same capacity at the Fairmont Hotel. He had been trying for some time to convince the Swigs, who owned the hotel, that Charles Pierce would be a sellout in the world-famous show room. The cavernous, opulent space with its Venetian murals and rococo decor had been the scene of many performances by the likes of Marlene Dietrich, Carol Channing, Ginger Rogers, Joel Grey, Lena Horne, and many others.

At last the Swigs were convinced, and Charles Pierce opened on July 3, 1984, in what he called "The Men's Room at the Vatican"—or "The Pope's Dressing Room"—the fabulous Venetian Room! Scott Beach, *The San Francisco Examiner* music critic, reviewed Charles' performance under the heading, "Pierce Is a Winner with Bette Davis Eyes":

> . . . one of the cleverest and best entertainers in show business . . .
> a fearful challenge to bring this show to the Venetian Room . . .
> I've seen some big-name performers bomb there . . . But [Pierce]
> wowed them . . . Pierce had the audience in the palm of his hand
> . . . wanting more![1]

That was the first of Charles' engagements at the Venetian Room. The other two were in 1987 and 1988.

Between engagements at the Venetian Room, Charles performed at the Marines Memorial Theatre in San Francisco in 1985 in *An Intimate Extravaganza*. It was well-received in spite of the venue's lack of an intimate cabaret ambience where the audience could sit at tables and enjoy drinks.

In 1987 Charles starred in *A Night to Remember* at the Louise M. Davies Symphony Hall, with the San Francisco Gay Men's Chorus and special guest artist Barbara Cook. The most memorable occurrence of the evening was when Charles, as Bette Davis, lit a cigarette onstage and was confronted by a fire marshal who announced that there was no smoking allowed in the building! Charles was taken aback, and for once was left speechless—and smokeless!

Each time Charles appeared at the Fairmont Hotel, he was ensconced in the sumptuous Singapore Suite, which consisted of a living room, bedroom, and bath, with a small refrigerator for snacks and cold drinks. Located by the hotel's luxury tower, his rooms faced a wrought-iron trimmed balcony reminiscent of the buildings along New Orleans' Bourbon Street and overlooking the Transamerica Pyramid in the distance.

One of the unusual features of the Venetian Room is that there are no dressing rooms adjoining the stage. Artists appearing there were forced to apply their makeup in their suites, dress, and take the elevator all the way down to the kitchen, then walk to the edge of the large platform stage. There is no proscenium and no curtains. Charles solved the problem of space for his quick changes by having a tiny black phone-booth-sized area erected at stage right to hold his wigs, costumes, and props. It allowed his assistant to be out of the audience's sight, but still close at hand when a change of costume was necessary. Charles still had to make up in his suite and wear his opening gown down in the elevator to the kitchen. Often, guests of the hotel were startled to be confronted in the elevator by a six-foot man in drag! Can you imagine those great ladies, Lena Horne, Marlene Dietrich et al., picking their way around the huge ranges and vats of scalding soup to make their "glamorous" entrances?

Each night, Charles sailed on stage, making *his* glamorous entrance. Jesse Hamlin put it this way in a *Datebook* review dated July 5, 1984:

> . . . gliding across the Venetian Room stage in his customary platinum wig, bosom-filled red and gold spangled gown, mock ermine coat, and rhinestone necklace, heavy enough to anchor the *Enterprise* . . . an orgy of laughter—One of the funniest men to ever wear a girdle . . . Pierce can conjure up Joan Crawford

with the mere stretch of his lips . . . he sketches the persona magnificently with a sweep of the arm, the bulging eye, the telling movement of the neck or hip, a snippet of raucous laughter, then uses the character he has created to display the brilliant wit of Charles Pierce . . . Now if only Charles would add Nancy Reagan to his repertoire.[2]

Or as music critic Philip Elwood summed it up in his review in *The San Francisco Examiner* of August 26, 1988, during Charles' last engagement at the Fairmont:

> Charles Pierce, one last time . . . Pierce says that his two week run in the Venetian Room is his last such booking . . . the Fairmont presentation is, thus, something of a "farewell show" . . . Wednesday night's performance began sensationally. . . . He'd been announced as "the blonde that Hollywood forgot," and as he bowed (looking for all the world like a Jean Harlow-era bombshell in a ravishing red and silver striped dress) his necklace fell off. As he tossed a flower to the audience, he dropped his mike. Plop. No more sound. "Well," he pouted in his best Bette Davis inflection, "I don't need a mike," and he began . . . tossing off jokes and comments . . . if, indeed, he is quitting long engagements for awhile, he at least can note that he quit while he was ahead.[3]

Charles carried on without the necklace or the mike until they were replaced, and he was back hitting his stride. Pianist Joan Edgar, tuxedo-clad, and the Dick Bright Orchestra accompanied him with verve.

Mick La Salle in *The San Francisco Chronicle,* August 25, 1988, was also impressed:

> Pierce came out in a shoulder-length blonde wig and a black dress with silver appliques all over it . . . For me, the key question is this: Does he make an appealing woman? . . . the kind you would respect, or have a laugh with? That kind of thing.[4]

Evidently one woman in the audience thought Charles was convincing as a real woman. She and her husband were probably members of the Lions Club convention that was in town. As the couple was leaving after Charles' show, the woman turned to her husband

and said, "Well, she's not very pretty, and she's awfully tall." Charles just chortled when I told him that.

Cynthia Robins, of *The San Francisco Examiner,* reviewed the show and interviewed Charles on August 25, 1988:

> Charles Pierce . . . swoops on stage like a red-sequined Firebird. Flapping a cape studded with flashing lights ("Be careful with that, it's my pacemaker") . . . off stage, (Pierce) is a benign coun-tenance. As docile and sweet and retiring a gent as you'd meet at a Sunday social somewhere in New England. With his sandy hair, lanky body, and impish face, he looks more like a character out of Booth Tarkington than the King of Drag, as former *New York Times-*man Clive Barnes was wont to call him.[5]

In the interview, Cynthia Robins quoted Charles about his show and about his coming retirement. Describing his material, he said:

> People say, "Oh, he does the same act all the time. He just goes on stage." I've heard that. But there isn't a day goes by that I'm not thinking about it or working on it or changing a costume or seeing somebody about new wardrobe . . .
>
> "You know, when I first started, I wanted to be an actor in films, and the night clubs came along and I was swept up into that part of my career . . . I'm not saying that I don't want to play in other cities. I'm phasing out before I become this tottering, old . . . drag."

Charles was always telling reporters that he had had it and that his gig at the Fairmont would be his final "Farewell Performance."

Charles continues his Cynthia Robins interview:

> I'm always saying things like that . . . this time it's the truth. This time I can't go back, I think the time has come. But remember, I'm not retiring . . . I'm "abdicating" . . . and no (more) schlepping!"

Cynthia Robins summed it all up at the end of the interview:

> In the future, fans will just have to watch Pierce totter as Bette and wobble, er warble, as Kate closer to his Toluca Lake home. Back in Hollywood, where, after all, stars really belong.

I suppose Charles felt it was a good time to "abdicate" now that he had played the Venetian Room. It was comparable to playing the Palace Theatre in New York City. As Judy Garland sang when she opened there for her triumphant engagement, "Until you've played the Palace, you might as well be dead!" The Venetian Room was, as Charles wrote to his mother, "Top o' the World, Ma!" That was the famous line James Cagney screamed from the pinnacle of a gas refinery tower in the film *White Heat,* just before he was engulfed in flames. Indeed, Charles had reached the "Top o' the World" by appearing in the Venetian Room. As I sat there watching him perform, I thought back to those early days when I passed the hat so that Charles could get to San Francisco—and now he was here! He seemed to be really serious about ending his career, although I felt he had many more triumphs in the future. He did only one more important "Farewell Performance," at our old alma mater, Pasadena Playhouse. At the Playhouse he had come full circle, and farewell! Neither he nor I could predict that it really would be his very final performance, and that within months he would be diagnosed with a fatal illness.

31

Wild at The Ballroom—
Farewell to New York City

When Charles Pierce played The Ballroom in Manhattan, *The New York Post* for Wednesday, May 20, 1987, reported:

> Guest of honor at The Ballroom the other night, at the performance of female impersonator Charles Pierce, was one of his subjects: Lucille Ball. . . .
>
> Lucille Ball . . . laughed hysterically and accidentally dumped her mineral water onto Harvey [Fierstein's] lap, who announced: "Lucy was laughing so loud she wet *my* pants!"[1]

Charles takes a beat to preen in his glittering red-and-white sequined gown:

> This dress kept me out of the war. I won't say which one, but Grant took Richmond—and Richmond loved it!

More banter, a quick change, and he's Mae West in a stunning sequined gown, draped with a black cock-feather boa.

> Ooh, I was fourteen before I knew French was a language. If I could find a man as butch as Princess Stephanie, I'd marry him. She's so butch she rolls her own tampons. I saw her jump-start her dildo.
>
> Ooh, sex is like air. It's suddenly important when you're not gettin' any. I walked into a bar here in New York City with ma parakeet on ma shoulder. I said, "I'll go home with any man who can guess the weight of ma parakeet."
>
> One guy spoke up. He said "Two thousand pounds." I said, "Close enough. Let's go."

Ooh, I was brushin' up on ma old nursery rhymes: Hickory, dickory, dyke—oh, sorry, ma tongue got caught—in ma teeth. Rub-a-dub-dub, three men in a tub. Ooh—mmm. Pass the bath salts and call me Jacuzzi, with the accent on coozey!!"

Next he's Joan Collins, black wig, blue sequins, and spraying the air with an ornate perfume bottle. "She" goes offstage right, returns with a lavish white fur stole, and drapes it on the piano. She goes to the right again and returns with a slightly smaller white fur stole which she also drapes on the piano. Her last stole is very small, about two feet square. She holds it up as if it were a dead animal:

For the poor. I don't sing and I don't dance, and I don't tell jokes. And don't you dare say I can't act! Oh, you said it. Men are like diamonds. They can never be too big or too hard. I was doing my act in Tijuana, but my donkey died. I headed for Hollywood—wouldn't you if your ass gave out in Tijuana?

A brief pause, and Katharine Hepburn makes her way through the audience carrying her spindly calla lilies. Reaching the stage, she complains:

Oh, those gay rapists of the East Side. One held me down while the other did my hair.

As Gabrielle Chanel she comments on her father:

Daddy had a high voice. A toilet seat had fallen on his throat when he was a child—and someone was sitting on it.

Now comes the "piéce de résistance"—Charles Pierce as the incomparable Bette Davis:

(To the front row) I need a cigarette! *(A man hands her one. She is outraged)* LIT! *(She throws it back at him. He lights one and hands it to her)* Thank you! Oh, look! It's that old bag—lady, Tallulah Bankhead.

Charles performs the famous bitch fight between the two rivals:

TALLULAH: Bette, dahling, if you ever become a mother may I have one of the puppies?

BETTE: You are one of the puppies. You're like doggie-doo. The older you get the easier you are to pick up.

TALLULAH: Is it true when you were born the doctor slapped your mother?

BETTE: Tallulah, Tallulah, Tallulah! Your mother named you "Tallulah" because she couldn't spell "blech!"

TALLULAH: Really, Bette. Acid wouldn't melt on your face.

BETTE: Tallulah, you're such a smart ass I'll bet you could sit on an ice cream cone and tell me the flavor.

TALLULAH: You know, Bette sweet, I once had an affair with a buffalo—you could be my daughter.

BETTE: Is that your face or did your neck throw up?

TALLULAH: Dahling, if that's your skin you've outlived it. I suggest either moisturizer or wood filler.

BETTE: If those are character lines on your face you must be studying to play Quasimodo. You really should go to India. They worship cows.

TALLULAH: Is that a girdle you're wearing or a retaining wall?

BETTE: I'll have you know I have the body of a sixteen-year-old girl.

TALLULAH: Well, you'd better give it back. You're wrinkling the hell out of it. Like an accordion left over from Lawrence Welk.

Now after a brief moment, Charles returns as himself—something he's never done before—handsome in a smart black tuxedo with a red flower in his lapel and a red handkerchief in his breast pocket, he tosses out mementos of the show:

> My impressions have always been created to pay tribute to the great stars of yesterday and today. Hopefully, with this presentation I've captured the essence of their greatness as a lasting remembrance with laughter and love. Without them, I'd still be a department store Santa Claus in Pasadena!

Charles wrote me about The Ballroom show to fill me in on all the details:

Toluca Lake
May 21, 1987

Dear John,

I am going to make this a short one as I just returned from New York City AT LAST! Lucy (Ball) was in—also Chita Rivera, Dorothy Loudon, Julia Meade (married to one of the producers), Hayden Rourke, Michael Kearns—oodles of show boys—and girls—.

My God! October 27th is Mother's birthday—a long way off too. Well, it will be here before we know it.

More as it comes up! Mmmm.

Charles

The next year Charles was again performing at The Ballroom when he received the shattering news on October 5, 1988, that his beloved mother Jessie had died. She had suddenly felt very tired, and, seated in her favorite rocking chair, succumbed to a massive heart attack. Charles was devastated, and he raced to Watertown immediately. He didn't even get to say good-bye to the one person he loved the most in all the world. I always feared the day when Charles would lose his mother—that he would be unable to go on. But he held up remarkably well and was able to return to the show and carry on. He wrote two letters to me at this time from the Shelburne Murray Hill Hotel:

October 13, 1988

Dear John,

The flowers you sent for Mother were lovely—just lovely! I was in complete control through Sunday and Monday—though I had private "spells"—better now, but a lot to go through in the coming months.

I will be in North Hollywood as of October 17th—for 10 days—then back to Watertown to see to "things." My Aunt Carolyn is looking after the house and details like stopping papers, mail, etc.

Thanks for thinking of Mother. I know she loved the flowers! I had the casket completely covered in a blanket of roses and baby's breath—plus *all* the flowers, and it looked like a beautiful garden and not a funeral. [The] organist played for hours before and after the service—all of Jessie's favorites, including "Hello, Dolly!" and "Ja-Da." So it wasn't too heavy.

The show here is a complete sellout. Check *Newsweek*—Monday on stands—they came in to photo "Joan Collins" in color!

Charles

October 17, 1988

Dear John,

In two hours I'll be off to L.A.—at last! When you read this I'll be home.

Received your lovely card with beautiful message. Thank you. I do not know how I did it—I simply did it! The audiences, both amount and reaction have been great. That's one reason, plus I did feel Jessie "close by," as you said.

May I say that_____, although he called me a few days after Mother's funeral, sent no card nor flowers—also no card nor flowers from _____ or_____—one other reason I kept the show going. They could have pooled their resources, it seems. I find that _____, of late is really frugal—okay, CHEAP—and _____ too. They both did an excellent job—notice I said *did*—past tense.

Flowers from "The West Coasters" were from you, Les [Natali], Bob and Richard, Don Kobus, the Hal Holbrooks [Dixie Carter], Gene Lott, and Fred Cavallini and Jon. I wrote Rio [Dante] a few days after Mother's passing.

Sorry Les couldn't make the trip—and you too. I really am counting the minutes to get out of here!

Peek in the *Newsweek*—I am "Joan Collins" on the Newsmaker page, I hear. Will get a copy at the airport. A photographer was sent in to take the picture after the show last Tuesday evening—in color.

Mum's the word, please, on my thoughts about _____, etc. I did mention it in a note to Les, though.

More later (my last letter from N.Y.C.)

Charles

Another short note from Charles after he was home in North Hollywood:

October 21, 1988

Home at last! What a relief! Thanks for the lovely flowers—so sweet of you to send them.

I am going to Watertown October 26th for a week to see about Mother's clothes, etc. What an ordeal to go through—I will do it all in stages.

Keep well!

Charles

The sudden death of his mother was, I'm sure, a terrible ordeal for him to go through, and one from which he never fully recovered. I believe it was that ordeal that caused Charles to begin thinking seriously about retiring. Perhaps something died in him when his mother passed away and he lost the joy of performing—and even the will to live. After he gave up his acting career, he turned more and more to his vodka martinis for solace, began to gain a considerable amount of weight, and became more reclusive. If dear Jessie had lived, I believe Charles would have continued his fabulous career much longer.

32

Is There Life After Drag?

When Charles Pierce finally retired in 1990 he began to write his autobiography. After completing a few chapters he decided to abandon the project. What he did write I thought was very clever as only Charles could write it, and I tried to encourage him to finish it.

"You should write my biography—after I'm gone," he told me. "And when you do, tell it warts 'n' all, dahling, warts 'n' all!"

The following is Charles' complete and original interview with himself as he wrote it:

* * *

Charles Pierce—Alive!—and Living Pretty
or
Is There Life After Drag?

From 1954 to 1990, Charles Pierce entertained nightclub goers from London to Hawaii. He can be seen acting on *Designing Women, Wonder Woman,* and other television reruns. He has several videos out in the stores. He recently turned down an offer to return to showbiz in a play headed for Broadway. He said, "Too much work."

For six years he and his partner Rio Dante performed at the Gilded Cage on Ellis Street in San Francisco. He co-starred with Harvey Fierstein in *Torch Song Trilogy.* He lives by himself in North Hollywood, drives a ten-year-old car, and has no pets. "Not even a goldfish." If anyone is interested, he has a Victorian house for sale in Watertown, New York. "Gay couples are moving there, believe it or not." For economy's sake, he was asked, as he talks to himself all the time, if he would put some thoughts down on paper. The following is the result:

Charles Pierce Interviews Charles Pierce

CHARLES: And when was the last time you were in drag? What show?

PIERCE: No show. I went to Phyllis Diller's Halloween party, not in ninety-five but ninety-four, as Norma Desmond. I went with Bea Arthur and she was also Norma Desmond. We caused quite a stir, I might add.

CHARLES: You may. But when was your last performance on a stage?

PIERCE: June 1994. I appeared in New York at Town Hall with an impersonation show that included Charles Busch, Milton Berle, and The Grand Court of New York, and they had as their guest the original Empress Jose (Sarria) from San Francisco. Also Randy Allen, who did Bette Davis as she looked in later life after a stroke. Oh, the sadness of it all. The gods can be cruel. Randy died twelve months later. His Bette Davis character was in an Off-Broadway play and he rehearsed right up to the first preview when he was unable to go on. He was replaced by a woman, and we know, as good as they might be, no woman can replace a man doing Bette Davis! The show opened and ran only four nights.

CHARLES: What do you think about the drag performers of today?

PIERCE: I don't. There are too many to keep track of. I do not wish to go into the history of drag. There are many books out that will give you all the information you need on the subject. I began my nightclub career in September of 1954. Yikes! Did I really say that? 1954. That was the year Elvis hit mainstream audiences. I hit the stage of a little club in Altadena, California, called Club La Vie. I worked in a tux with a box of props. A headband for Bette Davis at a dressing-room table or one of those pith helmets for Kate Hepburn in *The African Queen*. Naturally, I enhanced it with yards of veiling. I was paid the enormous sum of $75 a week *and* my evening meal, which consisted of a hamburger.

CHARLES: How are the drag performers of today different than, say, twenty-five years ago?

PIERCE: The drag artists of yesterday were "more in keeping with the situation." I think that's an expression from *A Christmas Carol*.

CHARLES: Please explain.

PIERCE: When I eventually started working in drag I wore gowns in keeping with my characters and the makeup. "Full face," as we used to say, was never overdone. No huge lips, glitter on the eyelids, rouge for days. I was an impersonator and not a "drag queen," which was a term we all loathed, and which unfortunately has become popular today.

CHARLES: I hate like hell to keep asking you to explain what you say. But would you? Isn't a drag queen an impersonator?

PIERCE: Without going into too much depth—I hate depthy interviews—and without too many of those "Well, in my day, etc.," I will tell you this. Up to the late eighties, the performers who worked the clubs and theaters in drag were Lynne Carter, T. C. Jones, Craig Russell, Dame Edna, Divine, Big Jimmy, Fel Andrews, Arthur Blake, and myself. We were never what you call drag queens. Then, a drag queen was not an entertainer but someone who had a job other than showbiz, who came home from work, got himself up in some outlandish costume or frock and went sailing off to a party or a drag ball. There is an odd line there, I know, but I will always draw it.

CHARLES: You had a line in the show about a drag queen, didn't you?

PIERCE: *(Suddenly turning into Blanche Hudson)* "Oh, Jane . . . how kind of you to ask." I said, "She's so dumb she thinks a drag queen is someone of royalty who walks slowly"—then I went into Queen Elizabeth's voice and said, "Over here, Margaret, and put that Cold Stream Guard *down*. You don't where he's been!"

CHARLES: *(Laughing—a little)* Well, I won't ask you to explain *that*. You did have some rather obscure material.

PIERCE: Still do. It's all on paper and I have stacks of old jokes. Maybe I'll publish *The Gay Joke Book* one of these decades.

CHARLES: Without going too much "in depth," what would you say was your greatest failing?

PIERCE: Trusting a lover. *(He thinks)* Trusting a lover with my love. That's why I am "living alone and I like it." That was a Sophie Tucker number, and Bette Davis had a song called "Single." Living alone is okay for awhile, but it's nice "to have a man around the house." Another song from my era.

CHARLES: Of course, you're not the only gay man who lives alone. I agree with you about lovers and the problem with keeping a lover.

PIERCE: No, no. I never kept anyone. They had to work or heave-ho.

CHARLES: I meant simply maintaining a relationship.

PIERCE: *(He rhapsodizes with gestures)* Ahhh, that glorious time when a stranger across the crowded room smiles at you and you feel as if you had been hit by lightning. What a jolt! *(Does a Bette Davis)* The first night together. The first night on the town together. A cozy restaurant with candlelight and wine. Holding hands under the table. Of course, that makes eating and drinking a little difficult, but who cares? You're in love. Then you're promising him trips to London on the Concorde. Off on the Orient Express to Venice, Rome, Cairo. Blah, blah. They either hang on thinking you are serious or they know that you are not, and so you end up brushing your teeth alone. If they do hang in there and keep calling, then suddenly you are plunged into depression and the worry of how to get rid of them. Unto thine own self be true—with a single ticket to Europe. Much cheaper.

CHARLES: What was your happiest time?

PIERCE: That's a tough one. *(Looks down at the floor, thinking)* Peaks. that's what I've had. Peaks and perks. And, of course, plenty of valleys.

CHARLES: I asked about your happiest time on this planet.

PIERCE: *(He explodes)* Oh, for God's sake! I hate interviews. When a burglar said to Jack Benny, "Your money or your life!" Jack said, "I'm thinking. I'm thinking." I think, without sounding like a mama's boy, I was happiest when I was with my mother. She was companion, advisor, and, let's just say, a wonderful friend. As to when I was happiest doing the shows? There were many wonderful engagements. The ones I felt most like I'd "made it" were the Fairmont Hotels (San Francisco and Houston), The Village Gate in New York, The Music Center in L.A., and, strangely enough, a supper club on the East Side in Manhattan called Freddy's. I did ten engagements over a six-year period and the thought always crossed—what's left of my mind . . . , "Hey, I'm playing the East Side of New York City." Loved it. But, of course, there were many other shows I did that gave me a real perk.

CHARLES: Like?

PIERCE: Incredible engagements at Bimbo's here in San Francisco and unforgettable shows at the Plush Room as well. *(Glaring)* Aren't these interviews limited to space? You know, I have other things to do today.

CHARLES: Wait. A few more. Please.

PIERCE: Keep begging. I love it.

CHARLES: What is your greatest achievement?

PIERCE: Living as long as I have.

CHARLES: Your greatest disappointment in life?

PIERCE: No great film role that could have been seen in the year 3000—and those lovers.

CHARLES: I think you are better off without them.

PIERCE: So is my bank account.

CHARLES: But you said you didn't keep any of them

PIERCE: Oh, you know—a dinner here, a theater ticket there. Never the Concorde or the Orient Express. Maybe someday? I'll invite myself. And meet a fellow traveler—with knowing eyes.

CHARLES: Do you like women?

PIERCE: I have told you. My mother was my dearest friend. She died in 1988. Of course I like women. I have a very pleasant relationship with Bea Arthur. We have more laughs than are allotted to most people. Bea is a true and loyal friend—and a great cook! I can't begin to count the happy times she's had me over to her beautiful home for dinner. She always entertains at Thanksgiving and Christmas and I'm always invited. She's my "bosom buddy" for sure! I have women friends in every city I played and to whom I write all the time. What about the women in my show? I know they said some pretty outrageous things, but if I hadn't admired them I certainly couldn't have presented them in just such an outrageous manner. And don't ask me to explain all that because I won't. So there.

CHARLES: Would you care to tell us more about the drag entertainers of the past?

PIERCE: No, I wouldn't. Don't want to sound like Gore Vidal, but I'm bored. *(He gets up and starts pouring himself a drink)*

CHARLES: May I ask, then, what are you drinking?

PIERCE: Vodka. Pierre Smirnoff. He's a friend of the night. May I pour you a Pierre?

CHARLES: No. However, I would like a Diet Coke.

PIERCE: You've got it. My friend Larry and I—oh, we call ourselves "The Vodka Vamps." Bea is one too. Now, I've read that Mary Tyler Moore belted down a few at a time. When I die I want to be cremated and my ashes sifted into an empty vodka bottle and then tossed off the Golden Gate Bridge. And throw in a little glitter while you're at it. As Norma Desmond said, "Let's make it gay!" Well, not about my cremation. She was referring to her pet monkey's casket lining. Aren't you up on the old movies? Do you know what I'm talking about? If not, then you're not seriously gay!

CHARLES: I—I—think so.

PIERCE: A gay man knows all the camp lines in movies from the past. With the writing of today there are no lines in films worth picking up on. I think the last one we bothered with was Faye Dunaway shrieking, "No more wire hangers—ever!" in *Mommie Dearest.* Sad, sad, sad.

CHARLES: Do you have any regrets?

PIERCE: Nothing like changing the subject abruptly.

CHARLES: Do you?

PIERCE: What do you want me to say? I regret never having won an Academy Award. I regret never having performed on a Broadway theater stage. I regret never having sailed down the Nile or made love in a sand dune on Fire Island. Never having found "just the right person"? Look. In a way, I have done all those things. That is, in the realm of my world. I have won many awards for my performances and shows I've been in. Besides the nightclub engagements around New York, I was at the Beacon Theatre on Broadway for one night in a fabulous show. *(Thinking)* In fact, it was two nights and we were S.R.O. in a three-thousand-seat house. I was with a variety of entertainers, including Sally Rand, in her seventies, and still doing her famous fan dance! "Frisco Follies" was a group at the time specializing in pantomimes. Monte Rock was there and also a version of Ballet de Trocadero. I came and went as mistress of ceremonies, at one point rising from the orchestra pit playing the pipe organ as Norma Desmond! If that show hit Broadway today we would have a run of two or three years. We were way ahead of our time. Even Anita Loos, who wrote *Gentlemen Prefer Blondes* and a lot of films, came on as *The Mystery Lady.* It was camp!

CHARLES: You have more or less explained the difference between a drag queen and a female impersonator, but what is a "Male Actress?"

PIERCE: That was a description I used for myself when I was in a play here in San Francisco. I played "Helen" in a two-act play, *Geese,* at the Cable Car Theatre on Mason Street. I was the mother of a gay boy in one act, and the other act was all about lesbians in the Deep South. It was 1969 and there was nudity for days! Shocking for its time. I didn't use the Male Actress billing for too long as other *(he stresses the word) impersonators* decided they would rather be Male Actresses, so they stole it from me. Then it lost its class and value to me.

CHARLES: Would you care to mention just who were the ones who, shall we say—"borrowed" the Male Actress billing?

PIERCE: I would not. Most of them are doing drag shows—*(he points upward)*—in the Big Gay Bar in the Sky.

CHARLES: So you think there is "life after drag"—up there?

PIERCE: In all seriousness, and my gut feeling, and that's with or without a girdle, I have my doubts about a life hereafter. I think there is something, but I am afraid that no one has come up with exactly what it is that we go to. A fade-out and that is it? Oh, it would be wonderful to meet up with everyone we've known in some idyllic setting. I certainly don't think the human body developed by itself. But that's another interview, isn't it?

CHARLES: For you, has there been a life after drag?

PIERCE: Most certainly. Too much life and too many dinners. I've put on fifteen pounds in five years. Jenny Craig, hold everything! I'm coming your way! When I walked off the stage of the Balcony Theatre of the Pasadena Playhouse on October 7, 1990—the closing night of my engagement there—I had no idea that would be my last performance with all the "ladies." I had decided to put the show on the shelf for the holidays and start up again in January 1991. However, I got involved in doing voiceovers for TV and never went back to nightclubs. Yes, I have done a few appearances hither and yon that were fun. I appeared with the Gay Men's Chorus of Los Angeles at Christmastime of 1993, and as I told you earlier, at Town Hall.

CHARLES: Plain and simple—you have retired.

PIERCE: *(Raises his hand)* Stop! I have abdicated!

CHARLES: Hmmm. Cute.

PIERCE: You are catching on. That's what Norma Desmond said to Bill Holden in *Sunset Boulevard*. Just like that, too.

CHARLES: So you did not retire, you abdicated. In other words, you are leaving the dresses, high heels, the wigs, and the makeup to those following in your wake?

PIERCE: You make it sound like I was a boat. Here's a toast to the Ru-Pauls, the Lypsinkas, and the Charles Busches. *(He raises his glass and drinks)* I won't be here, of course. But I would love to know what they'll be doing with their lives when they're my age.

CHARLES: And that is?

PIERCE : Can you keep a secret?

CHARLES: Oh, yes.

PIERCE: So can I. *(Gives a Cheshire Cat grin)*

CHARLES: You've used that as a closing for every interview you've given over the last thirty years. Please tell me your age?

PIERCE: There were two of me on the ark. I was the one with the beads.

CHARLES: *(Pleading)* C'mon.

PIERCE: I go way back. I was in charge of gathering up Marie Antoinette's head. She wasn't the only queen in history to lose her head over a basket, y'know?

Charles: No more bad jokes, please. Your age?

PIERCE: I remember breaking a heel getting off the *Mayflower.* That Plymouth Rock is a bitch to walk on.

CHARLES: Stop! Answer the question.

PIERCE: I was with the Pope the day he looked up at the Sistine Chapel ceiling that Michelangelo had been painting for forty years and shrieked, "Sweetie, didn't they tell you I'm switching to wallpaper?"

CHARLES: Your age, pleeeeze!

PIERCE: My Transylvanian fan club would be too upset. Let's just say I have led a long and—*(he pauses)*—fruitful life. I have been blessed knowing some wonderful, fun people. My work in nightclubs was not work. It was party time. When I first started in 1954 I couldn't believe I was being paid for having such a good time. That $75 a week shot up to $250 for my next engagement, and I still felt I was taking money I didn't deserve. I was really lucky to have been brought up in the thirties. I think of that quite often. Except for distant cousins, I am the last of my family. With so many friends gone and most of my family, the phone doesn't ring as often as it used to—*(makes a gesture of playing a violin)*.

CHARLES: A final thought?

PIERCE: Jessie, my mother, said from time to time, "If you're going to live, live pretty." Then she would immediately make plans to have the house redecorated or go out and buy a new dress and hat.

CHARLES: And you?

PIERCE: I'll stick with Mother. I'll live pretty—pretty gay! But do everything in a moderate way, from drinking to shopping to sex. Do not blow everything at once. No pun intended. When your own true love walks out the door leaving you flat, sure, get upset, but get over it fast! Who am I giving this sage advice? Dear Abby? Enough already. As Bo Peep—or was it Bo Derek?—said to her sheep, "Let's get the flock outta here!"

CHARLES: I never did get my Diet Coke.

PIERCE: *(A withering look)* Oh, by the way, I'm sixty-nine—always have been!

Charles mentioned Randy Allen, the young man who was on the bill with him at Town Hall in June 1994, and that Randy impersonated Bette Davis after she had a stroke. Earlier in May of that year, Randy Allen played a short gig at the Plush Room in San Francisco. Before he opened, however, Charles phoned me, enthusing over Randy's act, "You've got to meet Randy! He's terrific as Bette after her stroke. Meet us at the Hotel York and we'll grab a cab and brunch it up at the Patio Cafe with Randy and a reporter from the *B. A. R.* who will interview him."

When I arrived at the hotel, Charles and Randy were in the lobby awaiting the cab. I was really shocked that Randy was in drag with full-face "disfigured" Bette makeup, and that he and Charles insisted that Randy be addressed as "Miss Davis." No professional actor is ever seen off stage in the guise of the character he is portraying. That's why greenrooms were created, so that the actor can greet his public as himself, leaving his "character" in the dressing room. I was appalled that Charles would condone such behavior, and I failed to see why Charles was cheering for Randy. He usually loathed any performer who did any impersonation close to his own. All through brunch, Randy kept up the charade, talking in the affected tones of Bette Davis, and Charles and the reporter catered to his every whim, addressing him constantly as "Miss Davis." I didn't address him at all, and I was glad when the farce was over.

The night of Randy Allen's opening at the Plush Room, Charles "comped" me in, and the one-man (woman?) show called *P. S. Bette Davis* began. On and on it went until I was squirming in my seat. The endless shrill, monotonous inflections of what Randy perceived to be the voice of Bette Davis and the totally boring dialogue about "her" husbands and "her" pictures added up to what I would critique as a "bomb"! Of course, Charles was lavish with his praise, but I couldn't figure out why and never will. I'm sorry the poor fellow died of AIDS, but I have to be honest about his act. Really, why would anyone want to see and hear a "Bette Davis" who looked and sounded like the walking dead?

33

Charles Pierce: Male Actress

The late Herb Caen continues to get credit for coining the name "Male Actress" for Charles Pierce, but the truth is that Charles gave that title to himself. He used it first when he appeared as "Helen" in the play *Geese,* and then again as "Margo Channing" in the musical *Applause.* Charles phoned Caen and told him that he, Charles Pierce, was playing "real women" at last, and that he was now a "Male Actress." Of course, Herb printed the bit in his column, but didn't give Charles credit for the clever name.

Charles talked about playing "Helen" in *Geese* in his preceding self-interview, but he failed to mention his portrayal of "Margo Channing" in *Applause.* In May of 1974 Charles signed with Kimo Productions to star in the famous musical that had starred Lauren Bacall on Broadway. Stepping into Bacall's high heels to portray the fabulous "Margo" would be a terrific challenge for Charles, as he would be required to sing and dance.

Kimo, the producer/director, is a well-known entertainer in San Francisco, as well as the owner of the popular bar Kimo's on Polk Street. Rehearsals began with Kimo directing, Jean Martin, a brilliant choreographer from Hollywood, creating the dances, John Noles playing "Bill Sampson," and Tony Michaels of *Beach Blanket Babylon* as "Margo's" assistant. A gaggle of gypsies and extras rounded out the cast.

California Hall was not the ideal venue to stage a play. It had been built as a German beer hall/gymnasium with a level floor so that folding chairs had to be provided for the audience, making sight lines difficult. The polished hardwood floor bore painted markings used for basketball games. However, it did have a large proscenium stage with curtains and a wraparound, horseshoe-shaped balcony.

Kimo left the show soon after rehearsals began, and Charles found it necessary to take over the task of directing the show. A young Michael Biagi, just graduated from high school, was hired to do the music arrangements and conduct the orchestra. Later on, Michael accompanied Charles on the piano at the Plush Room and other venues. They remained friends right up until Charles' death. Michael has conducted orchestras for Tommy Tune and many others on Broadway and around the United States.

On a May evening in 1974, Kimo Productions presented *Applause* starring Charles Pierce, and the old California Hall was packed. The house lights dimmed, and when Michael Biagi struck up the overture, I was amazed at his skill and professionalism for a man so young.

Charles was brilliant as "Margo Channing," and the reviewers raved. He was totally believable in the role, and though he was not a singer or dancer, he went through his paces like the professional that he was. He and Jean Martin became lifelong friends, and she would always attend his San Francisco performances and entertain him lavishly at her beautiful Atherton home. One memorable time she drove Charles, his costume designer Herman George, and me in a stretch limo to her home. After serving us her favorite lasagna, she drove us back.

On Christmas of 1974, Charles opened at New York City's Top of the Gate, where he received an Obie Award and rave reviews. Then he was off to London aboard the Concorde with his mother Jessie seated beside him. She was sporting the lavish new Autumn Haze full-length mink coat Charles had given her for Christmas, and they were eager to begin their London adventure. Jessie was proud of her famous actor son and took his dressing in female attire in stride. After all, he had donned drag often as a child, and now he had a profitable career that afforded her luxuries she had only dreamed of.

When Charles opened at London's Fortune Theatre, the famous gossip columnist Suzy confided a saucy item to her readers:

> Charles Pierce, one of America's highly publicized female impersonators is the talk of the town in London . . . the British call him the new Bea Lillie. . . . Charles and Dickie (she's a lady) Gordon . . . are what you would either call a hot item or an improbable couple. Take your pick.[1]

A large photo of Charles as himself appeared in the column. Bea Lillie was, of course, the famous international comedienne and star of films and Broadway and London shows. A Canadian by birth, she became Lady Peel after her marriage to Lord Robert Peel in 1920. Once on stage in London when Noel Coward was heckling her from the audience, she stopped in midsentence and bellowed, "Will someone please toss Noel a chorus boy so I can get on with the show?"

One night at the Fortune Theatre, Charles' old chum, Boyd Ransome from the the Gilded Cage and Lazy X days, appeared in Charles' dressing room. He was agitated and haggard-looking, and he asked Charles to "fix him up" with a transvestite he'd seen talking to Charles the previous evening. Charles arranged the meeting, but when Boyd's wife, Beverly Ashton, discovered the tryst, and Charles' part in it, she blamed him instead of her husband.

Charles was the toast of London once again when he returned at a later date to open at the Country Cousin. More rave reviews! His last visit to Britain was October 30 through November 7, 1993, after his retirement. This time he visited not as an entertainer, but as himself. He was the host of a London theater tour sponsored by SOPAC Travel Marketing Inc., and in a promotional brochure to advertise the tour, Charles wrote an imaginary interview with Bette Davis:

BETTE: Charles, dahling, Tallulah tells me you're off to London to see some shows.

CHARLES: Yes, Bette, I am. It's going to be wonderful. I'm going to be the "ambassador escort" for a gay tour group to merry ol' England, which leaves October 30, 1993.

BETTE: Oh, how I love traveling with gay companions. You know how much I love England. Remember when I played the Virgin Queen? Hah! Who ever heard of a "virgin queen"? Well, light my ciggie and tell me more about the trip.

CHARLES: Well, we'll be met when we arrive at the airport—hopefully by a Beefeater—and then whisked off to the wonderful Mountbatten Hotel in delightful Covent Garden for a stay of seven glorious nights, enjoying a full English breakfast daily.

BETTE: Well, I know the Mountbatten and it certainly is "not a dump." What else will you be doing?

CHARLES: Our British guides will take us on a tour around London. Maybe we can find out if what all those tabloids are telling us about the Royal Family is true. Then we'll drop in on one of those cute little gay spots like Kudos for a smart cocktail.

BETTE: I never heard of a *dumb cocktail.*

CHARLES: I'll ignore that, Miss Davis. We'll go to a cabaret show at Madame Jojo's in Soho, and the young at heart, including me, can dance the night away at Heaven. We'll have a tour of Windsor, plenty of free time for shopping at Harrod's, and on Oxford Street see the Changing of the Guard, and enjoy lunches at one of those quaint pubs. And they're all easily accessible from the Mountbatten.

BETTE: That all sounds very festive. But Tallulah said you were going to see some of the shows in the West End.

CHARLES: I'm getting to that. My, you've gotten pushy. Ever since you played "Margo Channing," there's no living with you. First we have Dress Circle seating to see *Kiss of the Spider Woman.*

BETTE: Obviously, that's Joan Crawford's life story.

CHARLES: Bette! Keep Joan out of this. You did enough to her in *Baby Jane.* We're also going to attend the world premiere season of *Sunset Boulevard*—before it gets to Broadway!

BETTE: You mean Gloria Swanson is coming back from the grave to do a play?

CHARLES: No, Bette, she isn't. And you of all people should not be talking about coming back from any grave. Besides, this is the musical version by Andrew Lloyd Webber, and Gloria hasn't sung since she was at MGM.

BETTE: Charles, this really sounds like a fabulous trip. I really do think you should take me along.

CHARLES: You know I'd love to, but if you come, I'd have to take Tallulah, Mae, and Katharine. And I'd have no time for fun playing "ambassador escort" as me—Charles Pierce.

BETTE: Oh, I guess you're right. I know you're going to have an absolutely divine time, Charles. "Fasten your seat belts, gang, it's going to be a bumpy . . ."

34

Letters from the End of the Rainbow

On the night of September 4, 1988, when Charles Pierce took his final bow on the stage of the Fairmont Hotel's Venetian Room in San Francisco, he fully intended it to be his farewell performance. However, his actual farewell performance would be on the night of October 7, 1990, on the Balcony Theatre stage at the Pasadena Playhouse. During the interval between the two engagements, he kept me informed about his various activities as noted in the letters that follow—letters that truly came from the end of his rainbowlike career:

North Hollywood
Easter 1990

Hi, John!

This week has been so fucked up I can't remember if I wrote you right back about your letter to the B.A.R. concerning Pat Bond? I thought what you wrote in the letter was excellent, and I'm sure you will get lots of comments. Be sure to let me know. Someone will write and say, "I'm glad to be a dyke, an old dyke, and Pat Bond would have wanted to be known forever as an old dyke too!" I'll bet you ruffled a lot of feathers. Good! [The letter Charles referred to was one I wrote to the *Bay Area Reporter* defending Pat Bond's memory. She had just died and her obituary stated that she was "an old dyke." I wrote that she was much more than that, and listed her accomplishments as an actress, and so forth. There were no responses to my letter.]

Ralph Senensky—remember him?—and others are putting a documentary together on the Playhouse. It is moving very slowly as it is one of those projects that when they can get their cameras and crew together (all gratis) then they "shoot" an interview. They started out with me, and I was in the Balcony Theatre for four hours last Thursday. 1 p.m. to 4 p.m., being

225

taped sitting in one of the seats and answering Ralph's questions about Playhouse days, etc. Before that they showed me walking on stage with comments like, "This is where it all began—for me." That 30-second scene took them almost 2 hours to do!

Joan Cannon, who is the producer, said it won't be finished till September. I thought she meant my scene—so when I say "slowly" I mean just that! They are going to film around the Playhouse, and some of the other interviews will be with Earl Holliman, Barbara Rush, and Bill (oops) *Dabbs* Greer. It will last about 45 minutes. Joan said I will get a copy. I don't know exactly what the plans are for it, although I suggested making it available for the alumni—which, you would think was the reason for doing it!

About ten years ago Les [Natali] bought me this stationery for my birthday—a huge box with a thousand sheets and envelopes. Well, my dear, *this* is the *last* sheet after all these years of letter writing. Sad. Maybe you should save it for the Smithsonian?

Speaking of the Smithsonian—have you heard from Harvey Lee? Ha! I have and I'm sure you have too. Those minute detailed letters! Pleeze! One came today stating how much he tipped his hairstylist!—and how much tax he paid getting his typewriter fixed!!—and that his medicines make him constipated!!! HELP!!! He wants me to come to Little Rock where, believe it or not, there's a gay night spot—and do my show! Maybe they'd love it?!!

Hope your Easter was pleasant and basket-filled.

Charles

Harvey Lee had been a headliner in drag at Finocchio's in his younger days. He had retired to Arkansas in 1990.

North Hollywood
August 7, 1990

Dear John,

SLAP! SLAP! SLAP! That's me slapping the shit out of me for not getting to you sooner than this to THANK YOU FOR THE WONDERFUL TELEGRAM OPENING NIGHT AT THE PLAYHOUSE!!! It brought luck as you can see from the enclosed review! We have been a sellout from day one! This past week has really been something—hectic—and it took me the full week to adjust to "Playhouse Playing"—getting used to the theater and mostly the drive back and forth—I do not like the drive home at night on the freeway, although it only takes me 20 minutes.

The backstage is depressing with the ceiling in the green room exposed, and we have been putting up with a lot of heat—so it has been quite a contrast to the "glamour" of the Plush Room and York Hotel. Also I have been going through a period of energy withdrawal—better today—I was so anxious to get off stage Friday that, without knowing it, I cut that whole Joan Crawford mouth-bit and some of the ending. Saturday and Sunday were much better.

We are closing as scheduled on the 12th of August, and I'll return after four weeks on September 19th. At that point I will do FIVE nights a week, which will mean one less day to hit the freeways—and give me two days off. That will be a better time for us to think about you coming down for a day or two. With this heat and humidity I wouldn't want you to come for your own sake.

Tonight's audience will include Dom and Carol DeLuise, Gretchen Wyler, Bonnie Franklin, and SISTER SHEL—Shelley Werk in from Las Vegas. Bud Cort has written a film script with a part for her—so she's here for that.

Wonder what Gilmor Brown would say if he popped into the Balcony Theatre and saw the goings-on???

By the way, I hear Alan_____ was dreadful in *Bye, Bye, Birdie,* and he had the balls to ask Michael _____'s lover, "How much do you suppose the Playhouse is paying Charles?"

More later.

Charles

North Hollywood
August 22, 1990

Hello, John,

Now, get ready for this—Alan _____ had the balls to *call me* ON THE PHONE and pump ME about the Playhouse!! I simply told him I produced my own show there, and he should do the same thing! He is STILL talking about his one-man show—and he's been talking about that since 1950—and has never done it! He said his bad reviews for *Birdie* were the director's fault!!

GET READY—AGAIN! We are coming back to the Plush Room for six performances *only,* September 4th to 9th. They said they were still getting calls for the show and as long as I had five weeks off before we reopened at the Playhouse, and I had the show pretty well set—why not? I know that's the week after Labor Day so it could be a disaster—then again—we will wait and see. I will stay on in San Francisco September 10th and 11th to do another greeting card shoot for West Graphics, then back here, have six days to relax, and then open again at the Playhouse. We played to full houses and I didn't lose a penny—in fact, made moneeee—which Uncle Sam will relieve me of next April!

Thanks for the video of *The Letter* with Lee Remick. Much different from Bette Davis' version. One or two good shots of Peter Mintun in his oh-so-starched shirt playing something Gertrude Lawrence sang. I will have to ask him about that. I didn't think the actor playing Lee's lover was good-looking enough to shoot, did you? I think when Lee was trying to get away from his advances it looked like she was enjoying it all. She should have said, "Oh, it's a hot night—let me give you a blow job and send you on your way."

Old classmates who showed up for the show were Kenny Bartmess, who looks like God (white beard), Paul Curtis, Max Hodge, Ralph Senensky, Tyler MacDuff, AND Dabbs Greer who sent me a lovely note about the performance. Oh, yes, Bernie Wiesen who kept talking about my "energy"—yes, but what about the SHOW???

Celebs were Gretchen Wyler, Bonnie Franklin, Bea Arthur, Dom and Carol DeLuise, Eileen Brennan, AND Brian Kerwin looking tres good with wife-to-be!!

I will not be arriving till Monday, September 3rd. The show is pretty well set with everyone concerned, including the light people, having done it many times, so we will only have to have a "talk through" on Tuesday at noon. Maybe we can have din-din on that Monday eve?

Till later,

Charles

North Hollywood
October 29, 1990

Dear John,

I assume our letters crossed each other somewhere over Bakersfield. Glad to get yours and to know that everything is "peachy keen," as Gidget would say.

I am voting for Pete Wilson—what a wimp—but I'd rather he get in and mess things up than Diane. I have a picture taken with her when I was a "waitress" dressed as Bette Davis for a Cable Car breakfast fundraiser. Wonder if *National Enquirer* would like to use it if she's elected? Headlines could read: "GOVERNOR SEEN LUNCHING WITH FEMALE IMPERSONATOR. SECRET TRYST DISCOVERED BETWEEN DIANE AND "BETTE"—WHO IS A MAN!" Well, something like that.

The show "shedyool" (as Rio used to say) has come to a screeching halt, so I might as well sit back and wait now till the holidays are over. I will leave in two weeks to spend a week with my Aunt Carolyn in Watertown, then back here right after Thanksgiving. Probably spend a few days in NYC.

I am wondering if backers will come up with the loot to back the Broadway show? It would be a tremendous responsibility and I think I'd rather stick with our little operation like we do at the Plush Room. Too damned stressful!

M_____ F_____ has not gotten good reviews on his show in NYC—in fact, I heard John Simon's review was so bad it put M_____ into bed for two days, and he canceled his appearance. They put M_____ P_____ on instead and K_____, who was there, walked out after fifteen minutes—he said, M. P. wore baggy clothes, dirty sneakers, sat on a stool (sound familiar?), and the piano was an upright!

I did my smaller-than-a-cameo role in *The Butcher's Wife* with Demi Moore and Jeff Daniels last week. Fortunately, it was filmed at Warner Brothers, five minutes from the house. One day I was seen dropping paper in a street receptacle (six seconds, at least), and two days later called back for my "scene"—two lines with my poodle "Butch"—probably fifteen seconds! I can't figure out why, if the writers came up with this gay character, why give him so little to do? They flew one actor out from NYC for the street scene I was in last Wednesday. He comes up the subway stairs and stands on the corner. That was it! He flew back to NYC the next day to return in three weeks for the scenes in an office. Crazy! I heard I had another scene with the dog in the park where Jeff Daniels steps in doggie-doo, but that scene was cut. Just as well!

Must close now.

C

In a *Los Angeles Times* review dated August 2, 1990, two months before Charles' farewell performance at the Balcony Theatre at Pasadena Playhouse, columnist Don Heckman made the following comments:

> Pierce . . . opened a two-week run in a one-man show titled "The Legendary Ladies of the Silver Screen." . . .
>
> Best of all was Pierce's Bette Davis—a dramatically believable image. . . .
>
> (After a particularly raunchy remark he quickly ad-libbed, "Well, I guess we can forget about the National Endowment grant!")[1]

Charles returned to the Pasadena Playhouse in October of 1990 for what would be the final performance of his brilliant career. As he stood on the flagstone steps of the patio of his old alma mater, he thought back to that memorable day when Lola Loraine, the fabulous movie actress he had met on the train, had dropped him off at this very spot so long ago. Over the years, he had called the number she had given him, but he was unable to speak with Lola herself. Always it had been the silky purr of some female secretary or personal assistant:

"Miss Loraine is filming in Rome," or "Miss Loraine is at her home in Switzerland," or "Miss Loraine is unavailable at this time. She's sunning in Majorca." He had wished he could hear her throaty laugh, but he had finally given up, and he never saw her again. During his many performances he hoped that one night when he looked out over the audience he would see her sitting there chortling away at his jokes. She had advised him, "Go for the laughs," and that was what he had done, and it had paid off handsomely.

Now with the coming opening at The Balcony Theatre, he had come full circle—back to where it all began that long-ago day. He didn't know then that when this gig was completed, he would enter a new chapter of his life titled "Retirement"—but an ominous fate awaited him in the wings.

35

Farewell, Old Friend:
The Last Charles Pierce Show

In February 1997 Charles Pierce was diagnosed with prostate cancer. He suffered with that condition for approximately two years until his death on Memorial Day, May 31, 1999. Charles and I were in frequent contact either by letter or by phone, yet I had no idea he was dying slowly of cancer. I certainly was aware that he was ill, as he informed me almost weekly that he was suffering terribly from an enlarged prostate gland. Many times he was unable to urinate and would have to drive himself to the emergency room at a local hospital where a catheter would be inserted, allowing him to relieve himself.

He came to San Francisco in the fall of 1998 for an operation on his prostate gland to allow the urine to flow more comfortably, and I visited him at Mount Zion Hospital, while he was recuperating. He returned to his North Hollywood home a few days later, and when I phoned him there, he said he was feeling much better.

One day in April 1999 when I phoned, he was depressed and said he had lost all faith in doctors. I told him perhaps he should go to UCLA for treatment, but he didn't answer. Then he said he wished he could take a big pill and have it all end. I was shocked, and I told him he shouldn't talk like that. If I'd known he was so near death I would have understood. Later, in May, Les Natali phoned me that he had just talked to Charles by phone, and he said that Charles was feeling much better. I really thought he was getting well.

My very last conversation with Charles was on Saturday, May 8, 1999, and it lasted just nine minutes because his voice was hoarse and very faint. He said, "We had a lot of fun, didn't we?"

And I replied, "Yes, Charles, we did—and will again."

He said he was very tired and that he'd have to hang up. It was farewell—but I was unaware!

The phone call came at noon on Tuesday, June 1, 1999.

"Hello, John?" It was a female voice. "This is Joan Edgar." Right away I knew that Charles had passed away.

"Joan, it's Charles, isn't it?" I asked.

"Yes. He passed away last evening in his sleep."

"Oh, God. I didn't know he was that ill. What was it?"

"Prostate cancer."

Immediately, I phoned Bob Ross, the editor of the *Bay Area Reporter*. He, in turn, phoned Peter Mintun, requesting that he write a memorial piece on Charles for the paper. Peter felt he didn't know enough about Charles' long career, so he phoned Les Natali, who told Peter to call me, saying that I had known Charles since his career began. I gave Peter enough information to round out the article, which appeared in the *B.A.R.* on June 3, 1999, under the banner headline, "Charles Pierce Dies at 76," which was incorrect—he was 72. However, it was a very well-written and informative piece and covered all the highlights of Charles' career. In addition, obituaries appeared in *Time Magazine, The Advocate, The Los Angeles Times, The New York Times, The San Francisco Chronicle and Examiner,* the January 2000 issue of *Life Magazine,* and in *Life Magazine*'s special book *The Year in Pictures,* which featured a full-page photograph of Charles as Bette Davis. How proud he would be to know he was remembered with such glowing praise for his performances and his dazzling career!

One of the unsung heroes of Charles' tragic end was Charles' friend Don Lee Kobus. He left his home in Yucca Valley, California, to stay with Charles at Charles' home in North Hollywood, caring for him unstintingly from the beginning of Charles' illness until he passed on. Don's loyalty didn't end there. He carried out every one of Charles' dying wishes, seeing to it that the memorial service was carried out just as Charles had planned it. He attended to myriad other details, including overseeing the preparation of a lavish reception at the Beverly Garland Hotel in North Hollywood for a select group of invited guests after the memorial service. Don told me later how Charles had planned every detail of his memorial service. Sheet music of every description cluttered the quilt on the bed, and when Charles grew too weary to carry on, he'd badger Don with the various ways he, Charles, could commit suicide. He couldn't face the chemotherapy treatments that the doctors ordered, feeling he'd never be himself again after taking them.

"I could throw a rope over a beam and hang myself."

"There are no beams in the house—and you don't have a rope."

"Well, I could jump off the balcony."

"Not high enough. You'd break a leg and you'd be worse off than you are now."

"Then I could overdose on pills."

"No, you don't have enough of 'em."

And so it went. Each day Charles grew weaker, but he was able to complete what he'd started: the script for *The Last Charles Pierce Show*—his memorial service.

The service was held on June 19, 1999, at 1 p.m. at the Church of the Hills in Forest Lawn Memorial Park, Hollywood Hills, Los Angeles. Don Lee Kobus kindly sent me a color videocassette of the occasion. Due to my serious heart condition, I was unable to attend.

* * *

The videocassette begins with a beautiful shot of the Church of the Hills. With its white walls and tall, graceful spire, it resembles a quaint chapel right out of New England's *Peyton Place*. Interior shots show banks of flowers, a podium backed by a huge stained-glass window, and a large blow-up color photograph of Charles, in casual clothes, standing in a peaceful woodland setting.

Outside, the day is hot, sunny, and smoggy as sleek limos start arriving. Guests file into the chapel as Lori Andrews, the harpist, readies her instrument and Jackie Altier, who will sing at the service, also checks out the platform. An array of celebrities can be seen embracing, chattering, and taking their places in the long rows of pews. Flame-haired actress Carole Cook is one of the first to arrive, followed by Rip Taylor, actress Bea Arthur, pianists Joan Edgar and Peter Mintun, Franklin Townsend, singer Sharon McKnight, comic Michael Greer, actor Bill Irwin, and actress Alice Ghostley. The church is packed to overflowing as actor Michael Kearns begins the proceedings by referring to the service as *The Final Charles Pierce Show*. He encourages the gathering to laugh and applaud, as Charles wanted the service to be a "show." He also honors Don Lee Kobus as the man who stayed by Charles' bedside, caring for him to the very end. He says Charles was not a drag queen, but he was a control queen. He planned every detail.

Conrad Brin reads a poem by Ralph Waldo Emerson sent to Charles by David Lane, a spotlight man from one of Charles' nightclub appearances. It ends with the line, "To know even one life has breathed easier because you have lived. This is success." Brin also reads a bit of prose by Elisabeth Kübler-Ross, a psychiatrist, the meaning of which is that when we die, we shed our cocoon, and we are "free as a beautiful butterfly, returning home to God."

Allan Byrns reads the well-known verse by Edna St. Vincent Millay that begins, "And you as well must die, beloved dust" to the accompaniment of Lori Andrews' harp.

Jackie Altier, who had appeared in Charles' show *Anemic Faces of 1957* at the Hollywood Purple Onion, sings "Smilin' Through."

The next speaker is Elliot "Ted" Reid, who deviates from the prepared script to remark, "Look at this packed house—if Charles could see this! Imagine what he'd get for just the cover charge!"

Reid says Charles had instructed that there was to be "no extraneous ramblings on of speakers." Then he reads Charles' own words about his life:

> As I reflect back on my life and my lifestyle, I realize what a joyous and happy time most of it was. There was my work, which was really play. I had my mother, Aunt Carolyn, father, other relatives, and friends who were like family. I was always on the move. My life was enhanced by a fair amount of good health, and a loving family. Jessie, my mother, was the one person I wanted to be with. Also, my Aunt Carolyn was a terribly important person in my life. My father, at times distant, was still a wonderfully understanding man, and I know he loved me. He passed away from asthma in 1973.
>
> During the nightclub years, I would finish an engagement, return to my apartment, get things in order, and then fly off to Watertown, New York, to be with Mother and Dad. I must have made the trip from the Syracuse airport by car three hundred times! Watertown was always beckoning. When Dad died and Mother was alone, I made the trip more often. Then, like a ballet dancer, I knew my time was up, and I should leave the clubs. Mother had died the year before, and I had not fully recovered from her death. I retired the "act" in October of 1990. Mother died in 1989 and Aunt Carolyn in 1995. She was my support af-

ter Mother passed away. Since Mother's death and my departure from the world of nightclubs, life has been totally different. I had a few good retirement years after 1990 with trips to Europe and elsewhere. When Aunt Carolyn took ill in January 1995, I made the trip to Watertown to see about her upkeep. She had nurses and caregivers 'round the clock till July, when she, too, left my life. I was left her Victorian-style house and a substantial amount of money. Sadly, I had to sell the house, as I could not live there alone. I left the house for the last time in the fall of 1995, and a dear friend, Charlie Bill Dunham, took over the sale of the contents of the house. Charlie himself died a few years ago. I have a list of over one hundred friends who have died, all missed so much.

"Now," as they say, "it's your turn." In February of 1997 I was diagnosed with prostate cancer. Those of you who know, know that I love a vodka martini. Perhaps they did me in—while I was doing them. It is not true I am to be cremated and my ashes, with some glitter dust, be put in an empty Smirnoff bottle and tossed off the Golden Gate Bridge. What an exit.

Perhaps too—splashy?

I have had my share of good times, and certainly more laughs than are allowed. Some may not think this was right, but it was right for me. So to my endearing and enduring friends and relatives, as Eternity beckons, I leave you with these thoughts:

> Laugh my friends, and laugh my foes
> Mirth lightly comes and lightly goes
> And learns 'ere life runs blithely past
> He longest laughs who laughs the last

From my childhood. And again from Miss Millay:

> My candle burns at both ends
> It will not last the night
> But ah, my foes, and oh, my friends—
> It gives a lovely light!

Exit Charles with an old Irish lesson:

> —and until we meet again
> May God hold you in the hollow of His hand.

There is one more poem Charles asked Michael Kearns to read:

> A man may kiss a maid goodbye
> The sun may kiss the butterfly
> The morning dew may kiss the grass
> And you my friends—
> Farewell.

At the end of the service Charles had asked his beloved friend and "bosom buddy" Bea Arthur to read his favorite story. As she fights back tears, she reads:

> John invited his mother over for dinner. During the meal his mother couldn't help noticing how handsome John's roommate was. She had long been suspicious of John's sexuality, and this only made her more curious. Over the course of the evening while watching the two men interact, she started to wonder if there was more to John and his roommate than met the eye. Reading his mom's thoughts, John volunteered, "I know what you must be thinking, but I assure you that Mike and I are just roommates."
>
> About a week later, Mike came to John and said, "You know, ever since your mother came to dinner, I have been unable to find that beautiful silver gravy ladle. You don't suppose she took it, do you?"
>
> John said, "Well, I doubt it, but I'll write her a letter just to make sure." So he sat down and wrote, "Dear Mother, I'm not saying you did take the gravy ladle from my house, and I'm not saying you did not take the gravy ladle, but the fact remains that one has been missing ever since you were here for dinner. Love, John."
>
> Several days later John received a letter from his mother which read, "Dear Son, I'm not saying you do sleep with Mike, and I'm not saying you do not sleep with Mike, but if he was sleeping in his own bed, he would have found the gravy ladle by now."

Much laughter and applause follow her reading. Then, as Bea dabs tears from her eyes, and as Lori Andrews accompanies her on the harp, Bea sings, with great warmth and deep feeling, the lyrics to Sir Noel Coward's "I'll See You Again" from *Bittersweet*. The song completed, Bea raises her right hand in a sad gesture of farewell, as more tears well up in her eyes. It is an unforgettable and heartbreaking moment as the congregation breaks into applause, some wiping tears from their eyes.

The service ends, and the gathering moves on to Forest Lawn and the Columbarium of Providence, where a bright golden urn containing half of Charles Pierce's ashes rests before a large bas-relief plaque depicting the Madonna and Child, and above it the name "PIERCE" in large block letters. The remaining half of Charles' ashes was sent to Watertown, New York, for interment at his parents' graves.

Long-stemmed yellow roses fill a wicker basket nearby and, one by one, the mourners place them by the urn, some pausing to touch the urn, then moving on. Others, Peter Mintun informed me, placed roses on the grave of Bette Davis, which is close by. The long line of black limos moves quietly away, and *The Last Charles Pierce Show* ends forever!

Epilogue

Charles Pierce told me more than once that if I ever wrote his biography, it should be "warts-and-all." I have not emphasized those "warts," but you'll find them here, not to denigrate a great performer, but to paint a complete portrait of what the man was truly like beneath the makeup, false eyelashes, girdle, and gowns. A real human being not unlike the rest of us, with all the passions, emotions, triumphs, failings, and foibles that, in the final analysis, make up a human being. However, Charles, because of his remarkable talent, stood out from the crowd and caused those warts to fade into the background. Charles had "a talent to amuse," as Sir Noel Coward once said about himself. But Charles went beyond that. He completely captivated his audiences, for when he had fun, they had fun. When he was onstage, he owned it, and it could be intimidating to share that stage with him. Liza Minnelli often told of her experience when she appeared with her mother, Judy Garland, at the Palladium in London: "Suddenly, she wasn't Mama anymore! I was invading Judy Garland's turf, and I was terrified!"

I felt some of that whenever I shared the stage with Charles at the Gilded Cage. He was never unkind, but I knew it was his turf, and I knew not to overstep the boundaries!

I've never known a performer who could take command of an audience and hold it in the palm of his hand the way Charles could. He was never thrown by hecklers or other interruptions, and when he strode out onstage there was never any doubt who was in command!

There was nothing swishy about Charles either onstage or off. He was nimble and graceful and moved like a dancer, flashing those million-dollar gams, but he was always masculine, with his resonant, radio announcer's voice. He could distort that voice when it was necessary to coo and squeal as Marilyn Monroe, or to do Butterfly McQueen's "Prissy" dialect. He was an actor first—"an actor in a dress," as he called himself—and he proved it as Katharine Hepburn doing "Always Mademoiselle" from *Coco* and with the Bette Davis speech as "Margo Channing" about what it takes to be a woman from *All About Eve*. He could change instantly, chameleon-like, from high camp to heart-touching emotion.

I believe that deep down Charles was a lonely man, but he never whined about it. He'd often say to me, "I wish I'd had a brother or sister. You're lucky to have one of each." I think his constant search for sex partners had a certain amount to do with that longing for a close sibling or companion. He could never fill the agonizing vacancy left in his life by his mother's sudden death, and he never stopped loving her or his first love, David Hartley. He'd say, "Why couldn't David love me the way I loved him? Why did he treat me so bad when I loved him so much? It broke my heart the day he got married, and I never saw him again." With all his sexual encounters, he never found the soulmate he so desperately desired. His often-repeated phrase was almost like a mantra:

"Why can't we have lovers?"

"Charles, I don't want a lover," I'd reply.

"Well, tough shit—I do!"

"If you want a lover bad enough you'll probably get one." But he never did—not one that lasted.

That's a side of Charles people seldom saw. He had a loving heart, but he could put it aside when he strode out onstage and became his sometimes "heartless" characters. But that was all in fun—"just an illusion," as he sang at his show's finale.

When Charles Pierce finally hung up his drags and retired, he settled into a mundane routine. There were no fantasy trips racing through the night aboard the Orient Express to Venice, Rome, Cairo, and other exotic ports-of-call with a dream lover seated beside him. So, by his own admission, he turned more and more to his vodka martinis for solace while he pored over his stack of scrapbooks, reliving the lost moments of the past. The phone ceased to ring as often as it had in the glory days, and some of the so-called friends, the "star-fuckers," who had constantly hovered and sucked up to him when he performed in the spotlight of celebrity, even though they now lived nearby, were suddenly too busy to visit or phone. He did have loyal friends such as Bea Arthur, Virginia Grey, Alice Ghostley, and others who invited him to dinner, and others who corresponded regularly, and they were the friends he never forgot.

But Charles Pierce attained and lived his dream. He found his pot of gold at the end of the rainbow. He had a long, brilliant, and lucrative career that lasted over forty years, and he never had to use his unemployment insurance. That alone is a triumph in the unstable business called "showbiz." He did what he loved best, and he met a wealth of interesting and talented people along the way. How many female impersonators leave an estate of over half a million dollars when they depart this old world? A world Charles Pierce created for himself of style, panache, wit, and high camp. Charles did, and most of that money he "made the old-fashioned way—he earned it!"

Notes

Chapter 6

1. Viola Hegyl Swisher, "Chrome Plated Nader," *After Dark,* June 1978, p. 58.

Chapter 7

1. Interview, 1986. Anthony Slide, *Great Pretenders,* p. 147. Lombard, IL: Wallace-Hempstead. The interview is available on the Web at: <http://pages.prodigy. net/kevb/charles.htm>. Charles Pierce is interviewed by Peter Mintun.

Chapter 9

1. A full account of this episode is related by Shirley MacLaine in her book *Don't Fall Off the Mountain,* 1970, W. W. Norton and Co., Inc., New York, pp. 106-110.

Chapter 10

1. *Classic Images,* April 1998.

Chapter 12

1. Pierce wrote an interview with himself titled "Charles Pierce Interviews Charles Pierce," which was published in the *Bay Area Reporter* around December 1995.
2. *Variety,* 1962. Pierce sent me a brochure he assembled which showed clippings of these reviews, but no titles, authors, page numbers, or dates were given.
3. *Hollywood Reporter,* 1962.

Chapter 14

1. During the 1960s, Mrs. Elva Miller recorded albums under the name "Mrs. Miller," and her recording of "Downtown" was a hit. (See Capitol Records album #T2494, *Mrs. Miller's Greatest Hits.*)

Chapter 20

1. *The San Francisco Chronicle,* July 12, 1967.

2. Ibid.

3. David Perry, "My Bruncheon with Charles," *Bay Area Reporter,* September 1, 1988.

Chapter 21

1. John L. Wasserman, "On the Town," *The San Francisco Chronicle,* November 4, 1974, p. 44.

2. Paul Lorch, "Charles Pierce Quakes the Castro," *Bay Area Reporter,* 10(9), April 24, 1980, pp. 1-2; 4-5.

3. Paul Lorch, *Bay Area Reporter,* 10(9), April 24, 1980, p. 4.

Chapter 25

1. Curt Davis, Review, "Pierce Knows How to Dress Up His Act," *The New York Post,* November 1, 1979.

2. Howard Kissel, "Night Life," *Women's Wear Daily,* November 16, 1979.

3. Lee, *Variety,* November 7, 1979.

Chapter 26

1. David Perry, "My Bruncheon with Charles," *Bay Area Reporter,* September 1, 1988.

Chapter 28

1. Liz Smith, *The Daily News,* June 11, 1982.

2. Curt Davis, "Pierce: Master and Mistress of Disguise," *The New York Post,* May 14, 1984.

3. (no source)

4. (no source)

5. Rex Reed.

6. Key, "This Week in New York."

7. Chip Orton, "Nightcrawling."

Chapter 30

1. Scott Beach, "Pierce Is a Winner with Bette Davis Eyes," *The San Francisco Examiner,* July 4, 1984, p. E8.

2. Jesse Hamlin, "Good Old Girls," *Datebook,* July 5, 1984, p. 1.

3. Philip Elwood, "Charles Pierce, One Last Time," *The San Francisco Examiner,* August 26, 1988, p. C-12.

4. Mick La Salle, "Life's a Drag with Pierce, Thank Goodness," *The San Francisco Chronicle,* August 25, 1988.

5. Cynthia Robins, "Charles Pierce: Always a Lady, Never a Drag Queen," *The San Francisco Examiner,* August 25, 1988, p. D-1.

Chapter 31

1. "Wild & Wet," *New York Post,* May 20, 1987.

Chapter 33

1. Suzy, "Too Bea or Not Too Bea? Ask London," newspaper column, 1975?

Chapter 34

1. Don Heckman, "Pierce Dresses Up Balcony Theatre," *The Los Angeles Times,* August 2, 1990.

Chapter 35

1. Peter Mintun, "Charles Pierce Dies at 76," *Bay Area Reporter,* June 3, 1999, p. 1.